THE BOYCOTT

How Refusing to Play Opened New Doors

PATRICK GALLIVAN

Copyright © 2025 Patrick Gallivan
All rights reserved.

Disclaimer

During the course of telling these uncomfortable stories, there are times when quotes are used with words that would not have been our choice. We included them because leaving them out would detract from the story.

JP Publishing LLC

ISBN: 979-8-218-81520-2

CONTENTS

Acknowledgments *1*
Preface *3*
CHAPTER ONE: *The Boycott* *5*
CHAPTER TWO: *"Roll With The Punch"* *21*
CHAPTER THREE: *When Minorities Were Invited* *29*
CHAPTER FOUR: *Race Pioneers* *38*
CHAPTER FIVE: *No Blacks Allowed* *55*
CHAPTER SIX: *The Big Uneasy* *73*
CHAPTER SEVEN: *Traveling While Black* *95*
CHAPTER EIGHT: *Beatles* *106*
CHAPTER NINE: *Southern Traditions* *120*
CHAPTER TEN: *Life Experiences* *137*
CHAPTER ELEVEN: *Black Coaches* *144*
CHAPTER TWELVE: *Black Quarterbacks* *160*
CHAPTER THIRTEEN: *The Boycott, Part 2* *176*
CHAPTER FOURTEEN: *Take A Knee* *187*
CHAPTER FIFTEEN: *"Shut Up And Dribble"* *210*
CHAPTER SIXTEEN: *Closing* *224*
Endnotes *232*

ACKNOWLEDGMENTS

It has been said that it takes a village to raise a child. I cannot argue with that sentiment. It has also been said that writing a book is a process done alone. I do not know if I can agree with that sentiment. While it has been my fingers on the keyboard, many people helped me along the way. Thanks go to family, friends, and service staff at libraries and copy centers, as well as the many writers of previous books. While there are too many to name them all, I am indebted to all just the same. My family, Karen and Annie, who are my personal cheerleaders who provide much needed support and encouragement along the way. My brothers and sister are behind me one hundred percent with plenty of enthusiasm.

I am so thankful to all those who provided editing and comments on my preliminary drafts. Fellow author, Andy Piascik, read an early sample and provided very useful advice. I cannot thank enough the best editor in the business, Beth Rodgers. She provided endless comments and assistance, and I am deeply thankful for her work. She helped me produce a much better product for all to read.

Last, thank you, readers. I hope you enjoy this story that comes from the sixties. It is not always a happy story. There are parts that are really disgusting but it is a true story that actually happened, causing many men to stand up and say they weren't going to take it anymore. Athletes today owe these brave men and their teammates gratitude.

PREFACE

After I wrote *Pro Football in the 1960s*, a reader told me I missed a great opportunity. The civil rights challenges that gripped the country encroached into football, too, and I did not give that side of the story much attention in that book. It was meant to be about football, not politics, I reasoned. I hope to change that perspective within these pages. The sixties were a difficult decade with many events on different fronts. War was raging in Vietnam and civil rights demonstrations were happening across the USA. In 1965, 21 Black football players from the American Football League (AFL) took a stand against discrimination on the streets of New Orleans. They faced ignorance and ill treatment when attempting to use essential city services such as taxis, restaurants, and hotels. Local white residents were rude and offensive. It was another in a long line of discriminatory events in the lives of these men, but they had had enough and figured it was time to do something about it.

This generation of men were born about the same time as Emmett Till and had witnessed lunch counter protests and the deaths of civil rights workers in North Carolina. They were about the same age as the youngster lynched in Mississippi and as the lunch counter protestors. In just the past decade, these men—along with the rest of the country—had lived through the following:

December 1, 1955: Rosa Parks refused to give up her seat to a white person on a Montgomery, Alabama bus. Her protest resulted in the Montgomery Bus Boycott, which lasted 381 days.

September 1957: The Arkansas National Guard was called out to protect nine Black students who attempted to integrate Little Rock Central High School.

February 1, 1960: Four Black students from North Carolina A&T State University protested at the lunch counter in Woolworth's in Greensboro, North

Carolina leading to similar protests across the country.

May 4, 1961: The first Freedom Ride left Washington, DC for New Orleans to protest discriminatory practices in bus station accommodations across Southern states.

October 1, 1962: With a National Guard escort, James Meredith, a Black veteran of the United States Air Force, entered the University of Mississippi to attend classes.

June 11, 1963: Alabama governor George Wallace stood at the doorway of the enrollment office at the University of Alabama in an effort to block integration.

June 12, 1963: Civil rights leader Medgar Evers was murdered in the driveway of his Mississippi home.

August 28, 1963: Dr. Martin Luther King Jr. delivered his historic "I Have a Dream" speech.

September 15, 1963: A bombing at the 16th Street Baptist Church killed four young African American girls and injured others. Members of the Ku Klux Klan (KKK) were responsible for planting the device in an intimidation attempt.

August 4, 1964: The bodies of three civil rights workers—James Chaney, Andrew Goodman, and Michael Schwerner—were found in an earthen dam near Philadelphia, Mississippi. They had been murdered six weeks earlier by the Klan, were reported missing, and had been the subject of a long search effort.

All of these events attracted country-wide attention and showed the nation that we were not ready to all live together as an integrated society. Black athletes walked a tight line. In order to remain employed, they needed to go along and be quiet, even if they wanted to join the protest. At the same time, there were some examples of sports teams that formed a team with Blacks and whites working together and sharing a common locker room. Prior to the sixties, Black athletes and entertainers performed but kept quiet about the racism they faced daily. They did so to continue to do what they loved, but they needed to keep their thoughts to themselves. What happened in the sixties to cause this change? Why was it significant? What changed as a result?

CHAPTER ONE

The Boycott

Clearly something was not right. Big men, much taller than the average male, were standing at the curb right in front of a line of cabs and waving for the next in line to come pick them up. They could not be missed, though none of the cabs moved. They were professionally dressed but still ignored. These Black pro football players arrived in New Orleans for a game but could not get rides to their hotel. The best players in the American Football League came to New Orleans to play an exhibition all-star game. Delta flight 867 from Chicago arrived in New Orleans with Cookie Gilchrist, Jack Kemp, and Ernie Warlick from the Buffalo Bills, along with Art Powell of the Oakland Raiders aboard. Cookie snagged the pants of his new $150 suit and stopped at the Delta counter at the New Orleans airport to report it. The counter agent suggested the pants be patched. Cookie told the agent that the suit was brand new, it was expensive, and he did not want it patched. The agent told Gilchrist he must file a claim at Delta's downtown office. "You're not going to give us any trouble, are you, Cookie?" he asked. It was not clear if the agent was a football fan or if he had ever heard of Gilchrist, but his observation may have been accurate.

Gilchrist had a reputation as a malcontent during his playing career. That chip that Gilchrist carried on his shoulder came from the raw deal he was dealt as a teenager. Cleveland Browns head coach Paul Brown signed him to a professional contract when Gilchrist was nineteen years old before the league headquarters stepped in and said he was ineligible. Paul Brown should have known that rule. Colleges then backed out of scholarship offers because he signed a pro contract.

Gilchrist had no other option than to go north to Canada. He played two seasons in the Ontario Rugby Football League with the Sarnia Imperials and the Kitchener-Waterloo Dutchmen. He moved to the Hamilton Tiger-Cats of what would later become the Canadian Football League (CFL). In all, he played six CFL seasons with Hamilton, Saskatchewan, and Toronto. In eight seasons, from 1954 to 1961, he played for five different clubs. On the field, he was an impressive and productive player, even being named runner-up for the league's most outstanding player award in 1960. Off the field, he was gaining a reputation as someone who did not get along with others and who challenged authority. In 1962, he signed with the Buffalo Bills and was an impressive running back right away. He was the league's first 1,000-yard rusher with 1,096 yards over fourteen games that season.

After an impressive first season in 1956 with the Hamilton Tiger-Cats, Gilchrist had an opportunity to play for the NFL Browns with a stipulation: if he ended his relationship with a white Canadian woman. "The NFL would not accept interracial relationships," said Gilchrist. "Our relationship would be a public relations nightmare for them and that was a take-it-or-leave-it condition of their offer. While I would have loved to play back home on the NFL stage, I realized I loved Gwen more and saw a better future for us in Canada."[1] Along the way, Gilchrist had squabbles with every team for which he played. At that stop, he had money issues with general manager Jake Gaudaur, whom Gilchrist claimed reneged on a contractual bonus he was due with the Tiger-Cats. When he moved to the Toronto franchise, Gilchrist felt Argonauts' coach Lou Agase removed him from the game in favor of white players and said general manager Lew Hayman waived him due to a curfew violation. Gilchrist said that racial issues led him to initially decline induction into the Canadian Hall of Fame after his playing days were over. Trouble found Cookie Gilchrist everywhere he went.

On the evening of May 14, 1963, Gilchrist returned home after meeting with several friends in the Buffalo area when a marked police car stopped behind his car in front of his home. "The first thing out of their mouths was a stream of racial slurs," recalled Gilchrist. "They asked me how a nigger could drive such a nice car. I remember thinking to myself, how can police officers from a northern city still get away with conduct like this?" Gilchrist said he asked what he had done wrong, and one officer said he had passed through a stop sign three blocks back without stopping. When he questioned that account, he said he was attacked by the other officer with a nightstick. Several other police officers had arrived and joined in the fray. The police report claimed it took seven of them to take the big fullback down. "The next morning, I was transported to the courthouse to face seven charges, the most serious one was the felony assault on a police officer. I had the indignity of being transported to court in, of all things, a K-9 police vehicle and I was made to sit in the areas meant for the dogs."[2] Ultimately, Gilchrist said he was fined ten dollars for failing to stop at a stop sign and an additional fifty dollars for refusing to obey the order of a police officer. While he was waiting for the grand jury to meet, Gilchrist said he was followed by marked and unmarked police cars wherever he went. The Appellate Division of the New York State Supreme Court eventually dismissed the charge of felony assault.

What was Cookie Gilchrist like? "Cookie speaks at children's clubs for free and makes adults pay," recalled Cincinnati sports editor Pat Harmon. "He brags that he eats only one meal a day and friends say he snacks heavy with drinks and pastry and earned the nickname, Cookie, in between. He liked to call the Buffalo owner, Ralph Wilson, at midnight and demand a salary raise. But he was more dignified than other sports characters, Dizzy Dean and Walter Dukes, who did the same, he never called collect. He loves children and detests authority. Once he bought an airplane, took six flying lessons, forgot the plane, and bought a boat. He respects money but cannot manage it. He started a restaurant, then an appliance business, made money at the start and wound up in bankruptcy court. He was the greatest player in the Canadian Football League and was waived out of the league. He's an all-around athlete except for one sport—his friends say he can't swim a stroke."[3]

Back in New Orleans, Gilchrist and the other players made their way outside of the terminal to flag down a cab. Kemp, the white quarterback from the Buffalo Bills, waved first. A cab stopped for Kemp and his teammates followed him into the cab. The driver told the group he could take Black riders as long as a white person accompanied them and gave permission. Kemp told the driver that they were traveling together and the group proceeded to the Fontainebleau Motor Hotel, which served as the headquarters for the East squad.

Meanwhile, more players arrived at the airport and encountered the same issues. Black players Clem Daniels and Earl Faison followed the signs in the airport for ground transportation. They gathered their bags and made their way outside to look for a cab. Daniels raised his arm to wave at an approaching cab. He yelled,

"Taxi," but the empty cab drove by the two Black men standing with suitcases at the curb. Bobby Bell came outside with his bags and joined the other two. Despite another arm to wave, no cabs stopped for the three Black men. Finally, a Black porter approached the men and offered some advice. "Hey, you guys have to call a colored cab," he said. "They have to come from the city to get you."[4]

The annual all-star game was scheduled for Saturday, January 16, 1965, at Tulane Stadium in New Orleans. Newspaper accounts reported tickets were selling fast for the exhibition game. That was six months after President Lyndon Johnson signed the Civil Rights Act of 1964 and less than two weeks since the city hosted the first fully integrated Sugar Bowl game without incident. Syracuse, with eight Black players on its roster, lost to Louisiana State in that bowl game. Published reports indicated the Black Syracuse players encountered zero issues during their stay in New Orleans. The Civil Rights Act outlawed discrimination based on race, religion, sex, or national origin. It also marked the first Sugar Bowl that featured integrated seating.[5]

Many of the Black AFL players in New Orleans spoke of bad experiences dealing with racism. Some had found success previously living in an all-white world. Sid Blanks, the Houston Oilers rookie halfback, had captained the otherwise all-white Texas A&I team in 1963. He was the first African American to play in the Lone Star Conference and the first to receive a football scholarship. The treatment in New Orleans gave the 21-year-old pause. Was this his introduction to a new life experience in the South? He soon learned the reason. "I finally got a skycap to tell me, 'You need to get the right cab, because you're colored.' I said, 'What do you mean?' He said, 'They won't pick you up … It's a little different here. If you're colored, you just can't ride in any cab,'" Blanks said.[6]

"The white players were going out, getting in cabs and taking off, going to the hotels," recalled Bobby Bell, the Kansas City Chiefs linebacker and future Hall of Famer. "When the Black players would go out to get a cab, the white cabbie would say, 'No can do.' I guess we were out at the airport a couple of hours."[7] Boston Patriots fullback Larry Garron and others arrived at the New Orleans Airport and had to wait for a taxi despite 15 cabs lined up at the curb. Some of the players experienced issues even worse than being ignored. "What the cab drivers did," said Bills' trainer Eddie Abramoski, "was when the guys came in from the airport, they would take them out in the country, 15 or 20 miles, and tell them to get out of the car. Then they'd have to walk back."[8]

The West team was stationed at the Roosevelt Hotel, which had only been integrated weeks before following the signing of the 1964 Civil Rights Act. The East was housed several miles away at the Fontainebleau Motor Hotel. Once the all-stars arrived at their hotels, they unpacked, showered, and prepared for an evening on the town. They had heard about the excellent jazz artists performing at New Orleans clubs. At 4 p.m., San Diego cornerback Dick Westmoreland had showered and changed and was ready for a night on the town in the French Quarter. "I thought I was pretty sharp," said Westmoreland. "I had a nice brown suit on and some cologne: Aqua Velva or whatever it was in those days," he said. "Anyway, there was an elderly white lady on the elevator with us. She was looking kinda stern; she must have been 70 or 80. She made a statement as we were getting off. She said: 'What is that smell?' Like we were smelling bad or something to that effect. And I said (to myself): 'It's not me, because I have some cologne on.'"[9] Chiefs running back Abner Haynes, who along with Leon King integrated North Texas State University as the first Black football player, had issues with hotel guests and staff. "I get on the elevator to go to my room and the elevator operator says, 'You monkeys get in the back, so everybody can get in!' I said, 'You're an elevator operator and I'm a monkey.'"[10]

Black players were told things would be different during their New Orleans stay. "They told us bring your wife and kids," said Clem Daniels, Raiders running back. "There will also be a golf tournament. It sounded like a big picnic."[11] They had heard that before. The Supreme Court said school could be integrated in their 1954 *Brown v. Board of Education of Topeka* decision but not much had changed. The country struggled with the court's guidance over the next decade. By mid-1964, Congress passed the Civil Rights Act of 1964. This provided the federal government with the right to enforce segregation. Would that help? The Black players would see if French Quarter establishments were welcoming.

At 9:30 p.m., Art Powell called Cookie Gilchrist from the Roosevelt Hotel, where the West team was staying. "Meet you at the Dew Drop Inn, man," said Powell. Located in Central City, many considered the Dew Drop as an important and influential site for the development of rhythm and blues in New Orleans. Entertainers such as Ray Charles, James Brown, Sam Cooke, Ike and Tina Turner, and Otis Redding appeared there. Cookie got a cab outside the hotel. The white driver struck up a conversation. "Be careful in this town, boys," he told them.

After a couple of hours, Cookie Gilchrist, Abner Haynes, Butch Byrd, Bobby Bell, and Houston Antwine left the Dew Drop for a tour of other clubs. "You boys look like football players," the Black cabbie told the group. "Now that Abner Haynes, he's really something." . . . "Naw, he's terrible," said Cookie. "That Cookie Gilchrist, he's really great." . . . "You're right," agreed the cabbie. "Why, if I had him in my cab, I'd let him drive all night and not charge anything." . . . "You start driving, man," said Cookie.[12] The players chipped in two dollars each to tip the driver when they arrived back at the hotel.

New Orleans made no secret of its desire to land a professional football team. There were two leagues at the time. The National Football League had been around since 1920; the new American Football League had just finished its fifth season. The city made it clear to both leagues that New Orleans was available to host exhibition games with the goal of landing a franchise. City leaders were open to convincing an existing franchise to move to New Orleans but were also open to acquiring an expansion team. There were rumors about the Raiders looking for a new home city after years of dismal attendance in Oakland. Mayor Victor H. Schiro wanted his city to be big-league, so he created a municipal sports commission and put David F. Dixon Sr. in charge. He gave the group two tasks: (1) Construct a modern sports facility and (2) attract a professional football team. The city set out to attract a team by impressing the leaders in the leagues they could sell tickets to exhibition games better than other potential sites. When New Orleans was awarded the AFL All-Star game, some players were fearful of poor treatment in a southern city that was not used to hosting professional football. The city promised the red carpet would be rolled out for them.

Ultimately, Dixon was responsible for the concept and construction of the Louisiana Superdome and for the establishment of an NFL franchise in the city. Dixon provided his view of the all-star game boycott. "So, we decided to put on the AFL All-Star game, and we were promoting it pretty well," said Dixon. "We had about 20,000 tickets sold, even 25,000, which was pretty good in those days, and the AFL was really pleased. When players arrived in town, we were expecting a nice juice-up for ticket sales and nice gate sales, so we figured we'd be 35 to 40 and that was about 20,000 more than the AFL had ever drawn for an All-Star game We had integrated everything in town, but some of the taxi drivers wouldn't pick up Black people. Well, they do that in New York right now, you know, they drive right on past them. As a matter of fact, there's a joke always about it. A Black guy knows that he doesn't call for a taxi into those areas. It's a different area, you know, or whatever. Or he calls for it and uses his best white voice."[13]

"The first night we got there," recalled Ernie Warlick, "some of the guys said, 'Let's go down to the French Quarter.' I was a little skeptical, knowing where I was, but (white Bills' teammates) Jack Kemp and Mike Stratton said, 'Come on, let's go. Come on!' So, we all go down there and we were going into one of the places and the guy outside said, 'Come on in, everybody, come on in, hear the music.' He pointed at me and said, 'Not you—you can't go in!' I said, 'What do you mean?' He said, 'We don't serve your kind. You can't go in. Jack and Mike had already gone in and they came back and said, 'Come on!' I said, 'They won't let me in.' I said, 'The hell with that, we'll go find another place.' So, we went to another place in the French Quarter, then another place and ran into the same thing. So, I just said, 'Look, I'm going back to the hotel. I'll see you guys later.' So, I grabbed a cab—a Black cab—and went back to the hotel."[14]

"Art Powell went to Bourbon Street and they wouldn't serve him," said Elbert Dubenion, the Buffalo Bills' receiver. "Cookie Gilchrist came back to the hotel, woke me up, and said, "We're being discriminated. Get packed—let's go!' What was I going to do? I had to get up and go. I was ready to play in that All-Star Game. I didn't care about Bourbon Street or Jack Daniels Street—I didn't care."[15] Other players faced similar experiences. "We decided to relax in the French Quarter Saturday night and tried to catch a cab in front of the Roosevelt (Hotel, just off Canal Street)," recalled halfback Clem Daniels of the Raiders. Finally, we stood in the middle of the street and a cab stopped rather than run us down."[16]

Some of the Black ballplayers admitted they had a nice Saturday evening in New Orleans at a French Quarter nightspot owned by musicians Al Hirt and Pete Fountain. The players were introduced and received an ovation. "We were having a ball," said Ernie Warlick to columnist Peter Finney of the *New Orleans States-Item*.[17] It was in other parts of the city where many of the Black ballplayers recalled negative experiences in the city. "Several people shouted insults at us in the French Quarter," said Chargers' halfback Dick Westmoreland. "Doors were shut in our faces when we tried to enter several establishments. Wherever we went, people milled around us and some fellows—little guys at that—insulted us." Westmoreland said he was with two teammates, 320-pound Ernie Ladd and 270-pound Earl Faison. "Here

I was with these big men and the little guys were hurling insults at us," he said. "I was worried because Ladd and Faison have tempers. I suggested we go back to the hotel and they agreed, but then we couldn't get a cab to stop for us, so we had to walk back."[18]

"We arrived and there were some ballplayers, like Ernie Ladd, Earl Faison and they wanted to get a cab," said Bills' cornerback Butch Byrd. "No cab would pick them up. They wanted to go to the French Quarter. I wasn't there because I had gone to another bar called the Dew Drop Inn. That was my first time in New Orleans and being from a small town—Watervliet—that was really the big city. Other Black ballplayers had experienced some sort of segregation at the hotel and bias at the restaurant trying to get a meal and a taxi ride."[19] Many players told similar stories. "We weren't looking for trouble," said Westmoreland. "We were just sightseeing. Employees of some night spots milled around us as we walked down the street. We could plainly see that we were not wanted and felt it best to return to the hotel."[20] The treatment happened in the hotel, too. "Art Powell, Ernie Warlick (Buffalo Bills end), and I went into the dining room and Warlick went to hang his coat on a rack," said Daniels. "A woman sitting nearby screamed, 'Don't hang it near me.' Then I was walking through the dining room and another woman shouted, 'There's another one running around, just like little monkeys.'"[21]

Daniels said he was apprehensive about playing the game in New Orleans. He said all the players received letters from promoter David Dixon promising that there would be no discrimination. "I am sure he was sincere and I am equally certain that commissioner Joe Foss and others connected with the game were surprised by the unwelcome reception for Negroes. But the situation should have been checked out more thoroughly. The white players agreed with us and some of them told me beforehand they were worried for our sake."[22] Raiders' defensive back Dave Grayson joined several players including six-foot-nine Ernie Ladd of the Chargers in the French Quarter. The James Brown music that was playing attracted their attention. "Everybody come on in, come on in! yelled the barker out front. "Great show tonight!" The players moved to the door. The doorman, who had been so welcoming just a minute before, changed his tone as the players attempted to go inside. "Whoa, not your kind, we won't serve you. You can't come in.' The doorman had a gun in his waistband. He pointed it at Ernie (Ladd) and told him if he walked through the door, he was going to kill him."[23]

Gilchrist was awakened with the phone ringing at 10:30 Sunday morning. "You better come right over here," Art Powell told him. "The boys are having some trouble." Cookie called Ernie Warlick's room and told him. "I know," Ernie responded. "I got my bags packed. I'm ready to go home... Stop kidding," said Cookie. "This is too serious," replied Warlick, who assured his teammate that he meant business.[24] Cookie and the other Black players went outside the hotel to try to get a cab to the Roosevelt Hotel. A white driver stopped and walked to the phone. "I will call two colored cabs," he said. The players grew even more frustrated. Gilchrist went back into the lobby and ran into Bills' coach Lou Saban, who was coaching the East squad. "You see that?" asked Cookie. Coach Saban nodded that he had.

The coach drove some of the players over to the Roosevelt Hotel. The others borrowed Billy Shaw's station wagon. During the offseason, Shaw lived in Natchez, Mississippi and drove his own car to New Orleans. All 21 Black players met in the two-room suite of Earl Faison and Ernie Ladd (room 990 at the Roosevelt Hotel). Cookie, who had seen trouble off the field in Buffalo, was not an ideal spokesperson for the group. Warlick, with his gentle, outgoing personality, was one of the older players on either roster, and therefore was nominated to speak for the group. After two hours of discussion with players sharing stories of dismal treatment, most of the players voted to leave New Orleans immediately. Each squad had 29 players, for an overall total of 58. There were 21 Black players selected to participate in the contest (12 on the West squad and nine on the East squad), or about one-third of the total. Defensive back Dick Westmoreland was listed as an alternate.

During the meeting, they compared notes on the treatment since their arrival in the city and agreed to go along with the decision of the majority. Warlick was a big man at six-foot-three and 235-pounds with big hands. Those hands allowed him to be a pass-catching tight end during the sixties when pass-catching tight ends were uncommon. He earned the nickname "Hands." As spokesman for the group, Warlick issued a statement. "Because of adverse conditions and discriminatory practices experienced by the Negro players while here in New Orleans, the players feel they cannot perform 100 percent as expected in the all-star game and be treated differently."[25] Warlick phoned Commissioner Foss to advise him of the situation. "Actually, this came as a complete surprise to us," said Warlick. "We were led to believe that we could relax and enjoy ourselves in New Orleans just like other citizens. Maybe if we had been alerted to the fact that we wouldn't have run of the town, we could have avoided this unpleasant situation." After hearing from the players, Foss said, "I feel they are justified. You have 20 members of your ball clubs pull out and that doesn't leave you anything to do but cancel the game."[26]

Even before the official cancellation was announced, some of the Black players packed their bags and headed to the airport. "We're not wanted here so we are leaving," said halfback Clem Daniels of the Oakland Raiders, expressing the view of many. "We all encountered similar problems Saturday night. We were refused cab service and admittance to French Quarter clubs. We came here to relax and enjoy ourselves and put on a great game. You can't do those things under the existing circumstances."[27]

The players had received assurances prior to arriving in New Orleans. "Dixon assured me that New Orleans was ready in all aspects for a game between racially mixed teams," Commissioner Foss said at the time. "Evidently, it isn't. They contacted as many businessmen as possible and got them to agree to treat the Negro players well. But they just couldn't get to everyone. Negro players run into problems in nearly every city. But I guess what went on in New Orleans was more than they could be expected to take. I can't say that I blame them."[28] Warlick called Commissioner Joe Foss to let him know that the Black players voted to boycott the game. After consulting with team owners, Foss decided to take everything—All-Star Game, AFL Owners' meeting, and coaches get-together—to Houston. If it all was confusing to the average fan, it was pandemonium for the administrative staff of the Houston Oilers. They needed to plan all the details of playing a professional game, from concessions to advertising to ticket sales, in less than one week. But they did it! "The players called a committee meeting and decided that the incidents involving transportation and service were serious enough to warrant the walkout," said Commissioner Foss. "The players called me from the meeting—Ernie Warlick of the Buffalo Bills was the spokesman—and told me about their decision. I'm not critical of their action. They seemed to have adequate reason."[29]

The buses were in the parking lot waiting for the players to board and go to practice. "The bus was like a third empty," recalled Ron Mix, a white offensive tackle with the Chargers, and a future attorney. "And the coach said, 'Where is everybody?' Somebody said, 'None of the Black players are here." They're all in a meeting." Mix went to the room to talk with them. "So, I got off the bus and the first player I saw was Cookie Gilchrist. I asked him what happened and he said,

'It was almost impossible to get any cab to take us to the hotel. When we got to the hotel, they told us to enter through the back. We couldn't get admitted to any restaurants. Some of our players were turned away from a bar at gunpoint. We're not going to play in this game. We're boycotting.' I said, 'What about staying, because now we've got some national attention called to this. If we stay, then you've got a format.' Cookie said, 'No, the only thing that works is us leaving.' I said, 'Alright, I'll go with you.'"[30]

Mix joined the discussion and heard firsthand from the players about their experiences. According to reports, Mix thought he could convince the players to stay in New Orleans and play the game. "Look, we know we aren't going to change these people," Raiders' receiver Art Powell told Mix. "But neither are they going to change us. We must act as our conscience dictates." Mix countered that the public's impression may be one of a bunch of players who skipped town when the situation became difficult. "I suppose it would be better to stay here and by doing so imply that we accept such treatment for ourselves and our people?" countered Powell. "Do you want us to condone it?"[31] Serious discussions followed. "Some of the players thought we could accomplish more by staying and playing," said Daniels. "The majority didn't feel that way and I don't. We must draw a line somewhere. Possibly, as a result of the walkout, they may change their ways."[32]

"New Orleans, which was trying to get an NFL franchise, knew they would not get a franchise because of the national attention," Mix said. "They voted to desegregate the city. So, a bunch of Black athletes from the AFL desegregated a city. It's just kind of amazing."[33] City leaders claimed surprise as some recent sporting events were held without reports of discrimination. "Several Negroes played for Syracuse in the Sugar Bowl football classic New Year's Day," reported newspapers across the country. "Others participated in the Sugar Bowl track and basketball competition."[34] Little more than a week before, Jim Nance, who played for Syracuse in the Sugar Bowl, came away from New Orleans saying, "I'm going to tell everyone about the splendid treatment we received down there."[35]

"I was captain of the Eastern All-Stars," said Jack Kemp. "Abner Haynes was captain of the West. Obviously, we were discouraged, disheartened, and disgusted by the treatment of our teammates." The sides were not drawn along racial lines. Several white players immediately joined their Black teammates in support of the boycott. "Other guys said they were with us all the way," said Warlick. "Jack was with us and so was Lou Saban. He said, 'Whatever you guys do, I'm with you.'" The Bills coach agreed. "I was upset with what took place," said Saban, "but I figured if one was going to make progress, he doesn't take three steps back, he takes two steps forward. I told them, 'Not playing is not going to help us. I know what your feelings are and I feel just as bad as you do, but by walking away from it, that doesn't solve the problem. If we have to go to Houston, let's go and play the game. They lose if we don't play the game because they're displaying their talents.'"[36]

Early Sunday afternoon, the Black players from the East squad returned to the Fontainebleau Motor Hotel. Gilchrist packed and made a reservation on a 2:35 flight. Coach Saban came up to talk with him and a few other players gathered in his room. A call came from the Roosevelt Hotel asking the Black players to come over and meet with Dave Dixon, the game's promoter and a representative from the mayor's office. Due to the issue with catching cabs, Coach Saban offered to take one group over in his car. A Black bellhop offered to take off work and drive the others over to Roosevelt. The players met in room 980, which belonged to Chuck Burr, the Buffalo publicity manager who worked for the all-star game that week. Faison and Ladd did not attend as they told the group they were leaving town regardless. The players were joined by Dixon, Harry Kelleher, and Ernest Morial of the local NAACP. Gilchrist did most of the talking for the players and Kelleher pleaded for the city. Then the players, meeting alone, took another vote. This one was 16-3 in favor of leaving New Orleans. Three rookies cast the three dissenting votes, according to reports. Most of the Back players planned on leaving New Orleans Sunday.

After a day filled with meetings, Gilchrist had enough. Standing in front of the hotel, Gilchrist watched as five cabs drove past him while he attempted to get their attention. The sixth stopped. He got a ride from the Roosevelt Hotel back to the Fontainebleau Motor Hotel to pack his bags and head to the airport to leave. A snowstorm on the East Coast had made catching a flight difficult. To kill time, he watched television in an airport bar. Later that Sunday night, a telecast came on the television announcing the player revolt. "Suddenly, people are looking at me," said Gilchrist. "I can sense the hostility. For the first time in my life, I am scared. I've been brainwashed about the South."[37]

"The problem came when there was no organization for the exit from New Orleans," said Butch Byrd. "A lot of the Black ballplayers, including myself, were very nervous to get out. We knew this would have a major financial impact on people in New Orleans, so we didn't want to be the last ones out. I can remember going to the airport and just trying to find the next plane to Houston, because that's where we were headed. Fortunately, we didn't have to wait long, but I didn't have a flight in mind when I arrived. Subsequently, we did leave and to me it was a major positive response by Black ballplayers. It never had been done before and it had an impact. It was time. It was time for Black athletes to stand up for what was right. We took a stand and it turned out to be the right stand."[38]

Some critics discounted the players' decision. They said players would have faced discrimination in any city in the country. Mayor Victor H. Schiro said the players should have "rolled with the punch" and played in the game. He said he was disappointed with their decision. "If these men would play football only in cities where everybody loved them, they would all be out of a job today," he said. "Their reaction will only aggravate the very condition they are seeking, in time, to eliminate. We are a very cosmopolitan and tolerant city, but we are a southern city and there are times when personal reaction is unpredictable."[39]

"The false sense of full integration is what disturbed us most," said Ernie Warlick. "We all wanted to play the game. We're not part of any civil rights movement or anything like that. Our treatment was a real slap in the face." Other players commented, such as Clem Daniels, who said, "We went to New Orleans to put on a great game and relax a little. We were refused, abused, and not wanted. So, we left." Gilchrist added some illustrations. "The city rolled out the red carpet and jerked it from beneath us. Then it got mad when we didn't fall."[40]

The game was scheduled to be played in the 80,985-seat Sugar Bowl stadium at Tulane University. Event organizers hoped for a crowd of 60,000. Proceeds from the game, which was the first AFL all-star game scheduled in a non-league city, were destined to the Police Foundation, the Fraternal Order of Police, the National Police Association, and the Police Benevolent Association. Charles Chopin, part of a group of businessmen who supported the Fraternal Order of Police, said they planned on honoring the players at a banquet Thursday night. "We've got a big cake in the shape of a football on order and we'd like to know what's happening," he said when he first heard word of some upset players.[41] Profits from the game benefited the AFL Players Association. Nick Buoniconti, linebacker for the Patriots, disagreed with the players who refused to play. "As I see it, this hurt the league quite a bit," said Buoniconti when he first heard of the boycott. "I believe that this set back any negotiations with the National League for at least two years. It cost our pension fund $125,000 and it cost each of us money personally." Buoniconti said he felt "most of the Negro players voted to walk out to protect the three or four players involved. They felt that they had to back them up or let the three or four face some trouble from their own teams later."[42] Buoniconti made his comments before it was announced the game would be moved to Houston.

The AFL Players Association backed the players' action. In a formal statement, the Association asked that future sites for pre-season, All-Star, and other games sponsored by the league be investigated for discriminatory practices before the game sites were chosen. "A report on the degree of such practices should be made available to the players," according to the statement. Tom Addison, Boston linebacker and Association president, said his group prepared the statement after conferring with 10 Black players, including at least one from each of the league's eight teams.[43] Addison said the transfer of the game to Houston rescued the pension fund. "If the game had been canceled, all of our players in the league would have suffered," he said. "Our entire pension plan depends on the income from the All-Star game. Most of the Negro players had already left town before we first heard that they had voted not to play in the game. I called a meeting because I felt it was our duty to let the commissioner and the owners know how the representatives of all eight teams felt about the thing... We all agreed that the game should be played, if possible," continued Addison. "We sympathize with the problems of the Negro players and want them to be in the game. From what we could gather, there were eight separate and distinct cases of discrimination. These included transportation, refusal of admittance to clubs, name-calling, and things like that. I do know that half of the Negro players wanted to play the game here in New Orleans despite what happened."[44]

Many white players were sympathetic to their Black teammates. "It is a general feeling of regret that all the white players feel," said Patriots teammate Bob Dee. "I personally have never encountered anything like this and it's a rotten shame that it has caused so much trouble. But we are all in this together and certainly those boys are within their rights."[45]

Sports promoter David Dixon expected to see a huge loss due to the walkout. "Regardless of the right or wrong of the situation, the result is that a grievous injury has been inflicted on a city that has struggled sincerely not only to comply with the provisions of the Civil Rights Act of 1964, but before that, to reach a voluntary accommodation of the races. We seriously question the wisdom of the preemptory action which they (the Players) took to redress these alleged grievances."[46] At least one AFL owner felt sorry for the sports promoter. "I am truly sorry for Dixon," said Billy Sullivan, president of the Boston Patriots. "This just about wrecks all his hopes for an AFL franchise." Would it end the expansion hope in New Orleans? "Expansion is nothing immediate and is some time away as yet," said Commissioner Joe Foss. "Let the future take care of the situation so far as New Orleans is concerned. It is just a case of time." Dixon put a good public face on his disappointment. "To accept the actions of Sunday as a death warrant to our efforts is, in effect, to accept defeat of New Orleans, which we will not do," said Dixon.[47]

Butch Byrd, cornerback for the Bills, said he didn't think the players were thinking of contributing to the civil rights movement or making a political statement by their stand. "That thought never crossed our minds," he said decades later. "We weren't thinking about making history, so to speak. We just knew we were treated badly and we wanted to leave. We weren't out to correct anybody," he continued. "We were just thinking, 'They're showing us no respect. This is just pure hatred. We must get out of here." Byrd grew up near Albany, New York and played college football at Boston University. "Being from the North, I had never really experienced racism in that way," he said. "The Black guys from the South, they were scared to death . . ." Byrd attended the Sunday meeting in which players discussed the racist treatment. At 23 and in his first All-Star game, he was one of the youngest players in the room. "It wasn't acrimonious," Byrd said, "but there were two sides."[48]

At the end of the meeting, the Black players said they were going home. Ron Mix and Jack Kemp were two white players at the gathering. Both said they would support the Black players and refused to play. Many of the players went to the airport, got on planes, and returned home. When Byrd walked into his Buffalo home, his wife was on the phone with league officials. They told her the game had been moved and that he should get a flight to Houston. "I didn't even put my bags down. I walked right back out and to the airport and caught a flight to Houston," he said.[49]

On Monday, Joe Foss announced that the game would be played at Jeppesen Stadium in Houston. "Dixon assured me that New Orleans was ready in all aspects for a game between racially mixed teams. Evidently, it isn't," Foss remarked at the time.⁵⁰ Houston was the closest league city to New Orleans with a team office nearby to help with arrangements. It was an easy move for the players to get from New Orleans to Houston, about 350 miles away. Teams conducted their first workouts in Houston on Wednesday, only three days before kickoff, which was slated for 3 p.m. local time in Jeppesen Stadium. Some players still had not arrived, but coaches Sid Gillman of the West and Lou Saban of the East were hoping everybody would be ready to play by game time. According to the Associated Press, there were no reports of discrimination involving athletes in Houston since the Oilers began play and the Astros became members of Major League Baseball in 1962. All major hotels and taverns integrated several years before the game.

At 10:30 a.m. on January 11, 1965, AFL Commissioner Joe Foss called a press conference in the Imperial Suite of Chicago's Conrad Hilton Hotel. Foss spoke softly but emphatically about the reasons why he was moving the All-Star game from New Orleans to Houston. His talk was the exact opposite of the talk by the Bayou City mayor who was surrounded by another bank of press and television cameras. Reporters noted Foss looked tired, as he was up most of the night making alternative arrangements for the game. "The players called me about 8:30 last night and told me that they were seriously thinking of pulling out of New Orleans," said Foss. "They told me that the people down there had been insulting them in every possible way and that they didn't want to play in a city where so much prejudice prevailed." The commissioner told the players that he was behind them regardless of the decision. He said that decision was up to them. "But don't do anything hasty," he told the players. "Think this over for a while longer and then call me with your final decision. They said they'd call me back in an hour."⁵¹

The 1965 AFL All-Star game boycott was a landmark moment in American sports. Ancestors of these all-star players struggled to break barriers every day just to live ordinary lives. For the all-stars in New Orleans, an opportunity stood in the way. Essential services such as hotels, restaurants, and housing were locked to them. This was nothing new. Entertainment such as nightclubs, movie theaters, swimming pools, and amusement parks were off limits. In January 1965, this generation said enough was enough and they took a stand. Events such as the bus boycott, lunch counter protests, and civil rights marches led the way. The players decided it was time to take a stand and boycott the game in New Orleans.

CHAPTER TWO

"Roll with the Punch"

Reaction to boycott was swift and took the usual stances. White columnists in mainstream newspapers saw the boycott as an overreaction and thought AFL management should not have gone along with it. "We regret, of course, that the incidents that caused the offense occurred here," wrote editors of the local *Times-Picayune*. At the same time, they took the opportunity to criticize the players for "balking whenever they experience some unpleasantness." They ended by concluding, "It seems . . . some people were wearing their pride on their sleeves."[52] Some local columnists wanted badly to walk a fine line. Peter Finney wrote, "I'm not saying a little discrimination is all right," but went on to say that same thing. He suggested that the warm welcome at Al Hirt's nightclub should have made up for the other nightclubs turning players away.[53]

Many columnists in Louisiana and across the country expressed opinions on the boycott. "Some Negro players in New Orleans for the All-Star Game were making the rounds of dives in the French Quarter and were denied service," began Bill Carter, sportswriter for the *Alexandria (Louisiana) Daily Town Talk* in a January 14, 1965 column. "You might say they were looking for trouble and they found it. Then they called a meeting and voted to boycott the game. The AFL officials showed their lack of authority by going along with the players, without making an investigation and moving the game to Houston. New Orleans was left holding the bag—a bag full of pregame expenses . . . This was proof that the AFL is still a 'bush' league compared to the NFL . . . I hope the project to move the All-Star Game to Houston is a complete flop."[54]

Bill McIntyre, columnist for *The Times* in Shreveport, said the decision to move the game with less than one week's notice because of an alleged "mutiny" among 20 Black players proved the AFL was still in its infancy. The columnist, still peeved over losing the game, said the AFL no longer deserved a matchup championship game with the NFL. He cited a recent survey that found that most sports editors from the nation's 100 largest newspapers favored a matchup between the champions of the leagues.[55] After the boycott, McIntyre wanted to change his vote from yes to no. "When a tire goes flat on your car, you don't ship the whole chassis off to the junkyard. The AFL did," wrote McIntyre. "When a quart of milk goes sour in your icebox, you don't condemn the nation's dairy farmers. The AFL did. And one may ask, just why were the Negro football players in question so intent on living it up in the booze halls along Bourbon Street? We would have suspected that these were supposed to be athletes still in training on the eve of an All-Star Game."[56] Evidentially, McIntyre wasn't concerned about white players visiting night clubs before playing a game.

McIntyre continued, "The AFL's decision to take dictation from the 20 Negro players—and we will not dignify them by naming them here—reduces the players and the league to just one word apropos to sports: 'Bush.' And we couldn't care less how many thousands of dollars they shell out to the Joe Namaths of the future. Sports, as a word, is part of sportsmanship in the English language. But sportsmanship no longer seems to be part of sport. Not in the AFL."[57]

"The deplorable part of the New Orleans incident and all like it is that the bigots aren't punished," wrote national columnist Dick Young. "It is the innocent bystander who is punished. It is Dave Dixon, who will blow a fortune and it is the AFL and it is the many fine people of New Orleans; they are the ones who suffer ... Don't judge an entire town by some slob cab driver, because there are a lot of good cabbies and you don't say an entire city stinks just because some guys in some lousy gin mill insulted you, because there is something about a gin mill that makes it very easy to get insulted, whether you're Black or white, and when that happens you either fight your way out of the joint, or you find another gin mill ... There is a certain irony," continued Young. "It was not the majority that ruled; it was the Negro majority that ruled. In this historic southern election, the whites were not permitted to vote."[58] William N. Wallace of *The New York Times* called the players' walkout "a boycott without precedent in professional sports."[59]

"Those 21 Negro football players who refused to play in the AFL All-Star Game Saturday in New Orleans accomplished one thing: they caused their employer—the AFL—to lose at least $150,000," wrote sports columnist Bob Franklin in the January 16, 1965 edition of the *Delaware County Daily Times* in Chester, Pennsylvania. "Just what the sacrifice was made for is questionable . . . They won't be welcome in Houston's top night spots either. There's little difference between Houston and New Orleans as far as segregation is concerned. Perhaps the players got some satisfaction out of letting New Orleans know they don't appreciate being treated as second class citizens . . . In Houston, those players will go to the restaurants they choose to patronize and will be served with reluctance. Most taxis will take them where they wish to go and if they happen to enter a nightclub which caters to white trade only, they will be refused, regardless of what the law says. So, in the long run, they've accomplished little. All they've done is hurt the AFL, their bread and butter. In pulling out of New Orleans, these 21 players were being, in their own minds, gallant in defense of the Negro race. In going with them, the AFL was gutless."[60]

Enormal Clark, president of the Media Branch Chapter of the NAACP in Swarthmore, challenged Franklin's assertions five days later in a letter published by the *Daily Times*: "Mr. Franklin seeks to take to task the 21 Negro players who walked out of the AFL Pro Bowl game in New Orleans. For Mr. Franklin's information, those Negro players, in addition to being professional athletes, were American citizens and as such had every right to be treated the same as any other American citizen, no matter what city they were in. They had a right to refuse to perform in any city in which they were treated as anything but first-class citizens. Mr. Franklin might as well get used to the idea; this is the year 1965. Negroes simply aren't going to accept the things and conditions of even a year ago. It is now the Law of the Land that every American must be treated equally and we are determined to see to it that this law is applied everywhere. Mr. Franklin might as well get used to the idea: Negroes ain't acting like colored people anymore."[61]

Some of the criticism was leveled at the city of New Orleans and its collective inability to seize the opportunity within its grasp. "Well, it seems New Orleans has blown another big opportunity," said Phil Johnson of the city's WWL-TV in an editorial. "Of course, we're talking about the American League All-Star game . . . the one that was supposed to be played here Saturday. Well, it won't be. It has been moved to Houston. And New Orleans is left with an empty stadium and worse, a big black eye all over America. Now the obvious question immediately presents itself—why? Why did this happen? And the fact that 21 Negro players left town are complaining of discrimination isn't answer enough. To find the real answer you've got to go back a few years . . . back to the last time New Orleans blew a big opportunity . . . back to September of 1963 and the National American Legion Convention, which was supposed to be held here. Tens of thousands of Legionnaires were coming to town. And it was estimated that we would be $9 million richer by the time they left. This is, without a doubt, the single biggest convention in America. But it didn't come here because New Orleans could not guarantee unsegregated hotel accommodations. But only ten months later, New Orleans could and did—and still does offer unsegregated hotel accommodation. But it took a $9 million loss—and the Civil Rights Bill—for New Orleans to see in 1964 what it could not see in 1963. This is called learning the hard way . . . and it brings us up to date. Right now, it is popular to blame the loss of the nationally televised game on the 21 Negroes who walked out. So far, nobody has mentioned that perhaps New Orleans is to blame, also . . . just as it was then when the American Legion canceled out. If any good can come of this, perhaps it will be that this city must at least come face to face with facts. Either we are going to compete in this world of ours—as other cities are competing so successfully. Or we close ourselves off from the rest of America and remain the petty, provincial capital of limited opportunity and dubious culture which some seem to enjoy. But, of course, physically and economically, the latter choice is impossible. And the sooner all of New Orleans realizes this, the better off we will be."[62] *The Louisiana Weekly* published the WWL-TV editorial and said they agreed with the sentiment expressed. "We are, of course, convinced that had the mayor of New Orleans or one of his designees used television facilities to quickly and publicly apologize to the players for the actions of a few biased whites, the matter could have been settled to the satisfaction of all on Sunday," added the paper.[63]

"From the soap box, various horn blowers have blasted the tan (Black) players and have blamed them for grievous injury being inflicted on the city of New Orleans," wrote Jim Hall, sports editor for *The Louisiana Weekly*. "They say the 'Black Eye' inflicted upon our city by this group has left irreparable damage in our town, which will not soon be forgotten or forgiven. In one way or another, about everyone had dropped the hammer on the players, but no one has put the torch to the local brethren, who by their continued actions imperil the good name of our city and to a certain degree damage the process in race relations . . . We think the Negro players were right for not bowing to racial discrimination," Hall continued. "That jive of the 'players should have rolled with the punch' is for the kookaburras. For more than one hundred years, Negroes have been rolling with the punch. The case in point proves that Negroes today will not take the Sunday hate punches anymore . . . Let's put the shoe on the other foot for a while, we know it's going to hurt. In view of the fact that the city is trying to get on its feet to comply with the provisions of the Civil Rights Act of 1964 and march towards a progressive goal, why couldn't the cab drivers and Bourbon Street fellows have 'rolled with the punch?' That's a good question, but you can bet no answer will be given. Our brothers had the opportunity to 'strike a blow for nobility and muffed it.'"[64]

Jim Hall continued, "The wail of Louisiana Governor John McKeithen that the Negro players have been unfair in view of their having been provided with 'the finest accommodations,' is what is to be expected of Southern officials. They want to have the cake of segregation if they like, but the Negro is turning down half a loaf. The half loaf of partial acceptance is not better than not going on an empty stomach for a while to nurture one's human dignity. We think that Jackie Robinson scored a home run on that pitch. The whole story in a nutshell today is that average Joe Negro, whether he is a truck driver, longshoreman, or visiting athlete, wants no part of token integration. He wants to be accepted in full now. After one hundred years or more, we don't think Negroes are 'pushing things too fast.' They haven't pushed fast enough or far enough."[65]

A couple weeks after the boycott, *The Louisiana Weekly* columnist Jim Hall continued to write about the protest. He cited what some of the top Black athletes of the day were saying. Superior Court Justice Fred "Duke" Slater, a former football great, said the players showed great courage. "All of the Negroes were lifted and inspired by the stand they took," said Slater. "The city of New Orleans lost more than a million dollars in tourist trade because of the disgraceful treatment accorded these Negro athletes. And when you hit them in the pocketbook, there is a good chance of getting results."[66]

"Personally, I think the Negro stars deserve a great deal of credit," said Jackie Robinson, who knew personally of discrimination as the first Black player in modern Major League Baseball. "They are unwilling, as the Negro people are unwilling, to accept half a loaf. We have been through centuries of that kind of thing. It is easy for others to counsel patience when they have never known the daily experiences one faces, being a Negro not only in New Orleans but right here in New York."[67]

"Close observation on the scene by the writer lays the blame directly on city officials in the much-publicized cancellation of the 1965 AFL All-State game here (New Orleans) last week," wrote Butch Curry in the *Pittsburgh Courier*. The 20 Negro players involved did meet with racial incidents—isolated as they may have been—but even those isolated incidents could have properly been taken care of with normal advance preparations by the city as well as the promoters . . . The game was well publicized weeks in advance, even with the help of the mayor who appeared on local television several times appealing for fans to support the attraction," continued Curry. "But what the mayor and other city officials didn't do was to properly orientate local businesses—entertainment places, transportation firms, etc.—on what was to be expected from them. I believe that had they been called in weeks before, or contacted long before, of what was expected to make this game a success, last Sunday's embarrassing incidents involving some unconcerned cabbies and cheap French Quarter nightclub doormen might not have occurred . . . Dave Dixon and his group, sincere as any group of persons can be in desiring the game and its integrated aspects, overlooked this important item. Not intentionally, but accidentally, and their magnificent efforts went for naught because of a few unfortunate incidents that did not speak for the general citizenry of the town. It's tragic, but one must pay the price for a mistake. True enough, some cabs will transport passengers without regard to racial identity, some nightclubs in the French Quarter do admit patrons on a non-racial basis. But this was not relayed to the AFL All-Star players. Under current conditions as the city transits itself under the Civil Rights Act prepared lists of places to go and transportation to use would have been proper—perhaps would have prevented what happened . . . It gave New Orleans another setback in its struggle to regain its lofty national popularity. But it will recover as the forces of good have gradually overtaken that of evilness and racial hate. As painful as it was, the cancellation gained allies for the city's forces of good."[68]

The general consensus was the loss of the game meant the chances of New

Orleans getting a major league sports franchise—football, baseball, or basketball—appeared dim, if not gone. "I do not blame our Negro stars for doing what they did," said Foss at his press conference. "I doubt that New Orleans is ready for the big league. If they can't treat big leaguers with the dignity and respect that they deserve, then the city will have to suffer the consequences. "There's an old Dixieland standard which goes by the provincial theme, 'Do You Know What It Means to Miss New Orleans?' I don't know what it means to miss New Orleans, but I know what New Orleans means to me. They can have it . . . You may have gathered, if you're a regular reader of this column, that I don't like the South unless it's got a California after it . . . Once again, class, prejudice has no place in this country," he continued. "It's unfeasible from a Christian viewpoint, from a legal viewpoint, from a moral viewpoint, and from a moral viewpoint. The only thing it's good for is bolstering idiots' egos. They can't do anything else, but, by golly, they can keep Negro college graduates, professional athletes, high tax players, and generally gentlemen and respected citizens out of the Bourbon Street dives and taxicabs . . . Until the day when the meanest sharecropper in 'Bama and the dirtiest wino in Chicago are faster than Bob Hayes, run with a football better than Jim Brown, are more handsome than Harry Belafonte, smarter than Jimmy Smith, fool around with a baseball better than Willie Mays, and write better than James Baldwin, then there is no such thing as racial supremacy."[69]

On the weekend after the walkout, Mayor Schiro of New Orleans told a *Shreveport Times* reporter that he had received "a reef of letters from all over the country supporting New Orleans' position." The image of the city was not damaged and "certainly won't affect our plans for a professional football team."[70] He talked to various media with the same themes. "I think it was planned and organized," said the mayor. Mayor Schiro told the Associated Press that Commissioner Foss "acted hastily," and that the players did "themselves and their race a disservice by precipitous action."[71]

On July 5, 1965, Dixon announced that New Orleans was not interested in an AFL franchise any longer. The announcement came after the AFL had taken some hits. They lost out to the NFL for the city of Atlanta when the league awarded an expansion team as well as Philadelphia, when officials there agreed to finance a new stadium for the NFL Eagles and signed a ten-year lease agreement with the team. "With those two cities now firmly controlled by the older and more powerful NFL, the AFL had to start looking for another prize city and no doubt New Orleans was considered a plum," wrote a Louisiana columnist. "Pride is a wonderful thing to have and I believe that Dixon's pride had a lot to do with his attempt to land a National League franchise for New Orleans."[72] Dixon lined up another exhibition game August 14 with the Baltimore Colts and St. Louis Cardinals. He was determined to prove New Orleans was worthy of a professional team. He said he first dreamed of a professional football franchise for New Orleans while watching Tulane University play the University of Mississippi. "Tulane didn't have a ghost of a chance of winning, but they had Tommy Mason and were playing entertaining football. Some 60,000 people turned out for that game and just the week before that many were here for an Alabama–Tulane game. "I thought to myself that New Orleans was really hungry for football and we deserved a pro team."[73]

"Although the episode received little attention in the national press, it sent a clear signal to civic leaders," wrote Michael Oriard, a former NFL player and later a university professor who has written extensively about the business and cultural aspects of sports. "Through the combination of its economic clout and the collective influence of its Black players, professional football became a force for antidiscrimination. The NFL would not have to invoke this power again until 1991, when Phoenix lost a chance to host the Super Bowl after Arizona voters rejected the state holiday honoring Martin Luther King Jr. . . . The boycott in New Orleans by AFL All-Stars marked the end of pro football's official accommodation with segregation, when Black players were often housed separately from their white teammates on the road."[74]

In his series, "The Black Athlete," Jack Olsen quoted a white player who described the subtle forms of racial prejudice in the league: "I can say in complete honesty that I can never remember a coach mentioning a guy's race or color. I can't cite a single case of a player who was cut because he was Black. I can't remember a single Negro-white fistfight, except one or two that had nothing to do with race. But the prejudice is there. The league reeks of it. The way the teams are composed. The way the locker rooms are laid out. The way Negroes are criticized more than whites. The way they're not supposed to know how to play certain positions. The way the white players are allowed to boss them around and criticize them . . . If I were a Negro, I'd go nuts trying to fight it, because you can't fight it. Where do you start? It's like attacking a wall of mushroom soup."[75]

CHAPTER THREE

When Minorities Were Invited

When the National Football League began, there were minorities in prominent roles. The association was formed when managers of numerous professional clubs met in Ralph Hay's Hupmobile car dealership in Canton, Ohio in 1920. The group elected Jim Thorpe, the American Indian all-around great athlete, as the first commissioner of what was called the American Professional Football Association. Frederick Douglass "Fritz" Pollard, a Black running back, played and coached the Akron Pros to the league's first championship. Despite these early high profile successes, no team had more than a few Blacks at any time and, by 1933, the entire league had only two Black players (Joe Lillard and Ray Kemp). At the end of the season, they were gone, beginning a period of time where no Blacks played in the league until 1946. All the while, Blacks were still playing football. In Southern California, the UCLA Bruins went undefeated in 1939 with Kenny Washington and Jackie Robinson, who was famous for football long before he reached immortality on the baseball diamond. Washington finished the season with 1,370 yards, more than any other college player, and he was named second team All-American. Despite a strong college career, he wasn't drafted by any NFL club because of his skin color. He and Robinson joined the Pacific Coast Pro Football League, which allowed Black players to participate.

When Second Lieutenant Jackie Robinson was serving in an all-Black unit at Fort Hood, Texas, he refused to play football for the base team unless he could also play on its all-white baseball team. A commanding officer even threatened to order him to play football.[76] About a month after the D-Day landing in June 1944,

Robinson boarded a local bus and sat next to the light-skinned wife of a fellow Black officer. The driver told him to move to the back of the bus. Robinson refused and was arrested. Before the case came to trial, it received nationwide publicity. Black newspapers such as the *Pittsburgh Courier* asked why Black soldiers were asked to fight against foes overseas at the same time they could not defeat segregation at home.[77] The court found Robinson not guilty two months later. His all-Black unit, the 761st Tank Battalion, was deployed to Europe and suffered heavy casualties. Robinson did not go when a pre-existing bone spur in his ankle prevented his deployment. Had he joined the rest of his unit, he may have been killed or maimed and therefore unable to continue his athletic career, dramatically changing history.

During the war years, some NFL teams had reduced rosters. In 1943, the Pittsburgh Steelers and Philadelphia Eagles combined to form one team called the Steagles because they were short on players. The Eagles found enough players the following year, but the Steelers did not. So, in 1944, they formed a team known as Card-Pitt with the Chicago Cardinals. Despite the player shortage, no Blacks played on any NFL team. "For myself and for most of the owners, I can say there never was a racial bias," said Art Rooney Sr., owner of the Pittsburgh Steelers. Ray Kemp, one of the last Blacks to play in the league, thought differently. "It was my understanding that there was a gentleman's agreement in the league that there would be no more Blacks."[78] Many players put the blame on Washington team owner George Preston Marshall, who was known to support Southern attitudes regarding segregation.[79]

If the league were to change its stance, it would need some prodding. When Dan Reeves sought to move his Cleveland Rams to Los Angeles in 1946, he wanted to play in the Memorial Coliseum. It was a publicly owned building, so citizen comments were welcome. Halley Harding of the *Los Angeles Tribune*, a Black newspaper, rose at the meeting and reminded everyone that UCLA's undefeated 1939 team featured Black players Kenny Washington, Woody Strode, and Jackie Robinson. He wondered out loud how soldiers fought intolerance overseas during the war and yet the city considered leasing the publicly owned stadium to a sports league that refused to allow non-whites even a tryout. The protest had begun. In the end, the Rams signed Washington and Strode to play on their team. Neither had a banner year with the Rams. It had been eight years since Washington and Robinson led the Bruins to an undefeated season and Washington had undergone multiple knee surgeries. A running back, he carried the ball only 23 times for 114 yards, eighth best on the team. Strode was tenth in receptions with only four catches all year. It appeared that the team was having trouble with the fact that he was married to a Hawaiian woman. By year two, Strode was released and Washington remained as the only Black in the league.

At the same time, a new league named the All-America Football Conference (AAFC) was formed to compete with the NFL. In Cleveland, owner Mickey McBride hired Paul Brown, the man many considered the most innovative football coach of his day. While forming the Browns, Brown signed two Black players he was familiar with from previous stops, Marion Motley and Bill Willis. Motley, who played against Brown's high school teams, became the first Black to sign with an AAFC team in 1946. Willis had played for Brown at Ohio State. Strode, Washington, Willis, and Motley played in the AAFC and NFL before Robinson debuted in the major leagues.[80] "It's interesting, in a way, because he (Paul Brown) did it before they did it in baseball," said his son, Mike Brown. "I'm not sure why professional football is not given more credit for breaking the color line. It's always intrigued me that that was the case, though keep in mind that back in the '40s, baseball was the principal sport in the country. It definitely was the bigger sport. Maybe that was part of it, but it's almost forgotten . . . When he coached at Massillon Washington High School, he had many Black players on his teams. When he coached at Ohio State, he had many Black players on his team. When he coached in the service, the same thing was true. When he got to the Cleveland Browns, he looked around and he knew where he had better football players than he had with the Browns. Guys who formerly played for him. He didn't do it for any other reason than to make the team better. It wasn't to sell tickets in the sense of drawing people because we had a couple Black guys on the team."[81]

Although his son said Paul Brown wasn't a civil rights crusader, he followed a strict moral code. Bobby Mitchell, who played for Brown in the 1950s and 1960s, recalled an incident in Miami when the manager of a hotel informed Brown that the hotel would not accommodate Cleveland's Black players. "Paul Brown looked him right in the eye and said, 'No, our team stays together,'" Mitchell recalled. "They had words and finally Paul told them: 'I'll tell you what then. We'll just get back on the plane and go back home.' The manager said, 'You can't do that.' Brown said: 'Is that so? Our players stay together.' So, they relented."[82] Paul Brown led his AAFC team to a championship in his first season with Willis and Motley on the roster. He added another Black player, Horace Gillom, a punter and end who had played on Brown's high school team in Massillon, Ohio, the second season with the Browns. Since his coaching days at Massillon Washington High School in the 1930s, Brown did not have an issue with Black players on his teams. In his view, the best players played regardless of race. He continued that practice at Ohio State University, on to the Great Lakes Bluejackets during the war, and then with the Cleveland Browns.

When NFL teams gathered for the 1952 draft, half of the 12 teams remained all-white. After the Rams and Browns reintegrated football in 1946, the Detroit Lions, New York Giants, and San Francisco 49ers added Black players two years later. The Green Bay Packers integrated in 1950. With the third pick in the 1952 draft, the Chicago Cardinals selected Ollie Matson, the star halfback from the University of San Francisco. Two picks later, the Philadelphia Eagles selected Drake University quarterback Johnny Bright. Both men would be asked to integrate their new football teams. Matson signed with the Cardinals after running in the Helsinki Olympic Games, where he won a bronze medal in the 400 meters and a silver medal in the 400-meter relay. Bright turned down the Eagles offer and instead signed with the Calgary Stampeders of the Canadian Football League. The Eagles ended up with two other Black players that season. The Bears, Texans, and Steelers also added Black players in 1952, leaving the Redskins as the only NFL team to have never employed a Black player.

The college game experienced its share of racial segregation. It was significant in bowl games which, except for the Rose Bowl, were played in the South. Until the mid-fifties, bowl invitations were selected based on the racial make-up of the squads. Teams with Black players were asked to leave those players at home in order to accept the invitation. Late in 1948, when the bowl game line-ups were announced, fans of Lafayette College in Easton, Pennsylvania were ecstatic. Their team had not played in a bowl game for twenty-six years and were now selected to make a trip to El Paso, Texas and take part in the Sun Bowl. The cheering suddenly stopped when word spread that faculty rejected the bowl invitation because southern racial customs would have prevented senior halfback Dave Showell, an African American, from playing in the game. "It is fundamentally wrong," declared school president Dr. Ralph C. Hutchinson, "for any team to go and play a game and leave any player behind because of his race, color, or religion."[83] The team had earlier voted to accept the invitation after Showell told them he would not object to sitting out the game. The protestors' plea was simple: tell bowl officials we want to come and bring all team players, including Showell. Dr. Hutchinson accepted the argument and contacted bowl officials, who rejected Showell's participation and said a replacement team had already been contacted. The students could not be consoled and staged a civil rights demonstration, attracting further attention to their cause. National publicity embarrassed Sun Bowl officials and some residents of El Paso, Texas. It put the spotlight on the exclusion of African American football players from most college bowl games. It also showed that some football fans were willing to challenge the color line in sports.

In 1948, New Year's Day had risen to be the peak day in college football. Most of the top teams in the country were set to do battle in celebrated bowl games. Since most of the games were held in the Deep South, "southern traditions," including racial policies of the day, controlled the contests. In effect, Dixie could impose their racial views on non-southern teams. Before World War II, the bowl committees were largely successful, using their financial leverage to convince northern universities to leave their Black players at home and attend the game. After the war, many universities were willing to challenge that conformity.[84] Bowl games come and go. Four of the major bowl games were located in the former Confederate South where white supremacy rules prevailed: the Sugar Bowl in New Orleans, the Orange Bowl in Miami, the Sun Bowl in El Paso, and the Cotton Bowl in Dallas. The fifth major bowl game, the Rose Bowl in Pasadena, California, was the lone exception with a long history of inclusion. In 1916, the Tournament of Roses committee extended an invitation to Brown University, whose star player was African American, Fritz Pollard. Although Pollard met some discrimination in public accommodations, game sponsors made no attempt to block his participation. This was 1916!

The 1940 Cotton Bowl featured Clemson against Boston College. The bowl organizers controlled the rules and they informed Boston College that Black halfback Lou Montgomery would not be allowed to play in the game. Coach Frank Leahy disagreed with the stance, but the school accepted the invitation anyway. There was some past precedence: Montgomery needed to sit out two regular season contests that year, against Florida and Auburn. The following year, Boston College earned another bowl invitation, this time the Sugar Bowl in New Orleans. Again, Montgomery was not allowed to take part. The war years, with a campaign to defeat the Nazi doctrine of Aryan supremacy, seemed to bring some enlightenment. Northern teams were reluctant to bench their African American players for home contests against southern schools.

During the fall of 1948, the University of Virginia hosted an integrated Harvard team in Charlottesville. Progress was being made. The following January, the Cotton Bowl fielded a Southern Methodist University-Penn State matchup that was reportedly the first integrated contest held in the state of Texas. Penn State brought two African Americans, fullback Wallace Triplett and end Dennie Hoggard to the game. The following year, with the 1949 Cotton Bowl, the committee achieved a second integrated contest with an Oregon squad with three African American players, including starting halfback Woodley Lewis, coming to Dallas to face Southern Methodist. The Ducks squad stayed at a downtown hotel, but the three Black players stayed separately at private homes of Black Dallas residents.

In December 1946, the Sun Bowl association invited Virginia Polytechnic Institute (VPI) and the University of Cincinnati to face off in the annual bowl game. Cincinnati fans were excited to receive the first bowl invitation in school history. That enthusiasm was dampened when school officials were informed that senior Willard Stargel could not participate due to his race. That request was nothing new to the university; Stargel missed regular season games against Kentucky and Tulsa, the only two losses the Bearcats suffered. The story has a happy ending: Cincinnati was victorious in the Sun Bowl with an 18-6 victory over VPI.

In 1950, another incident involving a Black player occurred in El Paso. Loyola University of Los Angeles suddenly canceled its scheduled September 30 game against Texas Western College because local officials banned African American halfback Bill English from playing in the game. Some criticized Loyola for backing out of the game, but many in El Paso criticized the ban against Black players. Several civic organizations (Sun Carnival Association, the El Paso City Council, among others) urged the University of Texas board of regents to repeal the rule. They argued that the future of the Sun Bowl and Texas Western athletics could be in danger. The regents voted to repeal the policy specifically for Kidd Field in El Paso, but they retained the rule for other state universities. The Sun Bowl committee was happy because the pool of possible attendees was expanded with the rule. On January 1, 1952, Pacific halfback Eddie Macon became the first African American to play in the Sun Bowl when he took the field against host Texas Tech.[85]

Similar rules existed in Florida, where the state hosted the Orange Bowl every year in Miami. Traditionally, all athletic competitions had been segregated in the state over the years. In the late 1940s, the State Board of Control put the policy in writing. All state schools were prohibited from hosting integrated games in the state. Further, the Orange Bowl stadium facility, unlike many other facilities, lacked a segregated all-Black spectator section until 1950 when one was added in the east end zone. The topic hit national news when a scheduled game between Penn State and the University of Miami in 1946 was canceled due to the racial ban. Miami college students pointed out the contradictory stance of banning integrated sports at the conclusion of a war fought over Nazi Aryan beliefs. Over the next few years, several more games, both football and basketball, were canceled due to the race policy. Finally, in 1950, Miami city government permitted the University of Miami to host the University of Iowa in a football game. Iowa's team included five African American players and all of them saw action in the game. The first integrated Orange Bowl game took place on January 1, 1955, when there were two Black players on the Nebraska team during their 34-7 loss to Duke.

Things were worse in New Orleans than they were in Texas and Florida. Local customs enforced strict segregation in seating and other facilities at Tulane Stadium, site of the Sugar Bowl. By the late 1940s, tickers were imprinted with a statement that "this ticker is issued for a person of the Caucasian race" and any other person using it could be ejected.[86] The segregation issue got even more complicated in the fifties. By then, most northern teams had some African American players as did the marching bands and other fan groups. All were seeking attendance at games in the South when their teams played there. In an attempt at accommodating fans attending the January 1955 contest, Black fans were allowed to sit in one end zone while white fans were allowed unrestricted seating. That plan was in place when the Navy football team attended the New Year's Day classic against Ole Miss.

The Sugar Bowl was scheduled for January 2 in 1956 (since January 1 was Sunday) and Georgia Tech had agreed to play in the game against the University of Pittsburgh, which had a Black fullback and linebacker named Bobby Grier. Years before, in 1941, the Sugar Bowl invited Boston College, which had a Black player, but he was not allowed to play in the game due to the segregation policy. Pitt was acting like there was no segregation in the South. They insisted that Grier would stay with the team, including lodging, eating, and sleeping. Further, they agreed to sell 10,000 non-segregated seats, bring their band (inclusive of Black members) and travel in integrated railroad cars. If all that happened, the Sugar Bowl would be racially integrated for the first time. However, Georgia's Governor Marvin Griffin wouldn't hear of it. Amid fiery remarks, he asked the school's board of regents to withdraw from the game. "The South stands at Armageddon," he said on December 2, 1955. "The battle is joined. We cannot make the slightest concession to the enemy in this dark and lamentable hour of struggle. There is no more difference in compromising integrity of race on the playing field than in doing so in the classrooms. One break in the dike and the relentless enemy will rush in and destroy us."[87] Despite Griffin's stance, on January 2, 1956, Grier became the first African American to break the color line in the Sugar Bowl. Governor Griffin, in response to his receiving objections from residents, reversed his earlier approval and came out opposed to Tech's participation in an integrated contest. Thousands of protestors visited the state capitol and the governor's mansion voicing their support of Tech's participation in the bowl game. Ultimately, both teams played and Pitt made good on their pledge of the team sticking together by staying at Tulane University. Tech capitalized on a controversial pass interference call against him near the Pitt goal line to score the game's only points. Tech stopped Pitt twice near the goal without points even as the Panthers outgained Tech 311 yards to 142, but Tech was victorious 7-0.

One would have thought the game provided a huge step toward integration. Instead, lawmakers in the Louisiana State Legislature passed a law banning interracial sporting events in the state. That law limited the teams that the Sugar Bowl committee could invite and meant Major League Baseball teams could no longer hold spring training games in the state as the law prohibited interracial sporting contests and required segregated seating at all public events. Sugar Bowl officials voiced disapproval, claiming that the measures would damage sports programs in the state, but Governor Earl Long signed the bills into law. It is generally considered the legislation was a reaction to the 1954 *Brown v. Board of Education* decision.

In 1951, the University of San Francisco Dons won all nine of their games and were viewed as one of the top teams in the country. Bowls such as the Orange, Gator, and Sugar were all interested in the team. The team included eight future NFL players, including three future Hall of Famers—Gino Marchetti, Ollie Matson, and Bob St. Clair. All of the bowl invitations came with a condition: they would have to leave the team's two Black ballplayers, Matson and linebacker Burl Toler, behind. "We were all angry over the fact that they would even suggest that we would even consider doing that by leaving our two Black players behind," said Bob St. Clair. "These were teammates. These were brothers."[88] Two years before when the team traveled to Tulsa, Oklahoma for a game, Matson and Toler could not stay in the team hotel or eat with the white players in restaurants. The accommodation left the team feeling divided and they did not want to repeat that experience. They refused to go to any bowl that did not invite the entire team. The Dons stayed home. Soon after, the school ended the football program.

CHAPTER FOUR

Race Pioneers

In May 1954, the U.S. Supreme Court announced a decision of great significance for race relations. In a unanimous decision of *Brown v. Board of Education*, the court ruled that racial segregation in schools violated the Fourteenth Amendment which prohibits states from denying equal protection of the law. Chief Justice Earl Warren wanted the ruling to be unanimous, so he postponed the part of the ruling that outlined how the decision would be implemented. One year later, the Court announced a decision legal scholars coined *Brown II*, which attempted to complete the task. Although an exact timeline was not provided, the court said states must proceed "with all deliberate speed"[89] to integrate public schools. The states would be responsible for the implementation and the court asked them for a "prompt and reasonable start toward full compliance." The vagueness of the decision left the states plenty of space to ignore or, at the very least, slow down implementation. The decision ended the "separate but equal" precedent established 60 years earlier in *Plessy v. Ferguson*. In short, racial segregation in public schools is unconstitutional. Mississippi Senator James Eastland denounced the Supreme Court's *Brown* decision before a Citizen Council convention in Jackson. He said the justices "violated their oath of office" and the Citizen Councils were defending "the racial integrity, the cultural, the creative genius, and the advanced civilization of the white race."[90]

Another event generated publicity for the movement. Fourteen-year-old Emmett Till lived with his mother in Chicago. In the summer of 1955, Moses Wright, Emmett's uncle from Mississippi, visited Chicago. When it was time to return home, he invited Emmett to tag along and meet his Southern relatives.

Emmett wanted to go but his mother was reluctant to let him visit the South, as it was rife with segregationist policies he had not experienced. After much discussion and pleading, the teen convinced his mother. As any mother would, she told him to be careful. Summer meant cotton picking time and Emmett joined all the rest of the kids picking the crop. After a long day, a group of kids, relatives, and friends went to the corner grocery store to purchase some candy with their earnings. Till was a confident soul who bragged he could talk to all people. The other kids dared him to talk to the white woman behind the counter named Carolyn Bryant. In the South at the time, Blacks did not speak to whites unless they were responding. The story said Till may have even whistled, which is something he did to cope with a speech disability he had. In this part of the country, conversation between a Black man and white woman was frowned upon. A whistle was an even worse violation of the local social norms.

Carolyn Bryant was shaken and immediately told her sister-in-law, Juanita Milam, what had happened. She said a Black male she had not seen before grabbed her, held her, propositioned her, and whistled at her. To the Black youngsters, it may have been a prank gone badly but Bryant and her sister-in-law agreed to keep the incident from their husbands, fearing their reaction. Days later, Roy Bryant heard about the incident and asked half-brother J.W. Milam to bring his pickup truck over so they could drive out to Preacher Wright's home to scare the visitor from Chicago. Milam, bigger than his half-brother, also had more of a temper.

When Bryant and Milam showed up at Wright's house in the middle of the night, it was not a social visit. They demanded to see the "boy who had done all the talking." Emmett's aunt pleaded with the men to leave the boy alone. She even offered money. The two men ignored the pleas and took the boy. They kidnapped, tortured, and murdered the boy, then dumped the body into the Tallahatchie River. Lynching was not unheard of in this part of the country. It often happened to Blacks accused of violating social norms with white women. When that happened, the victims were usually buried quickly and police conducted only a brief investigation. As a general practice, local authorities, if not complicit, wanted to move on.

Before long, a youth fishing in the Tallahatchie River at Pecan Point discovered a badly decomposed body. Lower portions of the body were sticking out of the water as a fan weighing about 100 pounds was wrapped around the neck. A local police officer said the beating was the worst he had seen in eight years on the force. His tongue protruded from his mouth and was swollen to an excessive size. His right eyeball dangled from the skull, resting on his cheek. Only two teeth remained in his mouth. Above the right eye was a hole that looked like it was caused by a bullet. His right ear had been cut nearly in half. He had a cut across his head from ear to ear. It would have been difficult to obtain identification if it had not been for one piece of evidence. Police found a ring inscribed with the initials L.T. on one finger. His father, Louis Till, bought the ring in Italy while he was in the service. Mamie Till had allowed Emmett to wear the ring to Mississippi to show his cousins.

When word that a fourteen-year-old teenager visiting from Chicago had been lynched in Mississippi, it was headline news. Many living in Mississippi had heard of similar cases and figured this case, too, would be swept under the rug. The difference with this case was that Emmett Till had been visiting relatives in the South. A courageous woman, Mamie Till, would not accept the suggestion that her son be buried in Mississippi. Although she was told the casket containing her son's body should not be opened, she ignored that suggestion. Disgusted by what she saw, she allowed photographers from *Jet* magazine to photograph Emmett's brutalized body and requested an open casket at the funeral. The photographs found their way into other newspapers and magazines across the country. Quietly, some folks in Mississippi thought that there might be justice when Till's two killers were put on trial in the fall of 1955 despite the quiet objections of prosecutor Hamilton Caldwell, who doubted an all-white jury would convict any white man accused of killing a Black who insulted a white woman. In Mississippi, such offenses would be offered immunity from prosecution.

The trial of Till's accused killers was scheduled to take place in Sumner, Mississippi in the state's delta region. At the time of the Till trial in 1955, there were 19,000 Black people living in the county and not one was registered to vote. Strict segregation ruled the day in Tallahatchie County where cotton fields stretched from horizon to horizon. There were separate schools, separate eating places, and separate restrooms. There obviously was separation of duties as well because only white men sat on juries to judge their peers accused of crimes. Some locals were concerned about how the nation would perceive Mississippi based solely on the trial. Before it started, newspapers surveyed local residents; no one expected the two defendants to be found guilty. Their attorneys went even further; they expected a speedy decision. The trial lasted a week with plenty of witnesses and the all-white, all-male jury took slightly longer than one hour to return a not guilty verdict. One juror said later, "If we hadn't stopped to drink pop, it wouldn't have taken that long."

Till's death came a little more than three months before the beginning of the Montgomery bus boycott, which many cite as the first declaration of war against Jim Crow in the South. On the same day Senator Eastland criticized the Supreme Court's *Brown* decision, a seamstress named Rosa Parks refused to give up her seat on a public bus. Days before she made her historic stand by keeping her seat, Parks attended a meeting on the Till case at Martin Luther King's Dexter Avenue Baptist Church, where the Till case was discussed. The lead organizer of the meeting, T. R. M. Howard, wanted to make all of the attendees aware of the recent acquittal of Bryant and Milam. The men admitted that they kidnapped the boy but insisted that they questioned him and released him.

At the same time, Howard told the group that two voting rights activists had been recently killed in Mississippi and a third brutally beaten. He provided gruesome details and encouraged those present to keep faith in the struggle, though it was hard to endure. There were too many examples like Till and the voting rights activists, which made Blacks nervous. Too many people were killed without any legal remedy. Till's case seemed different. The attention given to the Till and other cases helped spread the word. They had hoped for a different outcome. Instead, the two accused were acquitted by the all-white jury. Four days later, when bus driver James Blake told her to move, Rosa Parks immediately thought of Emmett Till. "Rosa Parks would tell me how she felt about Emmett, how she had thought about him on that fateful day when she took that historic stand by keeping her seat," recalled Mamie Till years later.[91]

Martin Luther King, Jr. was the pastor at Dexter Avenue Baptist Church, which hosted the Howard talk that evening. King and family had moved to Montgomery the year before when he began his time as minister at the church. Parks first met King at a NAACP meeting in November 1954. He had come to speak about the *Brown v. Board of Education* ruling. Parks' first impression was to ask why they had selected him to speak, as he looked like a young college student. Once he started to speak, though, Parks knew the answer. He was eloquent and a very polished speaker who had the ability to get the audience's attention and hold it with his presentation. As she listened, Parks became discouraged. The description of Till's gruesome murder left her angry. She knew that he wasn't the only victim of lynching, but hearing about the brutal death of a teen left a huge impact. Years of activism left her weary that maybe things would never change.

"On December 1, 1955, I had finished my day's work as a tailor's assistant in the Montgomery Fair department store and I was on my way home," recalled Parks. "There was one vacant seat on the Cleveland Avenue bus, which I took, alongside a man and two women across the aisle. There were still a few vacant seats in the white section in the front, of course. We went to the next stop without being disturbed. On the third, the front seats were occupied and this one man, a white man, was standing. The driver asked us to stand up and let him have those seats and when none of us moved at his first words, he said, 'You all make it light on yourselves and let me have those seats.' And the man who was sitting next to the window stood up and I made room for him to pass by me. The two women across the aisle stood up and moved out. When the driver saw me still sitting, he asked if I was going to stand up and I said, 'No, I'm not.' And he said, 'Well, if you don't stand up, I'm going to call the police and have you arrested.' I said, 'You may do that.' He did get off the bus and I still stayed where I was. Two policemen came on the bus. One of the policemen asked me if the bus driver had asked me to stand and I said yes. He said, 'Why don't you stand up?' And I asked him, "Why do you push us around?' He said, 'I do not know, but the law is the law and you're under arrest.'"[92]

Parks was aware of the segregation laws in the city. Per the rules, all four Black people in her row would be required to stand so that the one white man could take a seat in the middle row. She knew of the danger in not listening to the demands of the bus driver. The sight of the driver walking toward a passenger with a pistol on his hip might encourage compliance. Bus drivers in Montgomery were allowed to be armed while driving. There were numerous cases of individuals being beaten or killed on buses. "I didn't even know if I would get off that bus alive," Parks said. Further, she "was resigned to the fact that I had to express my unwillingness to be humiliated in this manner."[93] Parks' arrest set off a yearlong boycott of public buses by thousands of Blacks, organized by King. The boycott ended when the Supreme Court declared Montgomery's segregation law unconstitutional. As a result of her actions, Parks lost her seamstress job, and her family suffered harassment and threats.

In August 1957, Raymond and Rosa Parks and Rosa's mother, Leona

McCauley, moved to Detroit, Michigan, where her younger brother, Sylvester, lived. Rosa Parks' life had been threatened in Mississippi and finding work wasn't easy. Parks went to take a hostess job at the Hampton Institute's Holly Tree Inn. When promised accommodation for her husband and mother never came through, she returned to Detroit at the end of the 1958 fall semester. The protest brought national prominence to King, who was barely 27 years old at the time. In the end, the court's ruling resulted in the integration of city buses in Montgomery, Alabama and elsewhere.

"Having to take a certain section [on a bus] because of your race was humiliating," said Rosa Parks, "but having to stand up because a particular driver wanted to keep a white person from having to stand was, to my mind, most inhumane. More than seventy-five, between eighty-five and I think ninety, percent of the patronage of the buses were Black people, because more white people could own and drive their own cars than Blacks . . . Over the years, I had had my own problems with the bus drivers," continued Parks. "In fact, some did tell me not to ride their buses if I felt that I was too important to go to the back door to get on. One had evicted me from the bus in 1943, which did not cause anything more than just a passing glance."[94]

"Twice daily, for most Montgomery Blacks, the Jim Crow buses served as a constant reminder of how far toward freedom they still had to travel," wrote historian Harvard Sitkoff. "Blacks had to pay the driver at the front of the bus and then enter through the door at the rear, however inclement the weather. They had to stand in the crowded back of the bus while seats were empty in the white-only front section. They could do little to constrain a vicious bus driver, no matter how abusive or violent he became. Then, in the last week of November 1955, the Interstate Commerce Commission banned racial segregation in all facilities and vehicles engaged in interstate transportation. On the first of December, Rosa Parks said no. Could they now do less? The trend of the law seemed unmistakable. The Parks incident had unified the Black community. For a while at least perhaps . . . maybe . . . The time had come to force Montgomery to change."[95]

After being booked by the Montgomery police, Mrs. Parks called E. D. Nixon, a railroad car porter and leader in the city's Black community. He ran the local chapter of A. Phillip Randolph's Brotherhood of Sleeping Car Porters and the local branch of the NAACP. Nixon and Parks had worked together for years in the local Black community. Nixon came to bail her out. Parks said later she was not planning to protest. She said she was tired of giving in as her thoughts went to Emmett Till. The white supremacy that existed led to bus segregation, lynching, and voting rights denial. It would not bring Emmett Till or any of the others back from the dead, but it seemed like the right thing to do. Some of the others on the bus exited in search of alternate transportation. Nobody on the bus offered words of encouragement or support.

The disgusting Emmett Till story took another bad turn when the two accused murderers confessed to the killing in a paid article with *Look* magazine. In 2004, the Justice Department and the Federal Bureau of Investigation (FBI) reopened an investigation. That inquiry was prompted when the central figure in the case recanted her testimony about Till's actions. Decades later, Carolyn Bryant Donham, the woman who accused Emmett Till of making advances, admitted to Duke University history professor Timothy B. Tyson that those statements were not true. Of her accusation that Till had physically and verbally harassed her, she told Tyson, according to *Vanity Fair*: "That part's not true. Honestly, I just don't remember . . . It was 50 years ago. You tell these stories for so long that they seem true."[96] Donham's allegation that Till whistled at her has also been disputed. On the stand in 1955, however, Donham claimed Till had said something "unprintable" to her and she was "scared to death," according to *Vanity Fair*.[97] "She told me that 'Nothing that boy did could ever justify what happened to him,'" said Tyson.[98] In 2021, the case was closed without any further charges being placed.

When Parks was honored with the Congressional Gold Medal in 1999, lawmakers called her the "Mother of the Civil Rights Movement." Congressional leaders honored her for her act of civil disobedience from more than four decades earlier. "She is the mother of the civil rights movement," said Rep. Julia Carson (D-Ind.), who pushed the legislation granting the medal to Parks. "It is a celebration of Rosa Parks, who is receiving the honor while she can still see it." The praise continued. "She sat, anchored to that seat, as Dr. King said, by the accumulated indignities of the days gone by and the countless aspirations of generations yet unborn," said President Bill Clinton. He continued, "Rosa Parks said, 'I didn't get on that bus to get arrested; I got on that bus to go home.'"[99] At her funeral, more memories were shared. "When the history of this country is written," Senator Barack Obama eulogized at Rosa Parks' funeral, "when a final accounting is done, it is this small quiet woman whose name will be remembered long after the names of senators and presidents have been forgotten."[100]

"Over the years, we would share so much appreciation and so much love," said Mamie Till-Mobley, mother of Emmett Till, about her relationship with Rosa Parks. "We would share something else, too. Something that had connected us for so many years. Something that should have brought us together so many years before. It was something that had made us hug each other so tightly when we met. Rosa Parks would tell me how she felt about Emmett, how she had thought about him on that fateful day when she took that historic stand by keeping her seat."[101]

Some modern football players recall the story of Emmett Till and how it influenced their lives. DK Metcalf, who was born in 1997 in Oxford, Mississippi, and has played in the NFL since 2019, said he first learned the story of Emmett Till's 1955 death when he was in fifth grade. The killing, which happened four decades before Metcalf was born, struck a nerve with people, especially those who grew up in the same state and looked like Till. Metcalf admitted that knowledge of the case may not have been the same for everybody. "I think a lot of people don't know about Emmett Till," he said. "He got brutally beat—to death, actually—by these white men for whistling at a white woman when he was down in Mississippi. They found him a few days later in the Tallahatchie River, which is, like an hour away from me, from where I grew up."[102]

Metcalf continued, "Emmett Till is really like a backstory of how cutthroat the world is, how racism has been going on for numerous years, been going on in America. And people think it just went on in the South. No, racism is going on across the United States. I'm sheltered because I am an NFL football player—and I'm a Black man first, though. And once I take this Seahawks jersey off, once I leave this football game, then I'm a regular Black man. How are my kids going to view the world? Because I know how I view it. This is not a new problem. We should have done something a long time ago. Just bring awareness to help your kids' kids. The world needs love right now. Say his name: Emmett Till."[103]

Metcalf's words were part of a 3-minute, 42-second video produced by the NFL with images ranging from those of the Ku Klux Klan to the 2020 Black Lives Matter movement. "When people are angry at what's going on in the world, you know it's nothing new in my eyes, coming from Mississippi. I've been around it my whole life. Never experienced anything firsthand. But I know what's going on in the world. I am not blind to the fact of any of it."[104]

If not for the Till case, others may have been influenced by the lunch counter protests of the early sixties conducted by college students of the same generation as the AFL All-Stars. Joseph McNeil thought of the idea as he was traveling back to campus in North Carolina after spending winter break with his family in New York. As he rode on the bus trip beginning in the North, he said he enjoyed the same freedoms as others on the first part of the trip but that all changed at the bus station in Richmond, Virginia. He ordered a hot dog but was denied service due to his skin color. Along with friends, he hatched a plan. He discussed the trip with friends and the four young men walked into Woolworth's store in Greensboro to carry it out. The four—David Richmond, Franklin McCain, Ezell Blair, Jr. and Joseph McNeil—were students at nearby North Carolina Agricultural and Technical College. They purchased a few items in the store and sat at the lunch counter and ordered coffee and doughnuts. The waitress said she could not serve them. They offered receipts to prove that they were paying customers. They insisted to her they had made purchases that very day. The manager arrived and told them that counter service was reserved for white customers. The four men refused to leave until they received service. They stayed the rest of the day and when the store closed, they promised to return the next day.

That was the beginning of a nonviolent protest strategy that spread across the country. Jim Crow laws included a particularly strong stance against whites and Blacks eating together. These four men were about the same age as Till when they read and saw photographs of Emmett Till, who had been beaten, shot, and killed in Mississippi at fourteen. "I remember seeing the picture of him when they pulled him out of the river," said Blair. "I never will forget that. It was chilling, bone chilling."[105] Till's murder created a generation of determined civil rights activists.

The next morning when Woolworth manager C. L. Harris unlocked the doors, the A&T College students returned. The first four were joined by sixteen other students. They sat at the lunch counter and ordered food. Again, the waitress said she could not serve them. They didn't argue. Instead, they quietly sat there, opened books, and read. They were neatly dressed and did not cause any trouble. Throughout the day, other students would arrive and take the place of the early arrivals who needed to go to class. The nonviolent protest was the method chosen by these students in Greensboro to protest segregation in the South. They continued the protest throughout the week. As word spread across campus, more protestors joined in. By Wednesday, the students occupied 63 of the 66 stools. By the weekend, there weren't enough stools to accommodate the protestors.

By the end of the week, word had spread so much that young, white people showed up at Woolworth's lunch counter. They wore blue jeans and leather jackets in sharp contrast to the well-dressed protestors. Once at the scene, the white youths taunted and harassed the peaceful Black protestors. When one of them attempted to set a protestor's coat on fire, he was arrested since police were standing nearby to keep the scene under surveillance.

Similar protests sprouted across the country. *New York Times* reporter Claude Sitton covered the protests from Raleigh, North Carolina to Montgomery, Alabama. Reporter David Halberstam covered protests in Nashville, Tennessee for *The Tennessean* and the national newsmagazine *The Reporter*. As more people learned of the protests in North Carolina, other protests sprang up in other stores. The sit-ins spread to 55 cities in 13 states.[106] "The sit-ins established a crucial kind of leadership and organizing of young people," said Jeanne Theoharis, a Brooklyn College political science professor. "They mean that young people are going to be one of the major driving forces in terms of how the civil rights movement is going to unfold."[107]

The four freshmen from A&T who started the protest at Woolworth's lunch counter in Greensboro, North Carolina in February 1960 demonstrated to the world that nonviolent protest could be effective and that everyone could participate. The movement spread across the country and, by the end of 1960, store managers in Greensboro, Nashville, and several other cities opened their lunch counters to Black customers.[108] One week later, a single Black student conducted Winston-Salem's first sit-in but was joined by twenty-five others in the afternoon. After that, sit-ins were held in Charlotte, Raleigh, and Hampton, Virginia. By February 17, sixty-six people were arrested at a counter protest in Nashville. Days later, 33 more were arrested in Richmond. Before the end of the month, demonstrations took place in Virginia, Tennessee, Texas, and South Carolina. Between February 1960 and February 1962, thousands of lunch counters, and other facilities in 150 Southern cities, were integrated.[109] They culminated with the Civil Rights Act of 1964, which outlawed segregation in public places.

"The mechanics of most southern lunch counter sit-ins had become routine by 1963," said Julian Bond, chairman emeritus of the NAACP Board of Directors.

"Peaceful Black and white protestors would calmly take seats at an eating facility reserved for whites only. Where laws forbade Blacks to sit at eating facilities reserved for whites, as was true in most of the South until the Civil Rights Act of 1964 became law, the Blacks were asked to leave. If they refused, police were called. Practicing what they understood to be Gandhian nonviolence, the protestors refused to strike back if struck."[110]

Months before the protest started, Martin Luther King, Jr. announced that "a full-scale assault will be made upon discrimination and segregation in all forms... We must employ new methods of struggle, involving the masses of our people."[111] The Greensboro Four saw the impact segregation had on their generation. "As kids, we always wanted to know what water from a white water fountain tasted like," said Ezell Blair Jr. "We thought it would taste like lemonade." By the time he reached adulthood, that wonder had turned to anger.[112] The protests continued with Freedom Rides, picket lines, and the March on Washington. The Freedom Rides started in the spring of 1961 when student activists from the Congress of Racial Equality (CORE) sought a way to demonstrate opposition to the segregation on interstate buses and inside terminals. They traveled on buses from Washington, DC to Jackson, Mississippi, meeting violent opposition along the way.

Just as the lunch counter protests were a nonviolent method used by college students to express their dissatisfaction with the current segregation practices in food service, another group of similarly aged people worked to integrate Mississippi's segregated voting system in the early 1960s. CORE recruited several hundred northern college students, mostly white, to work in Mississippi during the summer. The plan was to team the college students with local Black residents in an effort to register African Americans to vote. The initiative was called Freedom Summer. Less than 7 percent of eligible Black citizens had been registered to vote in Mississippi. Local reformers had labored for years for civil rights but faced intense and often violent resistance from segregationists in the state. The Student Nonviolent Coordinating Committee (SNCC) had made some progress in Birmingham and Montgomery, but segregationists were fighting to keep things the way they were.

For nearly a century, segregation prevented most African Americans in Mississippi from voting or holding elected office. While Freedom Summer was going on, the Imperial Wizard of the Ku Klux Klan (KKK) of Mississippi drafted their own plan, which called for Klansmen in Lauderdale and Neshoba counties to enforce opposition to integration with violence and intimidation. Just one week after the first group of volunteers arrived in Oxford, three civil rights workers were reported missing in Mississippi. James Chaney, a Black Mississippian and two white northerners, Michael Schwerner and Andrew Goodman, disappeared while visiting Philadelphia, Mississippi, to investigate the burning of a church. On June 21, 1964, they were arrested for speeding. The men were taken to prison and eventually released, but several KKK members followed them out of town. Through coordination with a deputy, who pulled them over, the KKK members following them shot them in a rural area.

The disappearance of the three civil rights workers struck fear in many of the volunteers, but the plan went on as scheduled. The three men were not immediately found, and local authorities speculated that their disappearance was just a hoax carried out by activists searching for publicity. The Federal Bureau of Investigation (FBI) investigated and posters were hung across the county in post offices, banks, police stations, and courthouses. As time dragged on and the whereabouts of three civil rights workers remained unknown, many feared that they were no longer alive.

As tips continued to come into the FBI, Klansmen got nervous. Finally, on July 31, an informant known as "Mr. X" told the FBI where the bodies were buried. The property was known as Old Jolly Farm and the location was a large earthen dam. They were buried by a bulldozer that was on site building the earthen dam on the property owned by Philadelphia businessman and Klansman Olen Burrage. Finally, on August 4, a team went onto the property and guided by pilots in the air, discovered the dam. Agents used their hands and tools to dig through the red clay in an attempt to discover the bodies. By mid-afternoon, the outline of a man's body was discovered. Workers kept digging and the other two bodies were also uncovered.

The effort to register Black voters was met with extraordinary violence including murders, bombings, kidnappings, and torture. Decades after the disappearance of the civil rights workers, the state of Mississippi charged Edgar Ray Killen for his part in the crimes. A part-time Baptist minister, Killen was found guilty of three counts of manslaughter on June 21, 2005, the forty-first anniversary of the crime. The events on national news programs brought increased attention to civil rights issues. Public outrage helped spur Congress to pass the Civil Rights Act of 1964 and the Voting Rights Act of 1965. "June 1964. Over 1,000 volunteers head to Mississippi to register Black voters," wrote Doug McAdam in *Freedom Summer*.

"By August 4 people are dead, 80 beaten, 1,000 arrested, 67 churches, homes, and businesses burned or bombed." Who were the volunteers who came to the South for this risky mission? In many cases, they came from wealthy families and had attended some of the top universities in the country. By and large, they had not experienced limitations based on race, like those that they had volunteered to help. They were generally liberal and sympathetic to the cause to which they had come. Gren Whitman, one of the volunteers, said, "it was simply the most important experience of my life. It really set me on a course in my life that I am still on."[113]

Other incidents sent shock waves through communities in the South. Sunday, September 15, 1963 started like any other Sunday. Addie Mae Collins, Denise McNair, Carole Robertson, and Cynthia Wesley attended Sunday school at the 16th Street Baptist Church every Sunday morning. The girls gathered in the restroom excited about their performance with the church choir. Addie Mae, 14, and Denise, 11, were about to sing while fourteen-year-old Carole and Cynthia served as ushers. Addie Mae was helping Denise tie the sash on her dress but, before she could finish, a bomb exploded. Klansmen had planted the bomb near the ladies' restroom in the church where the four girls had gathered. The four girls died, and twenty others were injured, which sparked similar outrage as the Till murder because children were involved. As Black people attempted to live their lives and enjoy public facilities such as restaurants, hotels, restrooms, and water fountains, they felt the pushback of those insisting on maintaining what they called their Southern traditions. It was code for racism. White supremacists responded with violence to racial injustice.

The 16th Street Baptist Church, located just blocks from the city's commercial district, served as a hub of activity in the African American community. As a meeting place, social center, and lecture hall, many civil rights meetings were held there. The media regarded Birmingham as the most segregated city in the United States during this time and Reverend Fred Shuttlesworth was driven to improve the racial climate in the city. Along with King and the Southern Christian Leadership Conference, Shuttleworth designed "Project C" as a desegregation campaign featuring a series of nonviolent protests and boycotts.

On May 2, 1963, students ranging in age from eight to eighteen gathered at the church to march downtown with a goal of meeting with the mayor about segregation. After leaving the church, police met the group and many protesters were jailed. By May 10, the "Children's Crusade" ended and thousands of children and adults had been injured by fire hoses and attack dogs deployed by "Bull" Connor, Commissioner of Public Safety. Soon the church became the focus of those opposed to civil rights and desegregation, prompting the bombing by KKK members. Children being attacked by dogs and knocked down by fire hoses did not look good in the eyes of the nation.

Looking back, an eight-year-old resident of Birmingham, Alabama said her life changed forever on that day. Former Secretary of State Condoleezza Rice thought her life took a different turn when a childhood friend died in the blast. "As an 8-year-old, you don't think about terror of this kind," said Rice, who recounted her memory of the bombing and its aftermath in remarks to a gathering in Birmingham as part of the 50th anniversary of the bombing. "There was no sanctuary [growing up in Birmingham]. There was no place really safe," she said. Rice said she has a treasured photo of her friend McNair accepting a kindergarten certificate from Rice's father, who was a pastor at another church. McNair's father had taken the photo. Rice said her personal connection was not unusual. "Everyone in the Black community knew one of those girls," she said.

Rice said the events of those days left a lasting impression. She used that experience as she attempted to construct a peace agreement in the Middle East. "I told them I know what it is like for a Palestinian mother, who has to tell her child they can't go somewhere," Rice said, "and how it is for an Israeli mother, who puts her child to bed and wonders if the child will be alive in the morning."[114]

"If you were Black in Birmingham in 1963, there was no escaping the violence and no place to hide," said Rice. "What I remember from this time is the sound of bombs going off in the neighborhoods, including our own. Clearly, leaders of the movement, such as attorney Arthur Shores, were singled out. His home was bombed twice in 1963 and his neighborhood became known as 'Dynamite Hill.' But the white 'night riders' and the KKK cared little about the role you played in the struggle; they were content to terrify any Black family they could. I can remember coming home from my grandparents one night. We had just gotten out of the car when we heard a loud blast down the street. In Birmingham that spring, no one had to think twice: a bomb had exploded in the neighborhood."[115]

Rice continued, "The images of [Birmingham Public Safety Commissioner] Bull Connor's dogs and fire hoses confronting unarmed, peaceful protesters in Kelly Ingram Park, located in downtown Birmingham directly across from 16th

Street Baptist Church, are some of the most indelible in American history. During that long, hot summer of 1963, Bull Connor even brought 'irregulars' from the backwoods of Alabama to do the dirty work that even the police would not do. My folks and I would watch them streaming down Sixth Avenue in pickup trucks adorned with confederate flags. Trying to intimidate us, they hung out of the windows and brandished sawed-off shotguns. The protestors met even these goons with dignity and reserve and refused to be provoked."[116]

Rice lived in Birmingham during those violent years when Bull Connor had his troops attack peaceful protestors, some of whom were children. "The only break from segregation came when we left Birmingham, which tended to be in the summer," recalled Rice. "When we would visit my grandmother and Aunt Theresa in Baton Rouge, we took the train, which provided integrated facilities. We would board the Silver Comet at about five in the evening in Birmingham, eat in the dining car, and sleep overnight in a bedroom berth. I can still taste the pudding served in the heavy silver ice cream cups and feel the excitement of getting into bed as the train rushed along the tracks. But when we returned to Birmingham, the only place to eat out was A.G. Gaston's restaurant and Mother didn't like to eat there because it was next door to a funeral home."[117] Those family trips formed the memories of her youth. "Once in a while we'd travel to Atlanta, about 150 miles away where there was a wider variety of Black restaurants and a nice movie theater. I can remember seeing Jerry Lewis' *The Nutty Professor*, on one such occasion, being treated to dinner at Pasquale's and then driving home since there was really no place to stay."[118]

When her father decided to attend graduate school, he encountered segregation. The University of Alabama was not an option because Blacks were not allowed. He soon learned that New York University had a good program, and he decided to drive the family to New York City. "The problem was that there was nowhere for Blacks to stay or eat until you reached Washington, DC. The only option was a picnic lunch of fried chicken, pork chops, bread, and potato chips to eat in the car. Mother would get up very early and prepare the feast. We'd leave before daylight, hoping to make it out of the deepest South before dark. This was in the days before the interstate highway system was completed and for a Black family some of the roads in Georgia and South Carolina could be pretty scary. When we reached Washington, DC, we were all excited to be staying in a new chain of hotels called Holiday Inn. The rooms were hardly luxurious, but they were clean and it was a relief to have a bathroom. My parents, particularly my mother, were not too keen to stop at the gas station restrooms for 'colored' because they were almost always putrid and foul smelling. If we couldn't find a reasonably clean bathroom when nature called, we just, shall I say, went in nature."[119]

Rice had been in her father's church the morning of the bombing. "Services hadn't yet begun at Westminster that Sunday, but the choir, elders, and ushers were already in the sanctuary," said Rice of the day the 16th Street Church was bombed. "I was there with my mother as she warmed up the organ. All of a sudden there was a thud and a shudder. The distance between the two churches is about two miles as the crow flies, but it felt like the trouble was next door. After what seemed like hours but was probably only a few minutes, someone called the church to say that 16th Street Baptist had been bombed. No one knew how many other churches might have been targeted. My father didn't try to conduct the service but somehow thought it was safer if people remained together in the church."[120]

Of the days after the bombing, Rice said, "The outrage would settle on our community, but at first we were just sad. Birmingham isn't that big and everyone knew at least one of those little girls. This was a deeply personal tragedy. Cynthia and Denise were from the neighborhood. I knew Denise best; though she was older, we would still play with dolls together. Her father was our milkman and a part-time photographer who worked at everyone's birthday parties and weddings. Denise had been a student in my father's first kindergarten. My uncle had been Addie Mae Collins' teacher and he cried like a baby when he saw her picture on the news and again when he saw her empty chair the next day."[121]

Rice went on to say, "The homegrown terrorism against Birmingham's children seemed finally to rock the nation's conscience. On June 11, President John F. Kennedy had delivered a historic address calling for an end to segregation and introduced a legislative package in Congress to do so. The proposed Civil Rights Act sought to atone for the systematic prejudice and oppression that characterized the South by banning segregation in public accommodations and allowing the federal government to join in state lawsuits to integrate public schools. Although this effort had begun months earlier, we believed the tumultuous summer of 1963—culminating in the horrific deaths of four little girls at the hands of violent extremists—would give the young president greater impetus to act."[122]

By the summer of 1964, the Civil Rights Act passed and segregation in public spaces was outlawed. "But it didn't matter," said Rice. "A couple of days later, my father said, 'Let's go out to dinner.' We got dressed up and went to a relatively new hotel about ten minutes from our house. We walked in and people literally looked up and stopped eating. But in a few minutes, perhaps recognizing that the law had changed, they went back to eating and we were served without incident. A few days after that, however, we went to a drive-through hamburger stand called Jack's. It was nighttime and as I bit into my hamburger, I told my parents that something tasted funny. Daddy turned on the car light. The bun was filled with onions: nothing else, just onions."[123]

Due to the desegregation campaign organized by Reverend Shuttlesworth, the city agreed to desegregate lunch counters, restrooms, drinking fountains, and fitting rooms. Stores hired African American clerks and jailed demonstrators were released. Not everyone agreed with the changes, and this prompted violence. A bomb exploded at the Gaston Motel where Martin Luther King, Jr. had been staying and another damaged his brother A. D. King's home. NAACP attorney Arthur Shores' house was firebombed. After Governor George Wallace deployed the National Guard to stop the desegregation of public schools, President John Kennedy seized control.

The same day as the church bombing, two boys—16-year-old Johnny Robinson and 13-year-old Virgil Ware—were murdered in Birmingham in racially motivated crimes. Robinson was shot in the back in an alley by a white police office, Jack Parker. Ware was shot off the handlebars of a bike by two white teenagers. Ware's murderers were convicted but a grand jury refused to bring charges against the police officer.[124] The bombing occurred just eighteen days after the 1963 March on Washington for Jobs and Freedom.

Racism came in many forms as Rice grew up in Alabama. "I'm five years old and going to see Santa Claus," she recalled. "Santa Claus is taking all the little white kids and putting them on his knee while holding the Black kids at arm's length. I remember thinking many years later: 'What a strange way to experience racism, from Santa Claus. Racism did infuse everything in life. But it also did not stop you from succeeding. It made you very tough. You learned to deal with tough circumstances."[125]

CHAPTER FIVE

No Blacks Allowed

Athletes viewed the plights of Emmett Till and Rosa Parks from a distance. They heard about entertainers having difficulty traveling and experienced similar experiences as they moved about; many may have had personal experiences with discrimination as integration came slowly. Most sports fans know the story of how Jackie Robinson broke baseball's color barrier. Every year on April 15, professional baseball teams honor Robinson on the anniversary of his major league debut by wearing his number: 42. Fewer people probably know that professional football integrated one year before baseball when four Black athletes joined professional teams. The Los Angeles Rams signed Kenny Washington and Woody Strode.[126] Washington signed his contract March 21, 1946, and became the first Black professional football player since the 1933 season ended. Their collegiate careers were long over, and neither was in his prime. The same year, the Cleveland Browns of the All-America Football Conference (AAFC) signed Marion Motley and Bill Willis. Over the years leading up to the merger with the NFL, the AAFC signed more Blacks than NFL teams. Both Motley and Willis were enshrined in the Pro Football Hall of Fame after their careers ended.

The Rams announced after the Washington signing that the star player would need surgery on both knees, which would be the fourth and fifth of his career. "A torn cartilage will be removed from the left knee and a growth from the right knee," according to an Associated Press story on April 11, 1946.[127] "They didn't let him in the football pros until he had a limp and needed a hearing aide," wrote *Los Angeles Times* columnist Jim Murray, with some exaggeration to make a point.[128] There was talk after the College All-Star Game that George Halas of the Chicago Bears was attempting to gain league approval to sign Washington, who stayed in the city for several days. What happened in 1940? "George Halas kept me around for a month trying to figure out how to get me in the league," recalled Washington. "I left before he suggested I go to Poland first."[129] Most historians blame Washington team owner George Preston Marshall as the primary enforcer of the Black blockade. "(Marshall) basically said you can't play in Washington with Black players," said Jim Rooney, the grandson of Steelers founder and owner Art Rooney. "My grandfather, new in the league, sort of followed the rule there, which he has admitted was the biggest mistake in his life. [Art Rooney] lived the life he lived and pushed hard in his own way, but he had a personality that was accommodating to a certain degree."[130]

Marshall marketed his squad as the "team of the South" and racial feelings were strong in the day. He even played "Dixie" at every home game. "Dixie" originated during minstrel shows of the 1850s but was adopted as a de facto anthem of the Confederacy. Not only did he refuse to play any minorities on his team, but he also did not want to see them on the field at all and risk alienating his customers. "His [Marshall's] strategy and his rationalization was that this was the only team in the South," said Len Shapiro of *The Washington Post*. "He had his own radio network all the way down to Florida that would carry his games. He would not integrate his team because he felt it would hurt him with his fan base in the South and even in Washington, which was segregated in the 1930s, '40s and '50s."[131] Not all historians agree that one man—Marshall—deserves all the blame. "There's a concerted effort to blame it on George Preston Marshall, that he forced the other teams to get rid of African Americans," said Damion Thomas, curator of sports at the Smithsonian National Museum of African American History and Culture. "But I think he's used as the scapegoat in many ways. I can't attribute it just to George Preston Marshall. The NFL grew out of the working class and some of the attempts to keep African Americans out of those industries in the 1920s and 1930s show up in the sports arena. I don't think those two things are separated."[132]

The Chicago Bears missed an opportunity. Bob Waterfield, an All-American and solid professional quarterback, had high praise for Washington. "Kenny was the best football player I ever saw in my life and that includes everybody I ever knew," said Waterfield. "He is also a great gentleman. If he had come into the National Football League directly from UCLA, he would have been, in my opinion, the best the NFL has ever seen."[133] Former Rams coach Bob Snyder agreed. "Kenny would have been the greatest player of all time," he said, "and that includes Thorpe, Nagurski, Nevers, and the rest if he had played in the National League as soon as he got out of college in 1939."[134]

The Rams are given a lot of credit for breaking the Black ban, but they should not receive applause for their dealings with Woody Strode. They nearly did not sign him because he was married to a Hawaiian woman named Luana. At the time, Hawaii had not gained statehood, so his wife was considered a foreigner, and interracial marriage was not accepted by a large segment of American society. "I had the ability to play in the NFL, but the Rams weren't concerned with that," Strode said. "They spoke badly of my marriage to a Hawaiian and I think if they had their choice, they would have selected somebody else. There weren't really glad to have me, so I spent considerable time sitting on the bench, collecting my $350 a week." He did not last long with the Rams; he was released before his second season even began. "It's not your ability," Washington told his friend. "It's your lifestyle. [Rams owner] Dan Reeves does not approve your marriage to Luana." Strode was direct in his assessment. "Integrating the NFL was the low point in my life," Strode told *Sports Illustrated* in an unpublished interview before he died. "There was nothing nice about it. History doesn't know who we are. Kenny [Washington] was one of the greatest backs in the history of the game and kids today have no idea who he is . . . If I have to integrate heaven, I don't want to go."[135]

The integration of pro football was much less celebrated than Robinson's historic breakthrough on the baseball diamond. At the time, baseball was considered the "national pastime" and received much more attention than football. By 1959, Black players accounted for only 12 percent of NFL rosters, according to Sean Lahman of *The Pro Football Historical Abstract*. "Initially, NFL teams were much quicker to integrate than their baseball brethren," wrote Lahman. "By 1950, thirty-three African American players had participated in the NFL, compared to just twelve in Major League Baseball. By 1952, eleven of the NFL's twelve teams had integrated (the Redskins were the lone holdout), while just six of baseball's sixteen clubs had broken their color barriers."[136]

In the post-World War II era, athletes traveling the country encountered racism much like Black entertainers faced. They were banned from eating in restaurants and lodging in many parts of the country, especially in the South. They generally could not stay in the team hotel, nor join the team meetings held there. In some cases, teams left the Black players home rather than face the issues traveling with the team in the South. Worse yet, if a Black player complained about the treatment received, he would be traded, released and, in some cases, blackballed from the league. There are six examples of athletes who faced difficulties attempting to play football during the late forties through the early sixties.

BOB MANN

A native of New Bern, North Carolina, Bob Mann played college football at Hampton Institute and the University of Michigan. His college playing career was interrupted by his Navy service during World War II. He was not selected in the 1948 NFL draft and signed a free agent contract with the Detroit Lions and later played for the Green Bay Packers. He has been recognized as the first Black player on both of those clubs, although Packers' team historian Cliff Christl noted that Walt Jean, who was of African American descent on his father's side, played in 19 games for the Packers in 1925 and 1926.[137] Bob Mann and Mel Groomes were the first two Blacks to play for the Detroit Lions in 1948, two years after pro football desegregated after 13 years of being an all-white league.

In his second season, Mann finished second in the NFL in catches, with 66, to Tom Fears of the Rams at 77 and led the league in receiving yards with 1,014 to Fears' 1,013. You might think that level of production would put a player in line for a pay increase, not a decrease. Despite his productive performance, Mann was asked to take a pay cut from $7,500 to $6,000 and he became a holdout when the Lions' summer practice began. When he refused to take a pay cut, he was traded to the New York Yanks in August 1950. The Lions had traded fullback Camp Wilson to the Yanks for future Hall of Fame quarterback Bobby Layne. Wilson refused to report and Mann was substituted. The Yanks released Mann three weeks later. When he was released, he claimed the NFL was blackballing him. Owners attempted to restructure salaries in 1950 because the AAFC merged with the NFL. This reduced competition and NFL teams attempted pay reductions. Without two competing leagues for players, there was no pressure to maintain player salaries.

In a series of moves, Mann lost his offseason job at Goebel, was traded from the Lions, and released from the Yanks. When people asked Mann about being let go by the Lions and then by the Yanks, with no other teams picking him up, he claimed he must have been blackballed out of the league. In response, Goebel President Edwin Anderson said that teams "want something more from an end than pass catching ability." Curiously, Anderson had ties to Goebel and the Lions. Mann did not make the team due to his "inability to block," according to Anderson. Mann was perplexed. "I must have been blackballed," said Mann. "It just doesn't make sense that I'm suddenly not good to make a single team in the league... Detroit sent me to the New York Yanks in payment for Bobby Layne, but I think the cards were already stacked against my continuing in pro football."

NFL Commissioner Bert Bell said that he never heard any owner describe Mann as "undesirable" and that there wasn't anything preventing him from catching on with another team. "When the Yanks asked waivers on Mann, twelve other teams could have picked him up, or he could have sold himself to any one of the twelve just as many other players have done."[138] He became the first Black player to play for the Packers when he signed on November 25, 1950, the day before a game with the 49ers at City Stadium. When he arrived in Green Bay, the city was primarily white. According to Mann, the only two Blacks in the city at the time were a porter for the Hotel Northland and a cook for the railroad. Art Daley, who covered the Packers for decades, recalled Mann's relationship with teammate Dick Afflis, a white guard who became better known as pro wrestler Dick the Bruiser. Daley said the Packers were staying at a Baltimore hotel that did not allow any Black guests. Mann was forced to go to another hotel; Mann was joined by Afflis. "They walked out of the hotel together and got outside and called a cab," said Daley. "The cab came up and the driver said, 'I can't take him because he's Black.' Afflis grabbed the cab driver by the shirt and he said, 'You take him where he wants to go.'"[139]

When Mann was named an honorary captain at a 1997 Packers game at Lambeau Field, he told the *Green Bay Press-Gazette* he did not have any problems in town. "Everyone treated me well," he said.[140] It was a different story when the team traveled to play games on the road. Daley said hotels in the South had restrictions back then but no such rules existed in Green Bay. "We had a problem going South," agreed Mann. "We went to New Orleans and played the Eagles and we had to stay in a private home. The lady was the best cook in the world. Boy, could she really cook. That lady cooked all those New Orleans dishes. One of them, I can't remember the name of it, it was baked fish and rice and it was just delicious. And the gumbo and the deviled crabs and fried oysters—just delicious. If you had to miss something, that's the way to miss it, I guess. We made the best of a bad situation. We should have been staying with the team, but it just ended up not being as negative as it could have been."[141]

Mann's family said that the integration of the game was difficult during those early years. "You might go to schools, or you might go to parties where there aren't many minorities, but to literally be the only one playing, the only one in town, I think that's a huge responsibility," said Marilyn Matthews, Bob Mann's daughter. "Those were indignities and injustices that he said were just politics, that he just had to deal with it and move forward because he was passionate about football and he was making a difference for people out there, the rest of America who was watching him."[142] After his playing career was over, Mann received a law degree from Detroit College of Law and went into private practice. "I went to law school when I got to be about 40 because I went to visit a friend of mine, a judge," recalled Mann. "I was watching the proceedings and I thought I could do that and do it as well as he could. I met and talked with him in the judge's chambers and he told me about law school and he sounded like he knew what he was talking about. It looked like something I could do and then it became something I wanted to do so I decided to go to law school."[143]

Eddie Macon

Eddie Macon ran track in high school and was drafted into the military during World War II. After the war, he joined the University of the Pacific track team. Coach Larry Siemering convinced him to join the Pacific football team, where he became the first Black player. On New Year's Day 1952, Macon became the first African American to play in the Sun Bowl in El Paso, Texas. Although he was the only Black player when he joined the squad, he said two more joined while he played there. Overall, there were only about a half dozen Black students at the school, he recalled. After college, he became the first African American to play for the Bears after Chicago drafted him in the second round (20th overall selection) of the 1952 NFL Draft. George Taliaferro had been a Bears draft choice in 1949, but he decided to play in the All-America Football Conference. When Macon arrived in Chicago, he immediately became the fastest Bear on the roster. He had been timed at 9.7 seconds for 100 yards; 21.2 seconds for 220 yards and 46.9 seconds in the 440.[144] Macon just missed making the U.S. Olympic team when he finished fourth in the 400-meter during the trials.

"I stayed at the YMCA off Wabash Avenue in Chicago when I played for the Bears because I couldn't afford to live anywhere else," said Macon. "It cost me $5 a week. Every week when I got my check, I sent most of my pay home to my wife and kids and kept a little for myself to live on. In 1952, I was the only Black player on the Bears and then the next year they brought Billy Anderson and Willie Thrower in and there were three of us." Emerson Cole also played one game for the Bears late in 1952. "I hardly had any social life at all," continued Macon. "The other players all lived on the North Side and I lived on the South Side. I used to take the tram up to Wrigley Field and then after the game or the practice was over, I'd take it back to the YMCA. The only thing I used to do was go to a little jazz club on State Street and get a whiskey sour for 45 cents. I'd sip on it for a couple of hours and talk a lot of talk and listen to the bands that played there. Then I'd go home to my humble little abode at the YMCA."[145]

Macon recalled, "After I played with the Bears for a couple of years, I had the chance to go to Canada to play for the Calgary Stampeders and my old college coach Larry Siemering. In the end, it cost me a lot of money. At first, I got more money in Calgary than I made playing with the Bears, but George Halas thought I was a traitor. He sued me and the Stampeders and I basically was blackballed out of the NFL. To show you Halas's power, I also didn't play for two years in Canada because the Hamilton Tiger-Cats were trying to contact me back here in the States and the Bears wouldn't furnish them with contact information. They finally got hold of me in 1957 and I played in Canada for three more years. There were other players that had gone to Canada, like my old college teammate Eddie LeBaron. However, Eddie was white, as were the other former NFL players who went to Canada and they were allowed to return to the NFL and play. I contacted every team in the league and none of them got back to me. Even though I was the first Black Chicago Bear, I have never received any type of invitation to any year reunions, so to me the blackball is still in place. I thought about suing the Bears and the NFL back in 1955, but the civil rights movement was just getting into full swing and I could never get anybody to really represent me. We did pretty well in Hamilton and played for three Grey Cup titles, winning one."[146]

At the time, Canadian teams had a limit of only six Americans per team and players would go back and forth between the United States and Canada. Players from the NFL like Eddie LeBaron returned to their NFL teams after one season. When Macon attempted to return, he could not find an opportunity. He talked to Tony and Vic Morabito, owners of the San Francisco 49ers and they said they needed to talk to Halas first. Macon said they never called back. It was the same story when he heard the Browns and Redskins were interested. Neither opportunity went anywhere. Macon quickly learned that he was being blocked from the NFL, after leaving for one year to play for his former college coach.

"I talked to Halas's grandson once, but I never got an explanation about why his grandfather did what he did. I also asked him why I never got invitations to any of the reunions or other affairs the Bears have and he wrote and told me he would make sure I got invited. You know what? Halas's mojo is still working, the blackball is still in place, because I have still never gotten an invitation of any kind from the Chicago Bears... A lot of people advised me to sue Halas and the NFL, but I never could because you have to have money to fight a case like that," said Macon. "This was when the civil rights movement had started and everybody was talking about civil rights, but I never could find anybody who wasn't asking for a lot of money up front. I asked people to take the case and we would split whatever money we won but nobody would."[147]

Macon continued, "Canada was okay. Canadians like to think they are more liberal when it comes to race but, like I said, I've never had a day where I didn't know I was Black. When you're Black, you're Black and that's it. When I lived in Calgary, Blacks were treated the same as anywhere else I had been. As a matter of fact, if there were 140,000 people there, I'd say 100,000 of them were Americans. Oil was big and there were a lot of Oklahoma oil people in Calgary. Hamilton wasn't much different as far as race. Okay, but nothing special."[148] His teams enjoyed success on the field. "We had a lot of success in Hamilton," said Macon. "I enjoyed playing and we played in the Grey Cup all three years I was there. We won one and lost the other two. I was 30 years old when I first got there and I'd been out of football for two years, so it was tough, but I played well. I feel I could've been playing in the NFL if they had given me a chance. That's why I say going up there cost me a lot of money. Now you have collective bargaining and free agency and it's harder for them to get away with that kind of thing."[149]

"In 1960, the new AFL was looking for players and the Raiders came to Stockton, my hometown, worked me out, and signed me. I am proud to have been an original AFLer. I played defensive back and intercepted nine passes and made some All-Pro teams. After that first season, though, I had had enough. When the Raiders wanted to go with some younger players and try and help me catch on with another team, that was enough. I was thirty-four years old, so I went back to Stockton."[150] Macon left football and returned to work on the docks doing longshore work, a job he had done all the while he played football.

HENRY FORD

Henry Ford was born in 1931 in Homestead, Pennsylvania, which was a poor, Black community situated off the Monongahela River southeast of downtown Pittsburgh. With his mother and three sisters, he lived for many years in a two-room house with 15 other residents. The house had no running water, and the only toilet was in the rat-infested cellar. Ford didn't know his father growing up. Ford earned the nickname "Model T" early in his athletic career, based on his famous last name. At Schenley High School, Ford gained recognition as the quarterback and captain of the school's undefeated 1950 city championship team. He earned All City, All State, and All-American awards while in high school. The University of Pittsburgh offered a four-year athletic scholarship and Ford, eager to prove he could play with the best, quickly accepted. Although he was a skilled quarterback, he played defensive back primarily for the Panthers, who were not ready for a Black signal-caller. He did see limited action at quarterback, which is why some reports call him the first Black quarterback at Pittsburgh.

"When we went on the road, the Black players were separated from the rest of the team," he said of his playing time at the University of Pittsburgh. "There were times when I was ready to quit school, but instead I decided that I just had to step it up. I tried to figure out how I was going to get through it. It wasn't easy, but I did. It was the same thing in the pros. It was even like that after I got out of football. I majored in business administration and they just weren't hiring Blacks into marketing and sales jobs in the steel mills or the banks, and I couldn't get a job. I went to Duquesne Beer and couldn't get a job. I went to an interview at a company and all we talked about was my playing football with the Cleveland Browns and the Pittsburgh Steelers. It was rough . . . Probably the most memorable experience of that type at Pitt was when we went to Florida to play Miami," Ford continued. "There were four Blacks on the team—me, Bobby Epps, Chester Rice, and Bill

Adams. Tom Hamilton, who was the coach then, called the four of us to the back of the plane and started talking about segregation and stuff. He said, 'We're going into the South and you know how the South is, so we had to make special arrangements for you boys. You'll be staying at the Lord Calvert Hotel.' The coaches and the white players stayed at another hotel and that's where the team meetings were and we weren't even allowed to go to their hotel for the meetings."[151]

After four years at the University of Pittsburgh, the Cleveland Browns drafted Ford in the ninth round (109th overall selection) of the 1955 draft. The Browns won the NFL Championship that season, beating the Los Angeles Rams 38-14. After that one season in Cleveland, Ford was traded to Pittsburgh and played for the Steelers during the 1956-1957 seasons. Just as his high school and college teams had done, the Steelers trained in Ligonier, a white, upper class, mostly Republican town. It was on his way to training camp that he first spotted a girl he wanted to meet. He found out later her name was Rochelle Shamey. He asked the bus driver to stop, but the driver refused. He eventually made his way back to the spot and she was still there. At first, he could not believe his good fortune until he got close and realized she was not Black. At the time, interracial marriages were illegal and would be for another couple decades. Relationships between Blacks and whites were strongly discouraged.

Steelers management discovered the relationship and delivered the ultimatum: choose professional football or dating a white girl. They ordered Ford to stop dating Rochelle and Ford insisted his professional life was separate from his personal life. Forced to make a decision, however, Ford chose Rochelle. They married in 1960, which was a time when interracial marriage still wasn't legal across the country. The Supreme Court would made it legal in 1967.

After the relationship became known, the Steelers told Ford not to pack for the next game as he would not travel with the team to Minneapolis. When the rest of the team returned from the game, his career was over. "As to why I was cut, I know why," said Henry Ford. "It's because of my love for Rochelle. Me loving her and her returning my love, that was apparently too much for Steelers management. I thought my world was coming to an end. Being kicked off the team for something that had nothing to do with football or how I played the game caused me a lot of emotional trauma. Rochelle, too. But we believed our love and commitment would outlast the pain we felt, so we stayed together and from then on, I was blackballed.

Nobody called. No question about it, I was blackballed. Eventually I got a call from somebody in Arizona to come out there and coach and play quarterback for a semipro team called the Tucson Cowboys. A lot of ex-NFL players went out there and played. It was a good league, we had a lot of good players, but after two years that was it for me as far as playing football. I coached high school football here in California for many years, but that year in Arizona was it for me as a player."[152]

Milt Campbell

Sports Illustrated once called Campbell "the greatest athlete you never knew." That is a surprising title because he earned a silver medal in the decathlon at the 1952 Helsinki Olympics when he was only a high school senior. He returned four years later and won gold in Melbourne, establishing a new Olympic record and becoming the first African American to win gold in the decathlon in a summer Olympiad. Olympic filmmaker Bud Greenspan called Campbell "the greatest athlete who ever lived." Part of the issue was the era in which Campbell won the decathlon medal. The Olympics did not receive the television coverage that the games receive today, reducing familiarity with athletes. Not only would Campbell have benefited from another era, but he was also a man of another era. He alienated some people with his outspokenness about racial discrimination.

Campbell went to Indiana University on a football scholarship, where he put his name into the record book before he hung up his cleats. When he got a "D" in physiology, he was ruled ineligible and he enlisted in the Navy during the Korean War, although his service never got any further than Catalina. "I was a watch officer on the U.S.S. Neversail," he said with a big laugh. "We guarded San Diego." That service time—with the great job—enabled Campbell to put extensive time into decathlon training. "I was able to work out 7 1/2 to 8 hours a day," he admitted.[153] By the time the 1956 Melbourne games came around, he was fully trained. He bested Rafer Johnson at the games; Johnson was the world record holder at the time. He missed a world record by a mere 48 points. Campbell beat Johnson in seven of the ten events on the way to the gold medal. Johnson would return four years later and snatch the gold for himself. After winning the gold medal, Campbell turned his attention to professional football. Campbell, who stood six-foot-three and weighed about 220 pounds, spent 1957 with the Cleveland Browns. On any other team, Campbell may have been a feature back on offense. But the Browns had Jim Brown, who would go on to be one of the league's all-time best running backs. His stay with the Browns only lasted one year and he went to Canada where he played eight seasons for the Hamilton Tiger-Cats, Toronto Argonauts, and Montreal Alouettes.

He strongly believes that his NFL career ended due to racism when the Browns found out he had married a white woman. "I found someone I was in love with and she with me," he said. "Nothing you, or anyone else, was going to say was going to change me."[154] His marriage to the former Barbara Mount of Portland, Oregon lasted 25 years and produced three children until an amicable divorce. "Paul Brown called me into his office and said, 'What did you get married for?'" recalled Campbell decades later. "I looked him in the eye and said, 'Two reasons. Number one, I got married for the same reason you got married, I presume. And number two, that's not a question you want to be asking.' The next day, I got a notice to come to the office, where they handed me a letter saying my services would no longer be needed. When I got there, I waited a half day in Paul Brown's office to talk with him, but he didn't have the courage to come see me. And just like that, I was blackballed out of the league."[155]

He insisted without hesitation, "I was blacklisted because I had an interracial marriage. There's no other interpretation to put on it. I ran well, I blocked well, I was understudy to Jim Brown, I made him better by being there and he was my roommate. I was the world's greatest athlete by definition. I was everything they could want. What explanation would you have for cutting me?"[156]

WALTER BEACH

Walter Beach III was born on January 31, 1933, in Pontiac, Michigan, about 20 miles northwest of Detroit. In recalling his childhood, "Pontiac was Mississippi in the North," said Beach. "Segregated, there were five movie [theaters]. My father never went to the movies because he said he refused to go to a movie where he had to sit in the balcony and sit in the back and go up the back stairs and pay for that . . . As a kid, you know, I loved the movies . . . I was the age where I'd pull for the cowboys and hope that the Indians fail. But that was before I became conscious. I didn't recognize that I was an Indian . . . [It] was clear lines. In Pontiac, once you crossed Orchard Lake to come to the west side, you were in the white neighborhood. My junior high school, Washington Junior High School, was in an all-white community. Of course, we had to go to that school, but we could only go down one street . . . So, it was very segregated, so I grew up in that and I got all of my strength out of that from my grandmother and my mother and father and the community."[157]

At Pontiac Central High School, Beach lettered in football, basketball, and track. He also played baseball for the American Legion. After high school, Beach entered the Air Force as a cryptographic operator, enciphering and deciphering messages. After his military service, Michigan and Michigan State recruited him to play football. His mother was impressed with Coach Bill Kelly of Central Michigan so Beach went there. After his final year, he was selected to play in the College All-Star game in 1960. Beach brought good speed to the game, covering 100 yards in 9.6 seconds while at Central Michigan. The New York Giants drafted him in 1959, but he signed with the Hamilton Tiger-Cats of the Canadian Football League instead. He was released from that contract when he left to play in the College All-Star game. Beach then went to camp with the New York Giants but was released during training camp. He signed with the Boston Patriots of the American Football League and played mostly offense during his first season; in 1961, he switched to defense. He played in 12 games, starting 10 games at right cornerback. He expected to return to the Patriots in 1962, but an incident derailed those plans, and he was released from the team.

Why was Beach released from the Patriots? Even though the AFL was considered more liberal than the NFL, both leagues experienced Jim Crow segregation as far as hotel accommodations were concerned when they traveled South. Military barracks had integrated by then, but in pro football in the 1950s and 1960s, the white players would stay separately from the Blacks. In August of 1962, the Patriots were scheduled to play an exhibition game in New Orleans against the Oilers. Coach Mike Holovak posted separate itineraries early in the week prior to the game. The white players were staying at a hotel near the practice facility in New Orleans, while the Black players were sent to a hotel in the Black part of the city. When Beach presented the view he said was shared by all of the Black Patriot players—Rommie Loudd, Ron Burton, Houston Antwine, LeRoy Moore, Clyde Washington, and Larry Garron—he was labeled a troublemaker and released. Beach sat out the 1962 season before a friend, Cleveland Browns defensive back Jim Shorter, told him to contact the Browns about playing for the team. He did so and was sent a contract.

Beach signed the contract and made the team. He played in only one regular season game. The next season was Beach's best. But it nearly didn't happen.

While in Cleveland, Beach struck up a friendship with Hall of Fame running back Jim Brown. Browns' owner Art Modell explicitly told Beach that the team took a chance on him when they signed him. It sounded like a warning that management would be watching him carefully. "I knew racism was involved," said Beach. "I eventually was blackballed by the Browns too, but it took them a while. The only reason I stuck around so long was I had Jim Brown on my side. Art Modell may still have been angry with me about the plane ride the season before. On a flight home in 1963 at the end of the season, I was reading a book titled *Message to the Black Man in America*, by Elijah Muhammad. Art Modell saw me reading and he said, 'I don't want you reading that book.' I pretty much ignored him and kept on reading. When he passed by again a while later, Modell repeated, 'I thought I told you, I don't want you reading that book.' I told him, 'I thought you were joking. A man cannot tell another man what to read. I play football. I am under contract to play football, but no one can tell me what to read.'"[158]

During training camp in 1964, Beach was called into a meeting with Modell and the Browns coaches. He was told he was being released. Later, Jim Brown came to the dormitory to get Beach for practice. Beach told him he was cut. Brown told him to stay there in the room. A few minutes later, he returned and told Beach to get ready for practice. He was back on the team. Beach said he never received an explanation for the release or return. Brown said he told Modell that Beach was one of the best cornerbacks on the team and the team was not as good without him.

The following season (1965), Beach played in ten regular season games, starting in six. The Browns returned to the championship game but lost to the Green Bay Packers, 23-12. Beach intercepted one Bart Starr pass in the game. He had one interception in each of the championship games he played. He played in five games and started four in 1966, his last in the league. After Jim Brown retired in 1965, Beach figured he would not last long with the Browns. He played five games in 1966 and was cut. He never played again. "I was a threat to them," he said. "I was one of those who stood up against racism and they blackballed me." Beach sued the NFL, claiming that he should have been allowed to play for another team, extending his career. He won the case and had years of service added to his career, which helped his pension.

In 1967, Beach was among the group of African American athletes who met with Muhammad Ali after the boxer announced he refused to be drafted into the military and serve in Vietnam. The other football players were Jim Brown, Jim Shorter, Bobby Mitchell, Sid Williams, Willie Davis, and John Wooten. "We were men coming together around a moral and ethical issue," recalled Beach. "No one paid us any money to travel from all over the country to come together in Cleveland and basically put our careers in jeopardy by taking a controversial stand. We just did it."[159] Later, Beach attended Yale Law School and in 2014 wrote a memoir titled *Consider This*.

ART POWELL

Art Powell was released by the Philadelphia Eagles after a promising rookie season as a defensive back and kick returner. Powell said he understood the reason why he was released. He said he refused to accept the social norms of the Jim Crow South. "The challenges before me were social challenges," he said. "I chose to challenge then, while others chose not to. I made a lot of people angry. All I wanted to do was be a football player. The rest of this stuff was dumped in my lap."[160] The incident that ended Powell's Eagles career was a scheduled exhibition game in August 1960 in Norfolk, Virginia against the Washington Redskins. "We were told that colored players would not be allowed to stay with the rest of the team at the hotel," said Powell. "I chose not to play. The other African American players [Tim Brown, Ted Dean, and Clarence Peaks] said they were not going to play either—but they did. I was the one that ended up being cut."

The Eagles told the media that Powell was released because he was overweight and that his play against the Rams and the 49ers in preseason games was subpar. Eagles coach Buck Shaw said the decision was based on performance, not promise, but the media was skeptical. Bill Wallace of *The New York Times* wrote, "Just how or why this fellow, who ran a kickoff back 95 yards against the Giants last year, was waived out of the National League and no other club made a claim on his services is mysterious."[161] In fact, the reporter was stating how performance was not the reason for Powell's dismissal.

He signed to play with the New York Titans of the rival American Football League. "I get to New York and I'm just there to play football and mind my own business," he said. "But while I'm there they schedule a game in Greenville, South

Carolina. We get to the airport and it's my first experience with white and colored water fountains. The general manager came up to me and said I'm in charge of the Black athletes and that we'll be going somewhere else. The white players took a bus to the hotel and they sent us off to the boonies. If they were making a movie, this would have been the place—hanging moss trees, dirt roads, and flies bigger than your fist. You wouldn't send your worst enemy to stay in a place like that. So, I didn't play. I told the general manager and coach I wouldn't play. I said I didn't think that was team spirit. I said you can't tell me I'm a part of the team, then put me somewhere and not make me a part of the team until I get back to New York."[162]

Powell became one of the early bright spots for the Titans and the AFL. In his first season, Powell caught 67 passes for 1,167 yards and 14 touchdowns. History repeated itself when the Titans scheduled an exhibition game in Greenville, South Carolina. He suited up and sat by himself on the bench, listening to racial epithets from the bleachers behind him. "I heard things I had never heard before and haven't heard since and I can recall every word," Powell said. "People in those days were getting killed and I was sitting there in the wide open. You just don't know what's going to happen next; I just wanted to get out alive."[163]

Two years after he sat out of the exhibition game in Greenville as a member of the Titans, Powell, now with the Raiders, saw a potential problem when he saw the preseason schedule. The Raiders were scheduled to play the New York Jets at Ladd Stadium in Mobile, Alabama on August 23, 1963. "We received word that we weren't going to stay together as a team," said Powell. "In addition, they were going to rope off a section for the colored fans to sit in and the colored fans wouldn't be able to use the bathroom."

Powell decided he needed to take a stand. This time, Clem Daniels was willing to stand with Powell. The Raiders had a new coach, Al Davis, so Art Powell wasn't sure how he would react to Powell's protest. Davis canceled the game and moved it to Oakland. "Personally, I would like to thank Al Davis for not putting any pressure on the Negro players. We got full cooperation from the Raiders staff and the Oakland press."[164] Davis met with Powell, Bo Roberson, Clem Daniels, and Fred Williamson before moving the game to Oakland. "When it was decided to play the game in Mobile, we were given assurances that the seating would be integrated," said Al Davis. "It's unfortunate that it worked out this way, because we would have taken a big step—a step that should have been taken a long time ago." Davis said the

Raiders would not schedule any future games in stadiums with segregated seating.

A prototype for the big wide receiver, Powell stood 6 feet 3 inches, and weighed 210 pounds. He had the good speed and sure hands that teams looked for in receivers. He came to the AFL at the time the league offenses were looking to open it up and demonstrate exciting offenses to challenge the long-established NFL. Powell supplied the big plays that teams coveted. He led the AFL in touchdown catches two seasons and was voted to the league's all-decade team at the end of the sixties. He made an immediate impact when he signed with the Raiders, who went 1-13 in 1962 and in his first season helped the team improve to 10-4 by leading the league with 16 touchdown catches.

"I did not want to take a leadership position [in New Orleans] and after my experiences in Philadelphia. I didn't trust the other players on what they would say later," Powell said. "So, to protect myself I wrote up a paper that said everyone in this room is here voluntarily and nobody has been coerced and I made them all sign it. I said I would never get stuck being the bad guy again, but as it turned out I still got blamed. I got blamed for being one of the leaders, but I wasn't. I was just one of the guys. I was just taking care of myself and I had made up my mind that I wasn't going to play in the game."[165]

After the New Orleans situation, Powell was another of the Black players traded from the team he represented at the game. He said he wasn't traded due to the boycott. He had business interests in Toronto and requested a trade so that he could play closer to that city. He was traded to Buffalo in 1967 along with quarterback Tom Flores for quarterback Daryle Lamonica and wide receiver Glenn Bass. Powell caught 254 passes for 4,491 yards, a 17.7-yard average, and 50 touchdowns in four years with the Raiders, including 73 for 1,304 yards and 16 scores in 1963, when Davis began the process of turning the Raiders into a pro football power. Powell passed away suddenly in 2015 at 78, less than a year after his brother, Charlie, who played defensive end for the San Francisco 49ers and the Raiders for two seasons, died at 82. His views of life could be summed up in a few words he told a reporter during an interview. "The challenges that were before me were social challenges," Powell told the *Contra Costa Times* in 2007. "I chose to challenge them while others chose not to . . . I made a lot of people angry."[166]

Mann, Macon, Ford, Campbell, and Beach were some of the earliest Black players in professional football after the ban from 1934 to 1946 ended. Injustice found these players when they were in the league, usually due to social reasons off the field. Social causes were often the reasons protests not involving athletes gathered legs, but many Black players didn't want to risk losing their opportunity to play the game. When it came time to challenge the status quo, the scene changed to a city with deep roots in slavery, music, and cuisine. It was a city in many ways knowledgeable of the world but still hooked into Southern traditions.

CHAPTER SIX

The Big Uneasy

After touring New Orleans, many visitors come away with a one-word description—unique. The uniqueness of New Orleans might be traced to its roots. Founded by the French in 1718, the area came under Spanish rule in 1763, and the territory was sold to the United States in 1803 as part of the Louisiana Purchase. English traveler James Silk Buckingham visited New Orleans in 1841 and told people its shops, hotels, theaters, and restaurants reminded him of Paris.[167] During the 1940s and 1950s, some travelers were inclined to describe New Orleans as "America's Most Different City." Polk's 1940 New Orleans City Directory claimed the city was distinct with an active mingling of diverse people producing a city much more like a European city than one in the United States. One was apt to hear various languages and taste a broad range of cuisines a few short steps from one another. That blending of different backgrounds made it a destination city unlike any other throughout the continental United States.[168]

The center of the city features a blend of Spanish and French architecture and features some vibrant nightlife, especially during celebrations such as Mardi Gras, which has a history dating back to ancient Roman festivals. When Christianity came to Rome, religious leaders tried to soften the transition with a raucous party filled with drinking, feasting, and dancing. It traditionally occurs prior to Lent, a period of abstinence in the Catholic Church. Over the last few days leading up to Ash Wednesday, the population doubles in New Orleans with people looking for a party. Catholicism is the dominant religion in New Orleans and Ash Wednesday marks Lent's beginning. According to the Church, Lent is a six-week period of sacrifice and service leading up to Easter Sunday. It is a period of repentance. Ironically, the days leading up to that repentance are filled with overindulgence. Translated from the French, Mardi Gras means "Fat Tuesday," which becomes the last day of indulgence before the period of sacrifice begins. Carnival comes from the Latin "Carne Vale," which means "farewell to meat." Carnival is an event with Catholic origins beginning in the Old World and brought to the United States.

By 1840, New Orleans was the third most populous city in the country and was the largest city in the Southern United States from the Antebellum Era until after World War II. The city first became important due to its proximity to water, at the mouth of the Mississippi River and on the Gulf of Mexico. On average, New Orleans is generally between one and two feet below sea level. That downside makes the city vulnerable to flooding and, even today, it needs a complex system of levees and pumping systems to protect it. In August 2005, the city was severely affected by Hurricane Katrina, which flooded most of the city, killed 1,800 people, and displaced numerous others.

By the time Louisiana became a state in 1812, it was a hub of commerce that connected the Mississippi watershed, the Gulf of Mexico, the Eastern Seaboard, the Caribbean, and Western Europe—especially France and Spain. The history of the region is unique because it had what amounted to three colonial eras in rapid succession: the French, the Spanish, and the Americans. Each was associated with a different world power using a different language. Each brought new customs and laws to the region. Louisiana was founded by the French, but their colonization effort can only be considered half-hearted and brief. The Spanish followed and was a period of expanded trade, particularly with Cuba. Then the United States purchase brought new challenges.

New Orleans is a city so big it has numerous nicknames. Some of them are:
- "The Crescent City," referring to one of the first commercial sections of the city. The Mississippi River, after running norward takes a turn to the east. These turns formed a crescent shape where people originally settled.
- "The Big Easy" is the term (according to local legend) coined for the city by musicians in the early 20th century. A dance hall known as "The Big Easy Hall" was a popular music venue in 1911.[169] Others say it is a simple contrast to the busy, crowded "Big Apple" of New York City.

- "NOLA," an acronym for New Orleans, Louisiana.
- "Hollywood South" for its role in the film industry and pop culture. Numerous films are set or filmed in the city and surrounding areas. "Gone with the Wind" (1939), "Easy Rider" (1969), "Pretty Baby" (1978), "Wild at Heart" (1990) and "Runaway Jury" (2003).
- The French founded the city in 1718, so the earliest influences came from the French. The original grid pattern of the streets came from a French engineer and can still be seen in today's French Quarter. The French built many structures using native cypress wood and the houses were spaced out with gardens in between. Two large fires destroyed many of the French colonial structures during the Spanish period (1763-1803). As a result, codes were put into place requiring greater use of bricks and plaster. When these houses were built, the homes were close together, often with shared walls and courtyards. Since many of the buildings burned and were rebuilt when the city was under Spanish ownership, the architecture is mostly Spanish, not French like the name suggests. Even if the original buildings no longer stand, the French culture remains. Today, the old square looks much like it has since the late 18th century thanks to strict local preservation policies.[170] Latin American visitors feel more at home in New Orleans than in any other large American city because the stucco buildings next to narrow sidewalks with occasional cast iron and tropical gardens in interior courtyards remind them of colonial Spain.[171]

In the earliest days, settlers established trading posts on the land that today is known as the French Quarter. A marketplace developed naturally as a Native American gathering place for trading, forming alliances, and hunting that lasted centuries. The Choctaw named the area "Bulbancha," meaning "Land of Many Tongues," which indicated it was a gathering place for many tribes. The French Quarter itself sits on higher ground. This spot, with convenient access to Lake Pontchartrain through the Bayou St. John portage, made it a prime spot for settlement. As it was settled, land was cleared and housing built. The city was built on the backs of enslaved Africans and their descendants. These men, women, and children constructed the city's infrastructure, provided domestic labor, and built many of the homes still seen today. The first enslaved Africans were brought to the city in 1719, a year after its founding. About 6,000 people were captured on the West African coast, many from Senegambia, and brought to Louisiana during the French period. The Spanish brought in a similar number from Benin and Congo regions in the 1780s. When New Orleans became an American city in 1803, one out of every three people were slaves. By 1820, many considered New Orleans the center of the domestic slave trade.[172]

Over time, the numbers of free people of color increased and communities were built all over the city. By 1860, New Orleans had the largest free Black population in the Deep South. Most free people of color were French speaking and some even owned property. Free men and women of color were skilled artisans, entrepreneurs, teachers, poets, and activists during the Civil War and Reconstruction.[173] In 1812, the steamboat New Orleans arrived in its namesake city. Two-way steamboats traveled up and down the Mississippi River providing income for the city of New Orleans over the remainder of the century. The development of steam technology in the early 19th century propelled New Orleans into one of the largest trading ports in the world. Steamboats were utilized because they could navigate the shallow parts of the Mississippi River and the port handled trade from the Mississippi River as well as the Eastern Seaboard, Europe, the Caribbean, and Latin America.

There are many quirks that New Orleans offers that might not be readily found in other cities. It is the inventor of its own brand of jazz music with a faster, happier, less regimented beat. The earliest form was Dixieland jazz, which morphed into other forms and can be found in many of the nightspots across the city. The food choices range from a po' boy, which is a sandwich served on baguette-like bread and filled with fried shrimp, oysters, and Louisiana hot sausage, to red beans and rice, which comes from the local Creole culture. "So why does New Orleans have all these traditions?" posed Scott Beyer in *Forbes*. "Perhaps counterintuitively, it is because the city has long been a port and cosmopolitan hub, with different groups entering and staking out their culture." As Loyola University New Orleans historian Justin Nystrom wrote, New Orleans "was a French and Spanish city for a century before becoming part of the United States and this cultural imprint endured well into the 19th century . . . Generations of black and white rural folk moved here, but unlike the rest of the South, New Orleans was a major immigrant destination for the Irish, Germans, and Italians,' not to mention Haitians, Cubans, and other Afro-centric groups brought as slaves. 'It is a Southern city, a Latin city, and almost Northern city.'"[174] According to NewOrleans.com, while the city was still under Spanish rule in 1796, it was treated to a performance of "Sylvain," the city's first documented performance of opera. That wasn't a one-time deal as some would refer to New Orleans as "The Opera Capital of North America." The French Opera House or Théâtre de l'Opéra, hosted many performances from 1859 until 1919 when it was destroyed by fire. It stood in the French Quarter at the uptown lake corner of Bourbon and Toulouse Streets, with the main entrance on Bourbon.[175]

The civil rights movement came to New Orleans and the city reacted like many other cities in the country. Resistance to school integration, white flight, and a declining tax base led to inner-city neighborhoods that became impoverished and divested.[176] Individual freedom across races came slowly, but significant events occurred there. In November 1960, four girls—Leona Tate, Gail Etienne, Tessie Prevost, and Ruby Bridges—desegregated New Orleans public schools. These brave young women faced harassment and threats in order to attend school. Local chapters of CORE and the NAACP Youth Council rallied people to integrate businesses, protest unfair hiring practices, and register Black voters. Those brave protestors risked their lives testing compliance with federal requirements regarding desegregation in interstate travel. A civil rights group called the Citizens' Committee formed in 1891 to challenge the Separate Car Act, which had become law a year before. The law said railcars, including street cars, must be segregated. Homer A. Plessy, a member of the Committee, who was light-skinned and had attended integrated schools as a youth, volunteered to test the law. It was thought that his light skin color might help him intentionally violate the law and get arrested so the law could be tested in the courts. Plessy boarded a "whites-only" rail car at Press and Royal Streets to protest segregation laws and a cooperating police officer arrested him to get it all started. The case went all the way to the United States Supreme Court in 1896 when the high court established in *Plessy v. Ferguson* (1896) the principle of "separate but equal." That decision paved the way for many Jim Crow laws by establishing the legality of separate facilities by race and it wasn't until 1954 that the Supreme Court reversed that doctrine. Before 1954, social settings, even professional sports, were dominated by the separate but equal doctrine established in the 1896 *Plessy v. Ferguson* case, which originated in New Orleans.

In 1954, with the *Brown v. Board of Education* decision, the court ended formal segregation. African Americans participated in sports prior to the *Brown* decision but not in the Southern states. By 1956, in reaction to the *Brown* decision, a Louisiana statute was passed that banned mixed-race sporting events and mandated segregated audience seating. These laws prevented the progress of desegregation seen in other parts of the country and also prevented the Sugar Bowl from inviting nationally ranked teams with Black players from participating in the game. The *Brown* case was rooted in schools and New Orleans faced segregation. In 1900, the New Orleans school board decided to end school for Black children at the fifth grade.[177] It was a huge setback for Black people and some residents began efforts to change it. By 1909, they had won back six, seventh, and eighth grade. Attention turned to opening a Black high school, which had not existed since 1880. The school finally opened in 1917 when the Orleans Parish School Board opened McDonogh No. 35.

Many people point to Rosa Parks and the Montgomery Bus Boycott as the start of the civil rights movement, but it was going on long before that in New Orleans. Recall that Rosa Parks refused to give up her seat on a Montgomery city bus in 1955. In 1943, 17-year-old Bernice Delatte was arrested for violating segregation rules on a New Orleans bus. It is said Dr. Martin Luther King consulted with Baton Rouge organizers about tactics to deploy in his bus boycott.

Perhaps better known for Mardi Gras and its wide variety of food offerings, New Orleans also prided itself on sports. Before Major League Baseball integrated in 1947, New Orleans had several Negro League teams. The most well-known were the Black Pelicans, the New Orleans Eagles, and the New Orleans Crescent Stars. During Jim Crow, sporting events were segregated so these games were the only way Black fans could enjoy live sports. High school sports were another option but there weren't that many Black high schools in New Orleans before 1950.[178] Even before the NFL awarded New Orleans a franchise in 1966, Louisiana State University and Tulane University were powerhouses in college football. New Orleans has hosted the annual Sugar Bowl collegiate game every January since its inception in 1934. The Sugar Bowl ranked second only to Mardi Gras in the number of visitors it brought to New Orleans.[179] The Bayou Classic, one of the best known HBCU matchups, has been held in the city since 1974. As the sixties dawned, there were two professional football leagues, and the NFL was looking to expand its footprint from one dominated by the northeast and the Midwest into the South. The AFL started with eight teams and soon would add more. New Orleans wanted to be a candidate for a team and, to prove its worthiness, the city hosted an AFL preseason game held at City Park Stadium in August 1962. A sell-out crowd attended the game and 20,000 pledged to purchase season tickets if a professional football franchise came to town.[180]

After the 1954 *Brown* decision by the Supreme Court, some white politicians in the South took stances to overtly tell voters they planned on protecting white ways, which they called traditional Southern values. These concerns competed with the interests of those attempting to increase the presence of sporting events in the Bayou. Previous racial struggles felt by college football in New Orleans made it appear that efforts to gain professional sports of any kind would be a struggle. David Dixon did not think that way. He loved his hometown of New Orleans and wanted a professional sports franchise there. Some said he should pursue baseball, but he had another sport in mind. His love of sports grew out of the history of the gridiron. "Just up the road from us, LSU football under Paul Dietzel in the late 1950s had thrown gasoline on the football fire in Louisiana. Dietzel had won a national championship in 1958 and Dietzel was building a juggernaut football program in Baton Rouge, with over 90% of players from Louisiana," recalled Dixon. "I was happy for LSU, but as a Tulane guy, I thought about what could have been for Green Wave and how the people considered the 'smartest men in the room'—sort of speak—shipwrecked that for the school in the late 1940s."[181]

In November 1962, the *Times-Picayune* reported that the Oakland Raiders were putting finishing touches on an agreement to move the team to the Crescent City. Bob Roesler, sportswriter for the paper, said an authoritative source told him Dixon arrived in Oakland "with the purchase price in his pocket" and that "all things point to the fact that the sale has been accomplished."[182] Former LSU All-American Billy Cannon, at the time a member of the Houston Oilers, confirmed the story at a Greenwood, Mississippi Quarterback Club appearance. He told those in attendance that the deal was already approved to move the Raiders to New Orleans. The story was flatly denied by then Raiders Owner and General Manager F. Wayne Valley. "Don't you get the wire services down there?" questioned Valley. "I told them the club had not been sold."[183] It turned out to be a false alarm but was further evidence that Dixon was trying everything possible to get a team into "The Big Easy." The Raiders were struggling in the only home they had known since 1960. They were wrapping up a season in which they only won one game out of 14 played and were averaging only about 10,000 fans per game playing at old Frank Youell Field. It was considered a temporary location with a capacity of 22,000 fans for football and the team was hoping to land a larger, permanent stadium. According to Dixon's son Frank, his father had formed a group that had an agreement to purchase the team. "Dad received a phone call. The caller tells him that the Oakland Raiders are for sale. They had just finished 1-13 and weren't drawing. He flew back to Oakland and, with a handshake agreement, accepted an offer to purchase the team for $236,000. Dad had a group of 8-9 guys who would pool their money and sign the paperwork."[184]

"I had a deal in place with the ownership group in Oakland to buy the Raiders for $236,000 at the end of 1961," Dixon said. "Can you imagine buying a professional football team for $236,000? We came to a tentative deal, but the main owner at that time, F. Wayne Valley, he told me he given his word to the AFL Commissioner [Joe Foss] to talk to him before he did anything with the team, but I had the deal in place to buy the Raiders."[185] Behind the scenes, there were conversations in Oakland attempting to retain the team. With community support building, city leaders gained a commitment to build a new stadium. Oakland viewed a dual purpose arena as an investment that would attract a Major League Baseball team in the future. Sure enough, the owner of the Kansas City Athletics, Charlie Finley, moved the team to Oakland to play in the stadium in 1968. Dixon said he had a tentative agreement in place for the Raiders to move to the Crescent City with a temporary landing spot at Tulane Stadium, but Foss and the mayor of Oakland got involved and kept the Raiders in Oakland.

That wasn't the only team rumored to be coming to New Orleans. Dixon was watching the events in Dallas closely where the NFL had placed an expansion franchise team in 1960, and Lamar Hunt, founder of the AFL, had a team. He was thinking that only one team would remain in Dallas and the other would have to leave. He had been talking with both ownership groups so that he would be in a position to court them when the decision was made. Toward the end of the 1962 season, Dixon got a call from Hunt, who had decided to move his AFL team out of Dallas. Hunt told Dixon he had lost more than $2 million in his three seasons in Dallas and wanted to relocate. Hunt and Dixon had something in common: they both wanted desperately to put a team in their hometown. Dallas was Hunt's home, but the competition from the NFL Cowboys had proven that the city could not support two professional teams. Hunt sent Dallas Texans General Manager Jack Steadman to New Orleans. He met with David Dixon and wanted assurances that his team would be able to play in Tulane Stadium. He also wanted it to be kept quiet, as Hunt didn't want anyone to know he was considering a move until all the details were ironed out. Dixon presented to the Tulane University board that a "generic" AFL team wanted an agreement on a lease. In retrospect, Dixon called that a mistake. If the Tulane committee had been allowed to know it was Hunt, the son of a rich oil man, H. L. Hunt, they may have viewed the arrangement more favorably. In the end, Tulane said it would wait for an offer from an NFL team. That league had been around for decades, and many thought the AFL might not survive over the long run. "It's just flat awful we missed the chance to have Lamar Hunt own this team and New Orleans would have played in two of the first four Super Bowls," said Dixon.[186]

"Hindsight being 20/20, Dave [Dixon] should have pushed that deal through and I really think he probably could have convinced the Tulane group, if he had told them it was Lamar Hunt coming to New Orleans," Buddy Diliberto, a *Times-Picayune* sportswriter in 1962, said. "I know it has bothered him ever since but covering the NFL and AFL for the newspaper back then, it was not certain the American Football League would survive at the end of 1962. Many of the top people in the NFL thought they would financially fold. They thought the AFL was a 'Mickey Mouse League.'"[187]

When Lamar Hunt could not secure Tulane Stadium, he turned his attention to Kansas City. "That might be a naïve way to look at things," Hunt said years later. "Kansas City was very much a baseball town then and that stands to reason because they had a major league team. They didn't have a pro football team, and they didn't have any college teams that played right in Kansas City. But I understood there was a potential of a six-state area to draw from."[188]

On May 26, 1962, *The Louisiana Weekly* pointed out that any mention of professional football in New Orleans omitted any mention of integration. "New Orleans can't get a professional football team without integration," said the newspaper. "The hotels will have to be integrated because there is nothing these days like a professional segregated ball team." The players "have to eat together and travel together because they are a team." The Black newspaper cited the example of

Houston and Atlanta, which could not maintain segregation when they got professional sports teams . . . Atlanta and Houston have gotten over their segregation jitters and, thank God, hell didn't freeze over."[189]

On August 18, 1962, Dixon's Louisiana Professional Sports Inc. sponsored an exhibition game between the Houston Oilers and Boston Patriots of the AFL at City Park Stadium. Thirty-one thousand fans attended the game. On the field, it may have looked like New Orleans was an integrated city, but the integration ended there. The sponsors housed the African American players from both teams at Mason's Motel, a Black establishment, while the white players stayed at the Fontainebleau Motor Hotel at Tulane and Carrollton. Several players expressed displeasure at this arrangement and said they would not cross a picket line if demonstrators had formed one at the stadium. The promoters planned to maintain segregated seating inside the stadium, but a last-minute rush for tickets made that difficult. *The Louisiana Weekly* made their view clear with the headline "City 'Not Ready' for Pro Football."[190] The Houston Oilers featured Billy Cannon, former LSU back in 1958 and 1959 and a local fan favorite, in a game at City Park Stadium. The city thought hosting the game was an important step toward showing the AFL and NFL that they were ready for a franchise.[191]

On September 7, 1963, the city hosted a doubleheader of National Football League games and Jim Hall, sports columnist for *The Louisiana Weekly* called the event "an overwhelming success." Hall continued, "Outdated segregation went out the backdoor here Saturday night." All of the players, Black and white, stayed in the Conrad Hilton Motel near the airport. All seating inside the stadium was integrated and the Black media members were given places in the press box.[192] The only downside to the entire day was a severe thunderstorm that delayed the games and forced fans to seek cover under the grandstand. Seeing Blacks and whites gathered in tight spaces to avoid the rain caused Dixon to fear the worst. "I had a vision of Blacks and whites hammering each other under the overhang, the media reports that would result, the end of my dreams of an NFL franchise . . . I was so scared I was shaking." He rushed down to the stands to join the crowd and witnessed no issues. Dixon's fears were for naught. After the rain allowed the games to continue, the Dallas Cowboys upset the Detroit Lions, and the Chicago Bears defeated the Baltimore Colts.[193]

On July 2, 1964, President Lyndon B. Johnson signed the Civil Rights Act into law. He asked that all Americans join in this effort "to bring justice and hope to all of our people and to bring peace to our land."[194] At the time, cities in the southern United States were still struggling with segregation-integration issues. Sporting events were still governed by the "separate but equal" doctrine established in the 1896 *Plessy v. Ferguson* case.

The AFL player boycott generated thoughts that New Orleans was not ready for a franchise. In mid-August, the city got another opportunity to show the sports leagues they were ready. On August 14, the Colts and the Cardinals faced off in Tulane Stadium. When Cardinals owner Charles Bidwill arrived, he told the media that New Orleans, Houston, and Seattle were the chief cities under consideration for an NFL franchise, with Atlanta having been awarded an NFL team that began play in 1966. Bidwill was aware of the Black players' complaints and the subsequent loss of the game, but it sounded as if it would not hurt the city's chances. "We investigated and found there was wrong on both sides," he said.

Others were not ready to roll out the welcome mat to football fans. Jackson G. Ricau, president of the pro-segregation South Louisiana Citizens' Council, attempted to get the city to boycott the game. "This puts a terrific burden on proprietors who are forced to cope with a racial powder keg to satisfy the tastes of some sports fans who obviously don't see the dangers," said Ricau.[195]

The exhibition contests staged in New Orleans were not uncommon as, throughout the decade, AFL and NFL teams traveled to non-league cities to see which cities held games that were well-attended and, therefore, candidates for expansion. At the time, the Southeastern United States was an untapped territory for professional sports expansion. The problem: many cities in the region had state laws that tolerated unequal treatment of African Americans. In the 1960s, Americans witnessed the widespread use of lunch counter sit-ins to protest seating for white customers only. Protests were springing up across the country as people tested discrimination practices and compliance with federal regulations. Since 1955, Washington and Green Bay played a game that became known as the "Piedmont Bowl" every summer in Winston-Salem, North Carolina, but the game came to an end after Packers coach Vince Lombardi was refused service in a local restaurant. According to his son, Vince Jr., the hostess had mistaken his dark complexion, which had been made darker by the summer sun of training camp, for that of a Black man. Coach Lombardi was asked to leave. Still stinging when they played the exhibition game, Lombardi's Packers beat the Redskins 41-7 and he vowed to never again play a game in Winston-Salem, North Carolina. He never did. When he arrived in Green Bay, he told his entire team that he would not tolerate any hint of racism among his players. His efforts did not go unrecognized.

During the summer of 1968, *Sports Illustrated* ran a five-part series on racism in sports. In part four, Jack Olsen asked the all-important question: "Can there be such a thing as a professional sports unit in America that works together and lives together without racial discrimination?" Then he provided his own answer. He said there are two places where it all works. The first was the Boston Celtics, led by African American player-coach Bill Russell. The second was the Packers' Vince Lombardi. "Whenever racial questions are discussed by NFL players, the subject of the Packers arises," Olsen wrote. "In a league beset with racial confrontations, the Packers players get along. Success has something to do with this; a winner always finds life more pleasant than a loser. But more to the point is the attitude of the Packers' remarkable Vince Lombardi."[196]

Lombardi preached, "Work together, win together." When he arrived, Lombardi saw only one Black player on the team he inherited—defensive end Nate Borden. Five months into the job, Lombardi acquired Black safety Emlen Tunnell from the Giants. When the veteran ran into issues attempting to find suitable housing, Lombardi stepped in. He paid for Tunnell's room at the Northland Hotel. Gradually, he added more Black players. Lombardi had sympathy for those who were discriminated against. That experience in North Carolina wasn't the only time Lombardi faced racism. As an Italian American, he felt the fact that his last name ended in a vowel prevented him from getting a head coaching job sooner in his career.

In 1961, the Packers played an exhibition game against Washington in Columbus, Georgia. The city wanted both teams to arrive early and publicize the game. The all-white team—Washington—arrived early, but Lombardi kept his team back home until the day before the game because of the Jim Crow laws. His team stayed together—Black and white—at the bachelor officer quarters at Fort Benning. Lombardi returned to Columbus the following year and stayed again at Fort Benning. In 1963, Lombardi canceled his team's participation due to the segregated seating plan at the game. At the last moment, the game was moved to Cedar Rapids, Iowa.

Segregated seating was another issue NFL and AFL teams faced when playing exhibition games in non-league cities. Often, local regulations dictated where Blacks could sit within the stadium. In a 1960 exhibition between Houston and New York (the Oilers beat the Titans 30-14), Alabama state law required racial segregation at all public stadiums. The Titans' Blanche Martin told author William J. Ryczek, who wrote about the early sixties in the AFL, that the Black audience was confined to end zone seats at Ladd Memorial Stadium and the "rest of the stadium was virtually empty."[197] The following season, 1961, Victory Stadium in Roanoke, Virginia maintained segregated seating pursuant to state law. NAACP leaders urged the teams' Black players (12 Steelers and 7 Colts) to boycott the game. Four days before the game, four of the biggest names—John Henry Johnson, Lenny Moore, Joe Perry, and Jim Parker—said they would not participate unless the NAACP gave them their okay to play. Commissioner Pete Rozelle said no player would be excused from playing in the contest. Community leaders relented and said Black fans could sit in any stadium section, so the players decided to participate.

When the Buffalo Bills beat the Houston Oilers 21-14 at an exhibition game in Mobile, it was the last pro game played before a racially segregated crowd. Ladd Memorial Stadium was steadfast in its policy of separate seating by race. Blacks could only buy tickets in the end zone and could not use any of the park's restrooms. Another scheduled exhibition never happened. Five days before Oakland was set to play the Jets, four Black Raiders—Art Powell, Bo Roberson, Fred Williamson, and Clem Daniels—said they would not play in the game unless the restrictions were lifted. Charles Trimmier, the mayor of Mobile, worked to get things changed but the facility manager said, "We don't want four boys from Oakland to tell us how to run our stadium."[198] At the last moment, the August 25 game was moved to Oakland. Two players who threatened to sit out had good games: Daniels scored two touchdowns and Williamson tackled a Jets ball carrier in the end zone for a safety as Oakland won, 43-16.

Back in New Orleans, 71,218 fans attended the doubleheader exhibition in 1964. In 1965, 75,229 people saw the Cardinals defeat the Packers 20-7. "We wanted to prove to the NFL that we could support an NFL team in New Orleans and our only way to do this was to make an impressive showing with pre-season games," Dixon said. "In 1963, we were able to land a doubleheader exhibition event. It was only the second time in NFL history that the NFL had a doubleheader format. We got the Dallas Cowboys to play the Detroit Lions. I wanted New Orleans to be the first Southern city to sell first-come, first-served football tickets. This was 1963, so the Civil Rights Act had not even passed yet in Congress. The Civil Rights Act was voted on, approved, and then signed in the summer of 1964. The state of Louisiana had their laws, but the NFL had their laws too and they made it clear to me that Tulane Stadium would have to be integrated. The NFL would not allow us to play in a segregated stadium. Joe Bernstein was our legal counsel and was tremendous in his help to land an NFL team, set everything up. At one time, Tulane Stadium had a section in the south end zone for Black fans to watch games. Maybe 5,000 seats at the most and that section was eliminated immediately. No matter the color of your skin, you could buy a ticket and sit wherever you wanted to."[199]

Dixon also recalled, "We were able to land another exhibition game in 1964 where the St. Louis Cardinals played the Green Bay Packers and we had over 75,000 at Tulane Stadium. It was the biggest draw in a non-league city at that time. And we had won over a friend in Vince Lombardi, the legendary coach for the Green Bay Packers and he was very influential behind the scenes. Lombardi loved New Orleans and was hooked on Barq's Root Beer. Can you imagine the conversation with Buddy Diliberto and Lombardi? But after Vince drank his first cold bottle, that was it and Coach had me set him with a distributor that would get him Barq's in Green Bay. He would be an advocate for us to sell New Orleans to the NFL crowd. And our friend Buddy Diliberto took him out to lunch leading up to the game and he got him. By golly, we had done it and sold the NFL on New Orleans as a football town. We wanted the next expansion team given and the Commissioner [Pete Rozelle] assured me New Orleans was in the hunt."[200]

By law, racial discrimination was not supposed to be a problem any longer in Atlanta's stadiums, hotels, and restaurants, but the San Diego Chargers reported issues just the same. The team was staying at the Atlanta Hilton and some of the Black players were asked to leave a pool hall located adjacent to the hotel. Ironically, the Chargers were owned by Barron Hilton, son of the operator of the hotel chain. *Sports Illustrated* reported on the incident and called it a factor in their 34-6 loss to the Jets.

New Orleans caught the nation's attention further as a six-year-old little girl attempted to integrate a previously all-white William Frantz Elementary School in the upper Ninth Ward. She became a symbol of school desegregation as she became one of the first to attend a formerly all-white school in the Deep South. Early Monday morning, November 14, 1960, Ruby Bridges wore a white starched dress, black shoes, and a bow in her hair for her first day at the new school. Her parents, Lucille and Abon Bridges, had moved to New Orleans two years earlier seeking greater opportunity. Like many other Black families during the fifties, they left a rural environment with a history of racial oppression for a big city that offered the potential for less discrimination and greater employment opportunities. All of the neighbors on the Bridges' block were African American. On this day, four United States marshals escorted Ruby Bridges to William Frantz Elementary School, four blocks from her home. In another part of the city, three other African American first graders—Gail Etienne, Leona Tate, and Tessie Prevost—were preparing to integrate another elementary school. They were given the opportunity after years of legal activism by the National Association for the Advancement of Colored People (NAACP).[201]

Bridges and the federal marshals encountered a crowd outside the elementary school as white protesters shouted racial epithets and threw objects as the marshals escorted Bridges into school. Once Ruby was inside the school, white parents went inside to remove their students from the school. This was not uncommon in southern cities across the country. In 1957, nine Black high school students enrolled in a white school in Little Rock, Arkansas. In a much-publicized case, President Dwight D. Eisenhower ordered federal troops to protect the "Little Rock Nine" as they attempted to go to school. Despite the widespread publicity, these same battles played out at other schools across the country.

Years later, Bridges recalled her first day at the new school. "I remember looking out of the car as we pulled up to the Frantz school," she said. "There were barricades and people shouting and policemen everywhere. I thought maybe it was Mardi Gras, the carnival that takes place in New Orleans every year. Mardi Gras was always noisy. As we walked through the crowd, I didn't see any faces. I guess that's because I wasn't very tall and I was surrounded by the marshals. People yelled and threw things. I could see the school building and it looked bigger and nicer than my old school. When we climbed the high steps to the front door, there were policemen in uniform at the top. The policemen at the door and the crowd behind us made me think this was an important place. It must be college, I thought to myself."[202]

John Steinbeck, author of *The Grapes of Wrath* and *The Red Pony*, won a Nobel Prize for literature in 1962. While traveling through Texas, he heard about the protestors outside the school and felt compelled to go there and write about the incident in *Travels with Charley*. "The incident most reported and pictured in the newspapers was the matriculation of a couple of tiny Negro children in a New Orleans school," he wrote. "Behind these small dark mites were the law's majesty and the law's power to enforce—both the scales and the sword were allied with the infants—while against them were three hundred years of fear and anger and terror of change in a changing world. What made the newsmen love the story was a group of stout middle-aged women who, by some curious definition of the word 'mother,' gathered every day to scream invectives at children. Further, a small group of them had become so expert that they were known as the Cheerleaders and a crowd gathered every day to applaud their performance."[203]

Steinbeck continued, "As I walked toward the school, I was in a stream of people all white and all going in my direction. They walked intently like people going to a fire after it has been burning for some time. They beat their hands against their hips or hugged them under coats and many men had scarves under their hats and covering their ears . . . It was apparent where the Cheerleaders were because people shoved forward to try to get near them. They had a favored place at the barricade directly across from the school entrance and in that area a concentration of police stomped their feet and slapped their hands together in unaccustomed gloves.[204]

"The show opened on time," Steinbeck recalled. "Sounds of sirens. Motorcycle cops. Then two big black cars filled with big men in blond felt hats pulled up in front of the school. The crowd seemed to hold its breath. Four big marshals got out of each car and from somewhere in the automobiles, they extracted the littlest Negro girl you ever saw, dressed in shining starchy white, with new white shoes on feet so little they were almost round. Her face and little legs were very black against the white. The big marshals stood her on the curb and a jangle of jeering shrieks went up from behind the barricades. The little girl did not look at the howling crowd but from the side the whites of her eyes showed like those of a frightened fawn. The men turned her around like a doll and then the strange procession moved up the broad walk toward the school and the child was even more a mite because the men were so big. Then the girl made a curious hop and I think I know what it was. I think in her whole life she had not gone ten steps without skipping, but now in the middle of her first skip, the weight bore her down and her little round feet took measures, reluctant steps between the tall guards. Slowly they climbed the steps and entered the school."²⁰⁵

"Once we were inside the building, the marshals walked us up a flight of stairs," said Ruby Bridges, picking up the story. "The school office was at the top. My mother and I went in and were told to sit in the principal's office. The marshals sat outside. There were windows in the room where we waited. That meant everybody passing by could see us. I remember noticing everyone was white. All day long, white parents rushed into the office. They were upset. They were arguing and pointing at us. When they took their children to school that morning, the parents hadn't been sure whether William Frantz would be integrated that day or not. After my mother and I arrived, they ran into classrooms and dragged their children out of the school. From behind the windows in the office, all I saw was confusion. I told myself that this must be the way it is in a big school. That whole first day, my mother and I just sat and waited. We didn't talk to anybody. I remember watching a big, round clock on the wall. When it was 3:00 and time to go home, I was glad. I had thought my new school would be hard, but the first day was easy . . . When we left school that first day, the crowd outside was even bigger and louder than it had been in the morning. There were reporters and film cameras and people everywhere. I guess the police couldn't keep them behind the barricades. It seemed to take us a long time to get to the marshals' car. Later on, I learned there had been protesters in front of the two integrated schools the whole day. They wanted to be sure white parents would boycott the school and not let their children attend.²⁰⁶

"On the second day, my mother and I drove to school with the marshals," continued Bridges. "The crowd outside was ready. Racists spat at us and shouted things like, 'Go home, nigger,' and 'No niggers allowed here.' One woman screamed at me, 'I'm going to poison you. I'll find a way.' She made the same threat every morning. I tried not to pay attention. When we finally got into the building, my new teacher was there to meet us. Her name was Mrs. Henry. She was young and white. I had not spent time with a white person before, so I was uneasy at first. Mrs. Henry led us upstairs to the second floor. As we went up, we hardly saw anyone else in the building. The white students were not coming to class. The halls were so quiet, I could hear the noise the marshals' shoes made on the shiny hardwood floors. Mrs. Henry took us into a classroom and said to have a seat. When I looked around, the room was empty. There were rows of desks, but no children. I thought we were too early, but Mrs. Henry said we were right on time. My mother sat at the back of the room. I took a seat up front and Mrs. Henry began to teach. I spent the whole first day with Mrs. Henry in the classroom. I wasn't allowed to have lunch in the cafeteria or go outside for recess, so we just stayed in our room."[207]

"The papers had printed that the jibes and jeers were cruel and sometimes obscene and so they were, but this was not the big show," continued Steinbeck in *Travels with Charley*. "The crowd was waiting for the white man who dared to bring his white child to school. And here he came along the guarded walk, a tall man dressed in light gray, leading his frightened child by the hand. His body was tensed as a strong leaf spring drawn to the breaking strain; his face was grave and gray and his eyes were on the ground immediately in front of him. The muscles of his cheeks stood out from clenched jaws, a man afraid who by his will held his fears in check as a great rider directs a panicked horse . . . No newspaper had printed the words these women shouted. It was indicated that they were indelicate, some even said obscene. On television the soundtrack was made to blur or had crowd noise cut in to cover. But now I heard the words, bestial and filthy and degenerate."[208]

As schools began to integrate, white parents were put in a difficult position. Even if they agreed with integration, they didn't want to put their children in danger by sending them to a school lined with angry people desperate to do something. Ruby Bridges offered an example. "Reverend Lloyd Foreman was convinced that integration was morally and spiritually right and was determined to keep his daughter, Pam, in the Frantz school. That November, the minister walked Pam to and from school every day. Very quickly the chorus of racists became obsessed with the Foremans. They taunted them without mercy . . . The Gabrielles were another brave family. Daisy and her husband, Jim, had several children, including a six-year-old named Yolanda. Mrs. Gabrielle had been in the Army during World War II and she refused to be bullied by the protestors. When I entered William Frantz, Daisy Gabrielle did not take Yolanda out of school . . . Yolanda came to school every day for three weeks. During that time, her family's home was attacked. Stones and rotten eggs were thrown. Windows were broken. Hecklers gathered in front of the house and threatened to hurt the Gabrielle children. Daisy's husband was about to lose his job. Though the police set up protection for the family and a wonderful New Orleans woman named Betty Wisdom offered to drive Yolanda to school each day, Daisy Gabrielle knew her daughter was still at risk. In the end, the Gabrielles gave up. They not only took Yolanda out of school but also moved the family to another state, a northern state where Daisy's husband had grown up. It was time to get away from Louisiana."[209]

"Then one afternoon, after the police had taken them through the mob, the child had looked behind her and suddenly became aware of the danger," added *Good Housekeeping* magazine. "That night she woke up screaming. When Daisy went to her, she was babbling about 'those ugly ladies; those ladies who yell so ugly.' Then Yolanda said her stomach hurt, that she didn't want to go to school the next day. Daisy held her in her arms, promising she could stay home, her heart heavy with the burden she had put on her family."[210]

At the same time Ruby was integrating Frantz Elementary, three Black girls named Leona, Tessie, and Gail were integrating McDonogh No. 19. "Some thirty minutes after the scheduled start of classes the marshals pulled up at McDonogh No. 19 with three pupils accompanied by parents, a man and two women," wrote *The New York Times*. "An angry roar went up for the whites among the mixed crowd of spectators. 'Kill them niggers!' shouted one man. The police rapidly moved the crowd off the sidewalk to a parkway in the middle of the street. The parents and the pupils, who were in pigtails and freshly laundered dresses, were rushed into the stucco building by the deputy marshals."[211] News accounts reported the dwindling attendance. On November 17, three Black girls and one white child were the only students at the McDonogh School No. 19, which normally had 467 pupils. Only three white and one Black at William Frantz School, which normally had 576 pupils.[212] "Near the end of the year, Mrs. Henry and I finally had company," recalled Bridges. "A few white children began coming back to school and I got an opportunity to visit with them once or twice. Even though these children were white, I still knew nothing about racism or integration. I had picked up bits and pieces over the months from being around adults and hearing them talk, but nothing was clear to me. The light dawned one day when a little white boy refused to play with me. 'I can't play with you,' the boy said. 'My mama said not to because you're a nigger.'"[213]

In addition to the hard news accounts in the nation's newspapers, some artists followed the story. Norman Rockwell, an American artist born in New York City at the turn of the century, was hired as cover artist for *Boys' Life* magazine when he was 18 years old. Over 47 years, Rockwell produced 322 covers for *The Saturday Evening Post*. "For 47 years, I portrayed the best of all possible worlds—grandfathers, puppy dogs—things like that," Rockwell said in an interview at age 75. "That kind of stuff is dead now and I think it's about time."[214] Rockwell had been known primarily for his idealistic cover art on *The Saturday Evening Post*. To many Americans, Rockwell's illustrations offered an identifiable and comfortable image of life in America during simpler times. He drew the images during complicated times of rapid change in the country and the images were viewed as sweet, nostalgic views of days gone by. "His paintings have human figures and storytelling, snoozing mutts, grandmothers, clear-skinned Boy Scouts, and wood-paneled station wagons," wrote Deborah Solomon in her biography of the artist. "They have policemen, attics, and floral wallpaper. Moreover, most of them began life as covers for *The Saturday Evening Post*, a weekly general-interest magazine that paid Rockwell for his work and paychecks, frankly, were another modernist no-no. Real artists were supposed to live hand to mouth, preferably in walk-up apartments in Greenwich Village."[215]

In 1963, Rockwell's relationship with *The Saturday Evening Post* ended and he moved to *Look* magazine, where his work took on a more edgy stance toward the hottest topics of the day. Rockwell's first illustration in *Look* appeared in the January 14, 1964, issue. *The Problem We All Live With* was spread over two pages inside the magazine. The illustration needed some explanatory text and received very little. Some readers may have wondered "What is this?" as they turned to page 21 and saw an African American girl—a six-year-old in a white dress and matching bow—walking to school. The only warning were the words, "Painted for *Look* by Norman Rockwell," which may easily have been missed.[216] She was escorted by four giant uniformed officers. The contrast was striking with a tiny Black girl in white dress escorted by giant protectors. The background demonstrates the controversy: the stucco wall is stained by a racial slur ("Nigger") and the letters "KKK" in the upper left. The girl appears confident and erect with eyes focused ahead, ignoring the violence around her. There is evidence of a tomato thrown at the wall and laying on the ground, which we can assume was tossed by a demonstrator.

A wire service photograph compares favorably with the painting. It appears that Rockwell loosely based his painting on that picture. Rockwell added the defaced walls and other details, but it was an attempt at pulling an event from the news headlines of the day. His selection of the lightly colored background makes Ruby's dark-toned skin the centerpiece of the artwork. In Rockwell's artwork, we see Ruby's face which displays her innocence, but he cuts off the marshals' heads. By removing their heads, we see them more as background to the centerpiece of the art, Ruby Bridges, who might appear as the only human representation in the view. Rockwell's frame of reference is low, which helps us see the events from Ruby's perspective. For a minute, we see the world from the perspective of a scared Black girl and not an angry white crowd.

Bridges said she never met Rockwell but expressed respect for his art. "Here was a man that had been doing lots of work, painting family images and all of a sudden decided this is what I'm going to do," said Bridges. "It's wrong and I'm going to say that it's wrong ... the mere fact that [Norman Rockwell] had enough courage to step up to the plate and say I'm going to make a statement and he did it in a very powerful way ... even though I had not had an opportunity to meet him, I commend him for that."[217]

The art was published three years after the day it chronicled. Rockwell may have been reminded of the day by John Steinbeck's memoir, *Travels with Charley: In Search of America*, published in the summer of 1962. In the book, Steinbeck travels across the country with his French poodle only to arrive in New Orleans on that November day and witness the shouting segregationists outside an elementary school. Rockwell could have been influenced by an account provided by the child psychiatrist Dr. Robert Coles. He and Rockwell became friends after being introduced by a mutual friend. At the time, Dr. Coles was a graduate student doing research in the Deep South and witnessed the scene outside the school. He had been driving to a conference in New Orleans when he happened upon the crowd of screaming people yelling insults toward a tiny, young child. For two years after that event, Dr. Coles provided regular counseling to Ruby Bridges and some other African American children trying to endure the strains of school desegregation. He published his findings in the October 1963 issue of *The American Journal of Psychiatry* and it is believed Rockwell saw the article.[218]

The Problem We All Live With was a sharp break from Rockwell's *Saturday Evening Post* cover art. Rockwell said that he had been directed by the *Post* to remove a Black person from a group picture because the magazine's policy dictated Blacks be shown only in service-related jobs. "The magazine was by no means alone in perpetuating racial caricature," wrote author Deborah Solomon. "Advertisements in newspapers and magazines were regular offenders. There was Aunt Jemima and her maple syrup; Uncle Ben and his long-grain rice; Rastus in his floppy chef's hat on the Cream of Wheat box, each of them smiling, teeth flashing against dark skin, as if nothing in their experience was more rewarding than cooking up hearty, starch-laden dishes for white folks."[219]

In *The New York Times Magazine* in 1971, Richard Reeves questioned Rockwell about the civil rights pictures he drew in the early sixties. Reeves admitted he was shocked that Rockwell did the pictures in the first place and said he did them only when race "was finally fashionable." Rockwell addressed the questions in his usual polite manner. "I was doing the racial thing for a while," he said. "But that's deadly now—nobody wants it." Rockwell's civil rights period was short in duration as people soon longed for the pictures shown on the old *Saturday Evening Post* covers of kids, dogs, and grandparents. "These days everyone is a little frightened and they want those good-natured human pictures again," he told *Good Housekeeping* in 1976. Were the good old days really better? "Yes, I would say so," Rockwell admitted. "We laughed a lot more in the old days."[220]

In 2011, President Barack Obama borrowed *The Problem We All Live With* for a special White House exhibition to commemorate the walk Ruby Bridges took to William Frantz Elementary School 50 years earlier. What did Bridges think of the painting? "The girl in that painting at 6 years old knew absolutely nothing about racism—I was going to school that day. So, every time I see that, I think about the fact that I was an innocent child that knew absolutely nothing about what was happening that day."[221]

CHAPTER SEVEN

Traveling While Black

In 1954, the U.S. Supreme Court outlawed school segregation in the *Brown v. Board of Education* case. Over the next few years, however, schools were slow to desegregate, as evidenced in Ruby Bridges' experience in New Orleans. During the fall of 1957, segregated schools in Little Rock, Arkansas were ordered to integrate but when Black parents appeared with their children, they were greeted by a mob of white adults shouting and spitting at the Black children. Arkansas Governor Orval Faubus vowed to keep the school white, and his words spread like wildfire in the media over the next few days. The Little Rock school board set a plan to integrate schools in this order: high school in 1957, junior high schools in 1960, and elementary schools in 1963. Many anticipated fewer issues in Little Rock than other southern cities because they said the University of Arkansas had been integrated since 1948—among the first universities in the South to integrate—and other school districts were slowly changing since then. In 1956, buses were integrated. Governor Faubus, like Mississippi's Ross Barnett and Alabama's George Wallace, rebelled. Faubus went on television and got the white mob riled up by warning that "blood would run in the streets" if Black students attempted to enter Central High School.[222] When nine students arrived, Faubus used state troopers to keep them out. An agitated mob was there shouting at the students. President Eisenhower sent troops from the 101st Airborne Division to escort the students to school. Brutality, bomb scares, and economic boycotts followed.

At the time Little Rock was heating up, trumpeter and influential jazz artist Louis "Satchmo" Armstrong was touring the country. On September 18, 1957,

Armstrong was in Grand Forks, North Dakota when he heard about the mob of whites yelling at the students in Little Rock. A local reporter then came into the room hoping to do a feature article about the visiting celebrity in town. He got more than he expected. Armstrong was riled up and told the reporter that President Eisenhower had "no guts" and he called Governor Faubus an "uneducated plow boy."[223] The news story hit the wire and Armstrong's words were widely quoted. Some wonder if the musician's statements caused President Eisenhower to act or if the Chief Executive had already planned on getting involved in the big tussle in Little Rock. Either way, other reporters wanted to know if Armstrong really said all those things. "That's just what I said and still say," Armstrong said as he reviewed a copy of the story. "It's getting almost so bad a colored man hasn't got any country," he added. "Don't get me wrong, the South is full of intelligent white people. It's bad the lower class who make all the noise, though."[224]

Armstrong called the strategy of deploying the National Guard to prevent school integration at Little Rock "a publicity stunt led by the greatest of all publicity hounds." He was referring to Governor Faubus. He said news stories cause confusion when he travels to other countries. "The people over there ask me what's wrong with my country, what am I supposed to say?"[225] Touring the country, as he did to play his music, Armstrong might have been a good person to ask about the pace of progress with integration. In 1957, that same year as Little Rock, Armstrong played at the famous Ryman Auditorium in Nashville, Tennessee before an audience that was all white in the balcony and all Black in the orchestra level.[226] Segregated seating during events was the custom of the day in Southern venues.

In December 1959, Armstrong was asked by a *New Orleans Times-Picayune* reporter why he had not played in his hometown for some time. "I'm accepted all over the world and when New Orleans accepts me, I'll go home."[227] He told *Jet* that he would not appear in New Orleans because mixed bands were illegal. "I ain't going back to New Orleans and let them white folks in my own hometown be whipping on my head and killing me for my hustle," he said. "I don't care if I never see New Orleans again."[228]

Perhaps a better view of Armstrong's stance on civil rights was put forth by writer Larry L. King, who interviewed the jazz musician for *Harper's Magazine* in 1967. "He was not eager to talk about civil rights," said King. "When I first mentioned the subject as he dried out between shows in the dingy dressing room at

Atlantic City, Pops suddenly began to snore. The next time he merely said, "There are good cats and bad cats of all hues. I used to tell [American trombonist] Jack Teagarden—he was white and from Texas like you—'I'm a spade and you are okay. We got the same soul—so let's blow.'" But another time, King wrote, "He approached the racial topic on his own," and provided some examples of what touring through the South had been like in the early days.[229]

In February 1957, sticks of dynamite exploded outside the concert venue in Knoxville, Tennessee, where Armstrong was about to perform. No one was hurt, but a five-foot hole was blasted in the ground at the bomb site. Seating in the auditorium was segregated with 2,000 white and 1,000 Black jazz fans on a Tuesday night at city-owned Chilhowee Park. Louis Armstrong refused to allow an explosion to interrupt his tour. "I've been playing the horns for 44 years and never had any trouble before," he said. Everyone heard the blast and heads turned. Satchmo only stopped playing his trumpet long enough to say a few words. "It's okay folks. It was just my telephone ringing," he told the audience in an attempt at downplaying the noise.[230] Armstrong and his musicians played for another twenty minutes before boarding their bus and heading for Columbia, South Carolina, the next stop on their tour, which continued without missing a beat. A reporter said Knoxville was only about 20 miles from Clinton, Tennessee, where dynamite damaged 30 homes the week before during school integration protests. "What's Clinton?" replied Armstrong. "I'll blow anywhere. The horn doesn't know anything about these race troubles."[231] When Armstrong saw television footage of the violence occurring in Selma, Alabama, he was in Copenhagen, and he told reporters "He got sick" watching it. He said white segregationists "would even beat Jesus if He was Black and marching along . . . I saw it on the TV screen how cops used clubs on women and children, how they clubbed the kid's head full force," Armstrong told news reporters. "I got it served nicely on the screen after my dinner and I got sick."[232]

"Before Black ballplayers and political activists became household names, musicians were the only Blacks able to attract white Americans' attention and Satchmo was the first to make it big." wrote David H. Ostwald in an opinion piece in 1991. "He was the first Black man to be featured in Hollywood movies made for white audiences, as well as the first to serve as host on a sponsored network radio show. The power of genius, combined with his loving manner, forced whites to rethink their racism, whether they knew it or not."[233] Armstrong seemed to be one Black entertainer who was able to avoid the barriers of segregation. In February 1949, he made the cover of *Time* magazine wearing a crown of trumpets. Edward R. Murrow featured the trumpet player in the 1957 documentary *Satchmo the Great*. He had hit recordings from 1920s to the 1980s. He knocked the Beatles out of the top spot in the Billboard Top 100 with his 1964 hit *Hello Dolly!* and he received a Grammy Award for Best Male Vocal Performance for that same song in 1965. "The true revolutionary that's not apparent," trumpeter Lester Bowie told Armstrong biographer Gary Giddins. "I mean the revolutionary that's waving a gun out in the streets is never effective; the police just arrest him. But the police don't even know about the guy that smiles and drops a little poison in their coffee. Well, Louis, in that sense, was that sort of revolutionary, a true revolutionary."[234]

Generally, Armstrong's music kept clear of political thoughts, but his 1929 recording "Black and Blue" said more than people may have thought. "I'm white inside, but that don't help my case 'cause I can't hide what is on my face." Some have called it the first Black protest song. But Armstrong's avoidance of race discussion only lasted until 1957 when the musician finally lost his cool over school desegregation. "The way they are treating my people in the South, the government can go to hell," he announced while canceling a State Department sponsored tour of the Soviet Union when he heard Governor Faubus ordered the National Guard to stop the integration of Little Rock's schools.[235] He had a few canceled engagements but suffered no long-lasting damage to his career after his outburst.

Black entertainers put up with segregated seating at their shows, as well as threats of violence and on-stage attacks. They also faced more issues when they got home. The February 19, 2015 issue of *The Hollywood Reporter* provided examples of issues faced by Black entertainers. "In 1948, Nat King Cole was one of the most popular musicians in America, with hits like "(Get Your Kicks on) Route 66," but when he bought a house in all-white Hancock Park, his neighbors sued to block the purchase. When that failed, they burned the N-word on his front lawn and killed his dog with poisoned meat. Cole resisted the attacks, and his family stayed there until the 1970s. The publication said he fared better than William Bailey, a World War II vet and science teacher whose house was bombed when he moved into a white Culver City neighborhood. Fortunately, Bailey and his wife escaped unharmed. The Bailey bombing was one of at least six against Black families who moved into white neighborhoods in the 1950s.[236]

Regarded as a laid-back performer, Cole sang with a smooth voice that was easy listening. He seemed to be the one singer whom everyone could enjoy. On April 10, 1956, Cole was performing at the Municipal Auditorium in Brimingham, Alabama. As he was beginning his third song of the evening, "Little Girl," five men ran down the center aisle and onto the stage yelling racial slurs. One of the assailants lunged at his knees, knocked over the microphone stand, and sent Cole backward into a piano bench. Editorials across the country expressed disbelief that racial hatred was so deep in some parts of the country that it took a violent form against a singer whom many viewed as highly likable. His chin was cut by the microphone stand and his back wretched in the fall. A crowd of 4,000 "whites-only" people attended that show as laws at the time said all audiences had to be segregated. After the attack, he returned to the stage and received a ten-minute standing ovation. "I just came here to entertain you," he told the white crowd. "That was what I thought you wanted. I was born in Alabama. Those folks hurt my back. I cannot continue because I need to see a doctor."[237]

After being examined by a doctor, he returned to the arena to perform the second show for the all-Black audience. "The King is preeminently a stylist—not only in his unique vocal delivery, but in the polished projection of a keenly-honed personality which hardly anyone else in the entire theater firmament even remotely resembles," gushed *Variety*.[238] Born in Montgomery, Alabama, the son of a preacher father and a choir director mother, he may have been destined for a life as a singer. By high school, he led his own band and in 1937, at age 18, he sold his first song ("Straighten Up and Fly Right") for $50 to Capitol Records. The record label made a huge profit on that deal. Cole's sweet voice, calm personality, and inviting smile made him the first Black entertainer with a national television show. Regrettably, he was forced to abandon the show in 1957 when producers could not find a national sponsor for the program.

Other Black entertainers faced their own issues traveling in the Jim Crow South. Ray Charles refused a concert in Augusta, Georgia in 1961 as the civil rights movement was near its peak and the city remained a hotbed of racial tension. The city remained segregated, and the Black community was not allowed to use the same facilities as the white residents. Fearing some sort of violence, the city refused to allow him to perform. The issue highlighted the fact that all people of color could be subjected to racist attacks. When Charles was told the seating would be segregated, he said he would not play. He was sued and fined for breach of contract.

Were the experiences of Armstrong, Cole, and Charles unusual or did other Black entertainers face similar issues during the '50s and '60s? *Billboard* magazine conducted a series of oral histories with many of the stars who traveled throughout the country during the period and anyone listening would answer affirmatively. "They were Black. It didn't matter if they were Miles Davis or [Charles] Mingus," said lead singer Eddie Levert of The O'Jays. "These are people that sat there, enjoyed the music and danced to it. But because you're Black, we cannot serve you. Because you're Black, we have to beat you. Because you're Black, we have to have systemic racism, which goes on for years and years . . . Back then, giants of Black music, from the Supremes to the Temptations to Sam Cooke, following in the paths of forebears such as Marian Anderson, Lena Horne, and Sammy Davis Jr., had to eat sardines from cans on the highway because they weren't welcome at white restaurants," wrote Steve Knopper in the *Billboard* story. "They couldn't use restrooms at small-town gas stations. They couldn't walk freely through the very Las Vegas casinos they were headlining. They slept on each other's shoulders in station wagons because they couldn't stay at white hotels. Police attacked their buses . . . When you would get on the road, you had two shows you had to do—the matinee show at 4 p.m. for the Black audience and the white show at 8 p.m. for the white audience," said Stax Records singer William Bell. "We did the exact same set. That's what was so weird about it. After we had a little more success in recording, we just started protesting: 'Wait, we are only booked to do one concert, not two concerts.' So, they would have the white audience on the floor in the bottom of the concert near the stage and then the Black audience upstairs in the nosebleed section. But at least we were doing one concert. So, it was just a little bit at a time that we made a difference."[239]

Traveling the country became really difficult for Black entertainers and any other Blacks who wanted to take a trip. It could become very dangerous. There was a useful tool available, which was initially called *The Negro Motorist Green Book* when it was first published by Harlem mail carrier Victor Green in 1936, but many just called it "The Green Book." His goal was to provide African American travelers with information on restaurants, gas stations, and other businesses that welcomed Black travelers. Jim Crow still ruled the day and his alerts were designed at helping advise Black travelers of "sundown towns," or those communities that explicitly prohibited African Americans from staying overnight. The guides were published from 1936 to 1967. The first book listed safe places near New York City. "Sundown towns were throughout the country; they were everywhere, even on Route 66," said Candacy Taylor, author of *Overground Railroad*. "When you have that reality, you need a guide. You need something to tell you where you could stay that was safe."[240]

A Jewish friend gave Green the idea for the guidebook after he showed him guides for avoiding "restricted" gentile-only places. Green's wife, Alma, was from Virginia, so Green reached out to fellow mail carriers to get tips that would make his family's travel back to Virginia less humiliating. Many small towns outside of the South had Jim Crow laws so he figured these tips could be helpful to other travelers. It was a lifesaver for many Black travelers. An African American who ended up in the wrong place—wrong hotel or wrong restaurant—could be beaten, shot, and on some occasions even lynched. "It was a lifesaving guide," said Rodneyna Hart, Louisiana State Museum Director. "From 1936 to 1967, most of that time overlaps with the Jim Crow era. During that time, it was a dangerous environment for Black people to live. And whenever you are traveling, you don't know the lay of the land. You don't know what perils exist."[241]

Green died in 1960, four years before Congress passed the Civil Rights Act of 1964, which prohibited discrimination in public accommodations. Except during World War II, the *Green Book* was published annually until 1967. After his death, publication continued with his widow, Alma, serving as editor. Maira Liriano, associate chief librarian the Jean Blackwell Hutson Research and Reference Division in the Schomburg Center for Research in Black Culture at the New York Public Library, reports 22 of the annuals have been digitized. The 1966-1967 edition has not been digitized because of copyright restrictions, but the library has a printed copy. "After the Civil Rights Act passed, you can't discriminate on race," said Liriano. "African Americans could go to any hotel and restaurant and couldn't be turned away. Once it was the law of the land, the *Green Book* was not necessary." Even though he did not live to see it, Green got his wish. He wrote in the earliest versions of the guide that he prayed for a day when they would not be necessary. "There will be a day sometime in the near future, when this guide will not have to be published," wrote Green in an introduction to one of the annuals. "That is when we as a race will have equal opportunities and privileges in the Unites States. It will be a great day for us to suspend this publication for then we can go wherever we please and without embarrassment. But until that time comes, we shall continue to publish this information for your convenience every year."[242]

The *Green Book* sold for twenty-five cents in 1940 at Black-owned businesses and Esso gas stations, which "were among the only gas stations that sold to African Americans" on a regular basis.[243] Esso stations were owned by the Standard Oil Company and Victor Green developed a relationship with James A. Jackson, a Black marketing executive from Esso, which helped provide *Green Book* with a distribution arm by selling the guides in their retail stores. By the 1940s, Esso was one of the largest businesses in the world and one of the most progressive when it came to its treatment of Black people. The book quickly became popular and helped traveling businessmen as well as families on vacation to avoid bad situations. By 1949, the book cost seventy-five cents and was 80 pages in length. It covered the United States, Bermuda, Mexico, and Canada. "Carry your *Green Book* with you," the book warned readers on the cover. "You may need it!"[244]

The *Green Book* was the most famous but there were other travel guides for Black people that sold during the century. The first Black travel guide, *Hackley & Harrison's Hotel and Apartment Guide for Colored Travelers*, was published in 1930, six years before the *Green Book*. Edwin Henry Hackley, an African American lawyer, and Sarah D. Harrison, secretary at Connecticut's New London Negro Welfare Council, created the guide that listed hotels and motels in three hundred cities. Hackley died soon after it was published and Harrison could not produce the book alone, so it only lasted two years, 1930 and 1931. Another Black guide, *Grayson's Travel and Business Guide*, premiered in 1937. The book's subtitle, *A National Directory of Hotels, Cafes, Resorts and Motels, Where Civil Rights are Extended to All* summed up the goal of the publication. The National Park Service published its own *Directory of Negro Hotels and Guest Houses in the United States*. *Smith's Tourist Guide*, started in 1940, the *Go, Guide to Pleasant Motoring* (1952-1959) and *Travelguide* (1947-1963) were other guides aimed at making travel easier for people of color.

An example of how routine travel could be made very difficult was the journey taken by Jackie Robinson and his wife, Rachel, from Los Angeles to Daytona Beach for his first spring training with the Montreal Royals. They could not have known it at the time, but they would be leaving a comfortable life in California for an unpredictable one in the Southern United States. Jackie's mother, Mallie, accompanied them to the airport to say goodbye. She handed Rachel a shoebox filled with fried chicken and hard-boiled eggs. Her experiences as a Black woman in Georgia taught her to be self-sufficient. The young couple protested, because they viewed the box of food as a sign of a time when Blacks were restricted when they traveled and unable to find access to food in foreign places. The younger Robinsons saw themselves as part of a generation that could fly on airplanes and travel across the country without restrictions. They would soon learn how wrong they were.

Robinson was expected to be at training camp on March 1. He thought if he left Los Angeles late on February 28, he would be in camp in Daytona Beach the next afternoon. He could not have anticipated the troubles ahead. The Robinsons landed in New Orleans in the early hours of the morning for what was supposed to be a four-hour layover. "As our American Airlines flight approached the New Orleans airport, we were paged and told we were being removed from the plane, 'bumped' as they called it, without explanation or recourse," recalled Rachel Robinson. "We went into the terminal and challenged the decision. As Jack's voice began to rise in protest at the counter, I escaped to the ladies' room, only to be confronted with "White Women" and "Colored Women" signs. Shocked and indignant, I rushed into the white ladies' room with such speed and determination that I was stared at but not stopped. I re-emerged, my self-esteem momentarily restored, and joined Jackie. It was clear that his appeal had failed. There were no more planes that day, so we proceeded to a seedy hotel, as directed. That evening we sat on the side of the bed and pulled out Mallie's chicken. As we quietly ate, I could feel humiliation and a sense of powerlessness overpowering me. More importantly, I appreciated Mallie's wisdom as never before."[245]

The next day, they boarded a plane for Florida. The plane stopped in the Florida Panhandle for refueling. It was at that stop that the Robinsons were removed from that flight, too. Frustrated with flights, they went to the bus stations and boarded a Greyhound bus for the remainder of the trip to Daytona Beach. They selected seats in the center of the bus and fell asleep. At the next stop, the bus driver woke them up and told them to move to the back of the bus. Jackie, who had once been court-martialed for refusing to go to the back of a bus, obeyed the driver. The bus ride was long—eight hours to cross the state from Pensacola to Jacksonville, where they waited inside a segregated section of a bus station for another bus that would take them to Daytona Beach. They arrived at 3 p.m. on March 2. The trip from California to Florida took more than forty hours. Wendell Smith and Billy Rowe of the *Pittsburgh Courier*, a nationally circulated Black newspaper, were waiting for them at Daytona Beach station. Rowe drove them to the home of Joe Harris, who was active in the Black section of the city and his wife, Duff, in the segregated part of Daytona Beach. The trip was tiring for Jackie Robinson, who expressed some interest in quitting Major League Baseball. He didn't care for the Negro Leagues but at least he was treated the same as everyone else.

Just how dangerous was travel for Black people? Lynching was a real threat. Those who study these terrible acts define a terror lynching as a horrific act of violence (not just a hanging) where offenders were not held accountable. In other words, the murders and tortures were done, and the perpetrators were never punished. On many occasions, the event was held at a public space with a large audience present. The public nature of the violence helped spread fear and ensure compliance. In effect, the existing criminal justice system turned a blind eye to the crimes. The Equal Justice Initiative, a nonprofit organization based in Montgomery, Alabama started by lawyer Bryan Stevenson, author of *Just Mercy*, produced a report on the history of lynching in America. The Equal Justice Initiative staff spent six years researching and documenting terror lynchings in America. The organization documented 4,075 racial terror lynchings in 12 southern states between the end of Reconstruction in 1877 and 1950. They also documented 300 racial terror lynchings in other states during the same period.[246] This total number of lynchings was significantly more than had previously been reported. Mississippi, Georgia, Louisiana, and Arkansas had the greatest number of lynchings. Right behind them were Alabama, Texas, Florida, Tennessee, South Carolina, Kentucky, North Carolina, and Virginia. Outside the Deep South, Oklahoma, Missouri, Illinois, West Virginia, Mayland, Kansas, Indiana, and Ohio also had lynchings.[247] "Racial terror lynching was a tool used to enforce Jim Crow laws and racial segregation—a tactic for maintaining racial control by victimizing the entire African American community, not merely punishment of an alleged perpetrator for a crime," wrote the authors of the report.[248]

The stories of lynching in this country are graphic and sad. Although hanging from a tree was the most common form of lynching, victims were sometimes tortured and burned alive. Often times, mutilated body parts—lips, teeth, fingers, internal organs—were removed and sold as keepsakes. Lynchings were photographed and transformed into postcards, which were sold as souvenirs. Thousands of people attended the lynching, which would be conducted in public at the courthouse square. Rarely, if ever, did anyone object to the terrorism happening in their hometown.[249] The stories of the lynchings were the ones that would turn your stomach. How could people be so cruel to another human being? "One particularly gruesome lynching was the murder of a nineteen-year-old pregnant woman named Mary Turner," wrote Candacy Taylor in *Overground Railroad*. "In 1918, she was hanged upside down from a tree and set on fire. While she was still alive, the mob cut open her stomach, ripped her eight-month-old baby from her womb, and stepped on the crying baby's head until it died. Turner's body was then riddled with bullets. No one was charged for the crime."[250]

CHAPTER EIGHT

Beatles

It wasn't only Black artists who took a stand against the segregation and outright racism entertainers faced on the road. In September 1964, Jacksonville's Gator Bowl adhered to segregated seating, restrooms, and water fountains established by city rules. In 1964, five days before they were scheduled to play there, the Beatles released a statement protesting segregation in the city's municipal facilities and refused to play unless Blacks were allowed to attend without being segregated. "I would sooner lose our appearance money," than play to segregated audiences, said John Lennon. The city relented and opened the arena to all.[251]

On June 5, 2020, Paul McCartney posted a reminder of the historic stand taken by the famous quartet from England. "In 1964, the Beatles were due to play Jacksonville (Florida), and we found out that it was going to be a segregated audience," wrote McCartney. "It felt wrong. We said, 'We're not doing that!' And the concert we did was to their first non-segregated audience. We then made sure this was in our contract. To us, it seemed like common sense."[252] That stand might not seem so bold today, but in 1964 it was a huge deal. In his post, McCartney celebrated Black Lives Matter (BLM) and said the Beatles refused to play in front of segregated audiences in 1964. His comments came following the killing of George Floyd while in police custody. "We all need to work together to overcome racism in any form," he wrote on Twitter. "We need to learn more, listen more, talk more, educate ourselves and, above all, take action . . . I feel sick and angry that here we are almost 60 years later and the world is in shock at the horrific scenes of the senseless murder of George Floyd at the hands of police racism, along with the countless others that came before. All of us here support and stand alongside all those who are protesting and raising their voices at this time."[253]

The groundwork for that stand actually was formed months before. After the group appeared on *The Ed Sullivan Show*, they planned a tour of multiple United States cities. For assistance, Beatles manager Brian Epstein contacted Norman Weiss, who was vice president of a New York talent agency named General Artists Corporation (GAC). The television appearance went well and the group was due to tour—32 shows in 24 cities in 26 venues in 33 days. Epstein selected cities all across the country, including some in the South, such as Montgomery, Charlotte, New Orleans, and Jacksonville. Epstein selected the locations based on the availability of venues, without regard to local laws and customs. Specifically, he had not considered the Jim Crow laws prevalent in the South at the time in his selection of concert locations.

Already on tour and during a break between the afternoon and evening concerts, the Beatles returned to their rooms at the Sahara Hotel in Las Vegas on August 20, 1964. Larry Kane had told the Beatles that a radio station in Miami reported that the management of the Gator Bowl was steadfast in maintaining segregated seating during the concert. The Beatles were indignant. They all agreed that they would not play in Jacksonville under those conditions. "We don't like it if there is any segregation or anything, because we're not used to it," said McCartney. "We've never played to segregated audiences before and it just seems mad to me. I mean, it may seem right to some people, but to us, it just seems a bit daft." He ended his comments by including the three other bandmates. "This is the way we all feel and a lot of people in England feel that way because there's never any segregation in concerts in England and in fact if there was, we probably wouldn't play them."[254] The reporter published his story and soon the whole country knew that the Jacksonville concert would not happen unless the seating changed.[255]

In June 1963, President John F. Kennedy sought legislation that would "give all Americans the right to be served in facilities which are open to the public—hotels, restaurants, theaters, retail stores, and similar establishments." After Kennedy's assassination, President Lyndon Johnson took up the crusade using JFK's desire to desegregate as motivation. The result: The Civil Rights Act was signed into law July 1964, which opened all public facilities to all people.

When the Beatles' final tour dates were being ironed out, the group sent contracts to the localities. The contract requested some items such as police protection and other technical items such as spotlights and microphones. One request stood out: in clause six, it stated that the "ARTISTS WILL NOT BE REQUIRED TO PERFORM BEFORE A SEGREGATED AUDIENCE." The line was not just included in Southern locations but was included for all locations from the start of their touring dates in 1964 and continued through their tours over the next two years. It became known as the "desegregation clause." The group included the clause only in contracts for the United States; it was not considered necessary in other countries.[256] Jacksonville might get a black eye in some reports of the 1964 concert tour, but the rider was in force the entire three-year slate of dates from 1964 to 1966, beginning with San Francisco's Cow Palace all the way to the last show at Candlestick Park in 1966. The Beatles' challenge to local seating laws came at a significant time in the civil rights battles. About that same time as the Jacksonville concert, Martin Luther King, Jr. led marches in St. Augustine, Florida protesting segregation in area schools. Another complicating factor with the Jacksonville appearance at the Gator Bowl was the fact that Florida had been ravaged by Hurricane Dora, leaving many residents without power in the storm's wake.

In 1966, McCartney reflected, "We weren't into prejudice. We were always keen on mixed-race audiences. With that being our attitude, shared by all the group, we never wanted to play South Africa, or any places where Blacks would be separated. It wasn't out of any goody-goody thing. We just thought, 'Why should you separate Black people from white? That's stupid, isn't it?'"[257]

The Jacksonville promoters were not to blame for the seating. Jacksonville's Gator Bowl was municipally owned and followed laws enacted by the city. Whites were allowed to sit anywhere, but Blacks were relegated to certain sections. Prior to the passage of the Civil Rights Act of 1964, it was completely legal for the city of Jacksonville and other cities to implement seating restrictions. By the time the Beatles were due to play the Gator Bowl on September 11, the Civil Rights Act had been signed into law. Some Southern cities were slow to implement changes to seating policies. The Cramton Bowl in Montgomery, Alabama and American Legion Memorial Stadium in Charlotte, North Carolina were two other locations where the segregated seating issue arose. Ironically, the Beatles were scheduled to stay at the Jacksonville's Hotel George Washington, referred to as the "The Wonder Hotel of the South." That hotel did not accept African American guests, even after the passage of the Civil Rights Act. The reservations were canceled prior to the entourage's arrival but it is not clear who canceled them—the hotel or Beatles management (GAC). The Beatles' traveling party included a support act with Black musicians and their practice was for all entertainers to stay at the same hotel.

Director Ron Howard mined archival footage to reveal the Fab Four's shock at being asked to perform for a segregated crowd in his 2016 film *The Beatles: Eight Days a Week—The Touring Years*. "We were kind of quite intelligent guys, looking at the political scene and, coming from Liverpool, we played with Black bands and Black people in the audience. It didn't matter to us," said Paul McCartney. "We played Jacksonville (Florida) and we heard that the whites and the Blacks were going to be segregated and we just went, 'Whoa, no. No way," he said. "And we actually forced them then, which is very early on in the 60s, to integrate. We actually even put (it) in the contract."[258]

During the Little Rock school desegregation of 1957, when nine Black students enrolled in a previously all-white school, white adults shouted threats and threw objects at young Black students attempting to enter the building. Footage was shown worldwide. It left an impression on a young Paul McCartney, who had not dreamed of the Beatles yet. In April 2016, Paul McCartney recalled the event as he welcomed two special guests backstage at his concert in Little Rock, Arkansas. McCartney invited two members of the Little Rock Nine—Elizabeth Eckford and Thelma Mothershed Wair—backstage. The song "Blackbird," which appeared on the Beatles' White Album in 1968, was inspired by the civil rights struggles in the American South. It is a simplistic production—McCartney's voice, guitar, and a basic timekeeping device for accompaniment. "I was sitting with my acoustic guitar and I'd heard about the civil rights troubles . . . in Alabama [where Rosa Parks refused to move to the back of a bus in 1955], Mississippi [where three civil rights activists were murdered in 1964], Little Rock in particular," McCartney told *GQ* in 2018. "So, that was on my mind and I just thought, 'It would be really good if I could write something that, if it ever reached any of the people going through all those problems, it might kind of give them a little bit of hope.' So, I wrote 'Blackbird' . . . In England, a 'bird' is a girl, so I was thinking of a Black girl going through this," he added, explaining that the message was 'Now's your time to arise, you know, set yourself free' . . . One of the nice things about music is that you know a lot of the people listening to you are going to take seriously what you are saying in the song. I'm very proud of the fact that the Beatles' output is always really pretty positive... it's always 'Let It Be,' 'Hey Jude,' 'Blackbird.' It's hopefully a good message. Hopefully, people out there will listen to it and think, 'It's not just me alone going through this . . . it's also something I can fix.'"[259]

Beyonce's cover of the Beatles classic "Blackbird" in March 2024 was profound to listeners who knew that the song was influenced by the Little Rock Nine and the integration of a previously all-white school in Arkansas. Her version was featured on her album titled *Cowboy Carter*. "This is the story of my life," said Melba Pattillo Beals, who was one of the nine students. She was only 15 years old when she enrolled at Central High School in Little Rock, Arkansas in 1957. She and her eight Black classmates were escorted by members of the military while they endured verbal and physical harassment by white adults. Beals said she didn't think the song was about the Little Rock Nine when it first came out. Instead, she saw the message as a broader commentary on the plight of Black people. "I didn't think it was about the Little Rock Nine, but I wondered if it was about Black pain." In her view, she thought "Blackbird singing in the dead of night" reminded her of how slaves relied on music to cope with the stress of daily life. Further, the lyrics "take these broken wings and learn to fly" and "take these sunken eyes and learn to see" captured Black Americans' strength and determination in a country that historically prevented them from succeeding.[260]

Just like the Beatles were the top of the entertainment world during this era, the Green Bay Packers were the top of the National Football League. Lombardi inherited a team what had won only one game the previous season (1958) and turned them into winners. By 1960, they were playing in their first championship. It would be Lombardi's only playoff loss with the team. They won the title the next two years (1961, 1962) and returned with three straight titles (1965, 1966, 1967). While the nation struggled with civil rights and integration, the Green Bay Packers were a successful organization that also got along without racial strife.

Willie Davis was raised in the South, served in the army, and spent two seasons with the Browns, so he had seen many different perspectives on racial relations. "I tell you right now, Green Bay would be totally, totally misled if they felt for a minute that Lombardi didn't blaze the way, open the way for Black players and build us into champions. I think the league started to look around and see these Black players make a difference in Green Bay. You saw them pop up more frequently in other places and, I think to that extent, it was definitely driven by him."[261]

"One thing that gives me enormous pride was my father's complete lack of prejudice and bigotry," said Lombardi's son, Vince Jr. "If you could play football, the color of your skin was immaterial . . . In my father's day, the most visible kind of prejudice was racial prejudice. It's more than a little shocking to look back to the state of race relations when my father finally got his chance to lead an organization. He came to the Packers already acutely sensitive to the insidiousness and the consequences of prejudice. Throughout his childhood and into his college days, he was frequently called a 'wop.' While a member of the Fordham football team, he was suspended by the college's president for fighting in the locker room. The cause of the fight? One of his football teammates suggested that Lombardi stand next to a third teammate so that everyone could 'see who was darker.' That was enough to get my father going. Both my father and his tormentor wound up in the infirmary. Vince Lombardi was convinced, briefly, that it was the end of his football career . . . Of course, he survived the suspension and went on to pursue his teaching and coaching careers," continued Vince Jr. "But as head coaching jobs came and went, he became convinced that he was still suffering for being swarthy, ethnic, and Catholic. He felt that people whose names ended in vowels—like his own—were far less likely to get the highly visible and prestigious jobs in football. My father's chemistry was such that he took prejudice as a challenge, an obstacle to be overcome. Fortunately, he had the drive and talent to succeed at this challenge."[262]

Gary Knafelc had spent five seasons with the Packers before Vince Lombardi took over. Knafelc provided a view of the team before and after Lombardi's arrival. "Coach Lombardi knew we were going to have a lot more Blacks in, so he brought Emlen Tunnell in to kind of help them along the way," said Knafelc. "Emlen was not only a great football player, but a great human being. He knew the right buttons to push on everybody. He never offended anybody, but he was such a high-caliber guy, everybody looked up to him: black, white, pink, or purple."[263] Boyd Dowler saw firsthand Lombardi's actions with players of all colors. "He didn't back off because a player was African American," said Dowler of Lombardi. "I think he was more concerned with whether he felt he could deal with the player; if he dealt with the issue, the team would deal with the issue. I think he felt comfortable enough and confident enough in his own leadership and in the fact that he was the main influence on the Green Bay Packers. He wasn't afraid of it; he didn't recoil with the thought, 'Oh no, no I don't want to get too many African Americans.' I don't think that bothered him one bit because he thought he was beyond that, above that, and he would handle it and he did. He couldn't have handled it any better."²⁶⁴

At his first team meeting as the new head coach of the Packers in 1959, Lombardi told the assembled team, "If I ever hear 'nigger,' or 'dago,' or 'kike,' or anything like that around here, regardless of who you are, you are through with me. You can't play for me if you have any kind of prejudice." By his second season in Green Bay, after he had established himself, Lombardi also let local restaurants and bars in Green Bay know that if his Black players were not going to be served at those establishments, then they would be off-limits to the white players as well. Lombardi saw the segregation that first season with the Packers. "Before Coach Lombardi came, we would go to Winston-Salem for two weeks; we would play the Redskins and then play the St. Louis Cardinals. We stayed at the Oaks Motel and at that time, there was segregation, so the Blacks could not stay with us . . . When Coach Lombardi came in, we went down there one year and, in fact, that was the year we used to go to the Holiday Inn for our meals and meetings and the Black players weren't supposed to eat with us."²⁶⁵ Tunnell took the Black players to the back door of the Holiday Inn to eat. "A guy at the hotel said, 'You can't do that,'" said Knafelc. "Somebody told the guy, 'Either he eats with us, or your repair bill will be quite extensive.'" He asked if they were serious. "We're serious," was the answer. "From that day on, they ate with us at all of our meetings and the next year we went to the Army camp. We all stayed at Fort Bragg because we could all be together. Lombardi was going to have none of that (segregation) nonsense."²⁶⁶

"When a restaurant in North Carolina, site of a preseason game in 1959, made the Packers' four African American players enter and leave by the back door, Lombardi made the rest of the team do the same," recalled his son, Vince Jr. "After those same four African American players were forced to sleep in separate accommodations from the white players' lodgings, my father took them aside as the team was climbing onto the bus and told them, 'I will never—absolutely never—put you guys in this situation again. If it means we play no games down here, that's the way it will be.'"²⁶⁷

"Coach Lombardi's policy toward racism can be summed up in two words: zero tolerance," said Willie Davis, Packers' Hall of Fame defensive end. "I can tell you truthfully that more than a few players were shown out of Green Bay because they weren't buying into Coach Lombardi's policy. I would say nobody had more impact in creating diversity in the NFL than Coach Lombardi. It was partly because he took a new approach—almost playing ignorant to any kind of racial tension in the league. Right from the start, he treated us as equals. We were just players competing for a spot on the team. He chose not to see color in an era where most coaches chose to look the other way in terms of Blacks. It was as if he felt the best way to fix the problem of segregation and racism in the league was to actually pretend it didn't exist—at least to us."[268]

True to his word, in 1961 and 1962, the Packers played Washington in Columbus, Georgia and the Packers stayed at Fort Benning, an Army post. The entire Packers team stayed there. "I remember in 1961, in Georgia, we could not stay in the same hotel together," recalled Jerry Kramer. "We ended up staying in the Army barracks at Fort Benning. It was not comfortable. We were big football guys and we had to sleep on cots. But we did stay together as a team. I also remember in Georgia that the Black players had to stay apart from the rest of the players in the back of the restaurant we went to. We all sat in the back and Coach Lombardi informed us if we went up to the front of the restaurant to order something like a burger, it would be a $500 fine. Vince made it clear that there was to be no discrimination." Another player confirmed the simple accommodations. "I remember going to Fort Benning in 1962, my rookie year," said linebacker Nelson Toburen, out of Wichita State University. "It was September and the barracks were not air-conditioned. It was miserable. But Coach Lombardi was adamant that we stay together as a team."[269]

On September 7, 1963, the Packers played the Redskins in an exhibition game that drew 13,500 fans to Kingston Stadium in Cedar Rapids. The game was moved to Iowa after the Packers pulled out of a scheduled game in Columbus, Georgia with segregated seating. Green Bay downed Washington, 28-17. According to Packers' team historian Cliff Christl, Lombardi traded defensive end Bill Quinlan, safety John Symank, and center Jim Ringo due to their racial biases. Quinlan was traded after a racist rant at the team hotel in Long Beach. Quinlan exploded after hearing teammate Willie Davis had been named All-Pro ahead of him. Quinlan was white; Davis was Black. Packers administrator Pat Peppler claimed in a 2005 interview that Ringo was traded after he called Lombardi an Italian epithet.[270]

"The Cedar Rapids game was my rookie year," recalled tight end Marv

Fleming. "I didn't go to Fort Benning the previous couple of years, but I do know that in prior years playing the Redskins in Georgia, there were some problems and the team stayed at the Army base so they could stay together. I grew up in LA and went to college in Utah, so being separate from my white teammates would have been foreign to me if we had played down South. In fact, when we played in Cedar Rapids, there were about three buses full of my supporters from Utah who came to cheer me on. The real reason I remember Cedar Rapids is because it was where I made the team. You have to remember that was my prime concern—not the fact that we moved the game. It was the last exhibition game before the regular season the next week. I got lucky because our regular tight end, Ron Kramer, got sick and I took his place and had a great game. After the game, Willie Wood came up to me and said, 'Welcome to the Green Bay Packers.' I asked, 'What do you mean?' He said, 'Look at how well you played compared to your competition.' I did actually play better than my competition for the spot behind Kramer, Jan Barrett."

Fleming liked Cedar Rapids because it presented an opportunity, but a starting lineman saw it differently. "The game in Cedar Rapids was nothing special," said Jerry Kramer. "There wasn't much of a crowd. We had played in a place like that before, against the Giants in 1959, in Bangor, Maine. I guess I didn't realize we played that game there because of the conditions for the Black players in Georgia. What Coach Lombardi did by moving the game was completely in his character, though."[271]

"I was not new to integrating the South," said Packers' linebacker Dave Robinson, who was inducted into both the Professional and College Football Halls of Fame. "At Penn State, I integrated the Gator Bowl in Jacksonville at the end of the 1961 season. I found something interesting. We were down in Jacksonville for ten days and the only time I felt comfortable was those three hours I was on the football field. Jacksonville was segregated, obviously. We stayed in St. Augustine, Florida at a place called the Ponce De Leon Hotel. I had a room to myself. There was an article in the paper about me integrating the Gator Bowl. I didn't know it at the time. I remember when they wanted me to go to the press room at the hotel, but I wasn't allowed to be in the lobby. I had to take a freight elevator and go in the back way so I would not be seen. We also got to meet the Gator Bowl queen. She was giving the players on both teams a kiss on the cheek as we were in line being introduced to her. She kissed the guy before me and after me, but not me.

It's been like this my whole life. I didn't start the game. Later on, I found out why. Some guy sent in a letter saying he was ex-military and was an excellent shot; if I was introduced before the game, he was going to shoot me."[272]

Lombardi first saw what his Black players had to endure when the team traveled to New Orleans to play the Steelers on August 13, 1960. When the team pulled up to the downtown hotel and the white players got off the bus, African American safety Willie Wood broke an unwritten rule by entering the hotel lobby. It was a hot and humid New Orleans day so maybe he just wanted to get out of the heat. He was quickly escorted out of the hotel by a Black porter. To add insult to injury, he attempted to hail a cab to go to the Black hotel but grabbed a white cab and had to be directed to a Black cab. At that moment, Lombardi swore his team would never stay in separate accommodations again.

"There were teams in the NFL when I came into the league in 1965 that had quotas for how many Blacks they would have on their roster," said Bill Curry, who went into coaching after his playing days were over at Georgia Tech, Alabama, and Kentucky. "With the Packers, it was different. On our forty-man roster we had ten African American players. Lombardi did not care about the color of your skin. He would have had forty Blacks on the Packers if that gave him the best chance to win. He cared if you could play football and whether you were a good person. He had a gift for getting all those different personalities and backgrounds to work together. Vince did not tolerate racism. With the Packers, if you said one racist thing, you were cut from the team immediately."[273]

"There was one other item I noticed when we went down South to play," said Nelson Toburen, Packers linebacker from Wichita State University. "I could see the attitude of our Black players change when we went South of the Mason-Dixon line. I think they felt they had to act a certain way or risk retaliation. They seemed to become a bit more fearful. I think it was more so that the Black players who had been raised in the South acted this way, as opposed to the Black players who grew up in the North and West, where they hadn't faced the Jim Crow stuff growing up. I cannot say I blamed them."[274]

In his later years, Lombardi described his stance on race by saying his players were not Black nor white, but "Packer green." He did his best to be color blind and to treat all his players equally. But he realized that the world they faced away from the Packers facility was not blind to the discrimination that they faced off the field.

The Jim Crow prejudice that Black players faced when the team traveled South enraged Lombardi. After that first preseason with the Packers, Lombardi vowed he would never allow his team to be split by race. Any hotel that would not accept the entire team would get no Packers. It was the last trip, to Winston-Salem, North Carolina, where the Packers faced the all-white squad from Washington, which may have sealed the deal.

Why did Lombardi feel so strongly? "I have already referred to his sensitivity to prejudice," recalled son, Vince Jr. "But at the dinner table one night, many years later, he told us another story. One night, toward the end of the 1960 preseason, again in North Carolina, he was refused seating by a hostess. Naturally dark skinned, he was deeply tanned after many hours in the sun out on the practice field. The hostess mistook him for an African American man and turned him away. The next time the Packers played a preseason game in the South, rather than abiding by the racist 'Jim Crow' laws of that time and place, my father quartered the team at Fort Benning. Benning had no air conditioning, but it was an egalitarian Army base. It was this uncompromising attitude, as well as his swarthy Italian complexion, that led the African American players on the team to refer to my father as a secret 'brother.'"[275]

Lombardi even had to deal with the interracial marriage issue. He did it in his own way, which was unlike how others in the league worked. Packers defensive end Lionel Aldridge feared he might be the next Black player released from the team after marrying a white woman. His wife, Vicky, recalled what happened. "Lionel went in to meet with Coach Lombardi because he had heard the first interracial couple that had gotten married in pro football had been blackballed from the NFL," she explained. "It was rumored to be Cookie Gilchrist and he ended up going to the AFL. Lionel wanted to find out from Lombardi what would happen if we got married. According to Lionel, Lombardi said, 'You know what, I don't care who you marry as long as you keep the Green Bay Packers team clean, your nose clean, and play good football. Don't worry about it—the same thing won't happen to you that happened to Cookie Gilchrist.'"[276] Most players were familiar with Cookie Gilchrist not being welcome to come to the NFL because he was married to a white woman. "I think part of Vince's open-mindedness toward Black players went back to his being denied service at a restaurant in the South because they thought he was Black," said Jerry Kramer. "He also broke down barriers in Green Bay. There was a bar and restaurant there that banned the African Americans on the team. It was a very popular place in Green Bay. Vince had a meeting the next day and informed everyone on the team the place was off limits."[277]

"Lombardi was also honest enough to admit that other factors contributed to harmony on his teams," said Vince Jr. "'One thing that has helped us,' he once commented candidly, 'is that we've been winning. When you're losing, it's easy to have discontented players—Black and white . . . If you're Black or white, you're a part of the family. We make no issue over a man's color. I just won't tolerate anybody in this organization, coach or player, making it an issue. We respect every man's dignity, Black or white. I won't stand for any movements or groups on our ball club. It comes down to a question of love . . . You just have to love your fellow man and it doesn't matter whether he is Black or white. If anything is bothering any of our players—Black or white alike—we settle whatever it is right away.'"[278]

Stein, Marc. "LeBron James Says He Doesn't Care if Trump Shuns N.B.A. Over Protests." *The New York Times*, August 6, 2020.

Actions speak louder than words and Coach Lombardi came through when a question of race came his way. Lionel Aldridge joined the Packers in 1963 after he was drafted in the fourth round out of Utah State. He was the first rookie to start on a Lombardi team right from the opening game. He had started dating Vicky Wankier, a white Mormon woman from Utah, when the two attended college together. Their relationship blossomed and Lionel proposed. "Word got back, not only to the campus, but to my hometown," recalled Vicky. "Things were very prejudiced back then. I was called 'nigger-lover,' a lot—but we kept it going and we became very good friends. Then, in his last year of eligibility, they did not allow him to come back to school anymore. So, he tried to get into another university in that area and they blackballed him."[279]

The bad treatment continued in Green Bay. "The first time I went back to visit him, we were engaged," said Vicky. "He and Bob Jeter shared a place—apartment if you want to call it—and I was staying at a hotel. After the game, we'd all gone to a party at Henry Jordan's and all of the wives were sitting in a circle and all the guys, of course, were over at the bar. I was sitting next to Dixie Taylor [who was married to Jimmy Taylor at the time]. She turned to me and she saw the engagement ring on my hand and asked me who I was here with and I told her, 'Lionel Aldridge.' She got up and moved to the other side of the circle and then really nobody talked to me... It was my very first introduction as not even a wife, but just as an engaged person to Lionel. From early on Kathy Grabowski and Mary Ellen Bowman took me in and really took care of me, made sure I was included in on all the parties and that I was a part of the organization from early on."[280] They did not get married until a couple years later. At that point, they had both heard about NFL careers ending due to interracial relationships so they were concerned.

The Packers' wives appeared to be a close-knit bunch in those days. They had a tradition of rotating watch parties in which the wives would gather at one of their homes. When Vicky's first turn came, she proudly laid out a nice spread of food, but when game time arrived, none of the invited guests appeared. She called around and heard a variety of excuses. The message was clear: she was being snubbed. On another occasion, she arrived at the Packers home game and went to take her seat among the Black Packers wives. They had given her seat away. Jim Grabowski's wife Kathy overheard and invited her to sit with her. The two would become longtime friends.[281] "About the last year of Elijah Pitts' playing with the Packers in 1969, we were all at a party at a hotel and Ruth Pitts came in, called me in, went to the bathroom, and said she had something to say to me," said Aldridge. "She apologized for how the Black women had treated me, how unfair they had been to me, she was so sorry and if she could do it over again, she would certainly try to make my life more comfortable up there."[282]

Vicky Aldridge is convinced that they would not have been married if Lombardi had been neutral or opposed to the union. She said Lionel loved playing football. After Lombardi gave his blessing, Commissioner Pete Rozelle came to Green Bay and tried to stop it. According to Vicky Aldridge, Lombardi stood his ground. Her parents even wrote Lombardi a letter and tried to get him to stop the marriage. Lombardi refused. Could anybody pressure Coach Lombardi to change his mind? "Absolutely not," said Lombardi. "This is my team. My team is who my team is and no one can tell me what I can and cannot do." Vicky Aldridge was thankful to have Lombardi on her side. "Coach Lombardi was totally a racial pioneer," said Vicky Aldridge. "He stuck his neck out for us and for his beliefs."[283] She continued, "I don't think he believed in any kind of racial discrepancy... I don't think he had anything—any care at all about color. I think he was color blind, as far as that was concerned. He came up and talked to me, he would ask me how things were going, make sure everything was going okay and always seemed to care, always seemed to be concerned and make sure that nobody was treating me really bad."[284]

After the rough treatment at college and initially at the Packers, Aldridge appreciated how Coach Lombardi treated her. A reporter wanted to know what she would say to him after all these years, given the opportunity. "Well, I don't know if I could say too much." she began. "I would hug him and kiss him and thank him so much and maybe kiss his ring like everybody else did. I know he was probably one of the greatest influences in my life, as a Packers wife and somebody that helped me stand up for my beliefs. A person that has that kind of power, that can help you back up your beliefs—gave me a lot of self-confidence, I could not thank him enough. He was the most wonderful man. I love him."[285]

CHAPTER NINE

Southern Traditions

When President John F. Kennedy planned a Texas swing in late 1963, his advisers were concerned. Many of the city's wealthiest citizens belonged to the John Birch Society, which was opposed to Kennedy, the United Nations, and many other issues they considered too liberal. JFK's advisers feared the city with good reason as handbills featuring Kennedy's picture and the headline "Wanted for Treason" were posted around Dallas. On the day of the president's arrival in the city, conservatives paid for a full page ad in *The Dallas Morning News*, accusing the president of being soft on Communism.

As the NFL expanded into Texas with the Cowboys, Black players met racism in Dallas firsthand. An early signee of the Dallas Cowboys when they were building their first roster as an expansion team, Don Perkins became one of the more heralded rookies on the team. At the University of New Mexico, Perkins rushed for more than two thousand yards in three seasons. Technically, the Baltimore Colts owned his NFL rights, but the expansion Cowboys, eager to build a team in a short period of time, signed him to a personal services contract before swinging a trade. He had been selected to play for the College All-Stars that summer in an exhibition game against the world champions. A broken foot in the practice sessions for that game ended his first season before it even began. Perkins came back strong in 1961, determined to win a starting spot and make amends for the missed opportunity the previous year. A dark-skinned Black man, Perkins had deep-set eyes and an impressive speaking voice. Although only five-foot-ten and 190 pounds, he consistently gained tough yards on inside runs up the middle. He finished that first playing season with 815 hard-earned rushing yards behind an offensive line that really wasn't that good. That level of production earned him second place in the NFL Rookie of the Year voting to Chicago tight end Mike Ditka.

When he first heard he would be joining the Cowboys, Perkins felt some level of excitement. He had some fond memories of his visits with relatives in Texas as a youth. Although he was raised in Waterloo, Iowa, his father hailed from Texas where some family remained. But his return as an adult to this part of Texas didn't bring back any fond memories. At the time, Dallas was the most racially divided city in which he had ever lived. For that reason, he left immediately after the season ended to return to Albuquerque, where his college football days helped him find a better job than would be available to him in Dallas. The only employment he could find in Big D was a job driving a truck.

The Cowboys were run by General Manager Tex Schramm, whose Los Angeles Rams teams had more players of color than most other NFL squads at the time. Most teams had a practice of stacking Black players at the same positions, so they competed with one another for a limited number of spots, which served to keep the overall numbers down. The Cowboys under Schramm had equal opportunity on the playing field, but off the field was another matter. Blacks roomed with Blacks and whites roomed with whites, which was common in the league at the time. To his credit, Schramm quietly arranged for the Ramada Inn at Love Field to drop its all-white policy for visiting NFL teams, which had been transporting their Black players to a run-down hotel in a Black part of Fort Worth prior to that negotiation.

Perkins faced discrimination in Dallas right from the start. After he landed at Love Field and attempted to hail a taxi from the airport, the cab driver informed him that he had flagged down the wrong cab. It was against the law for a white cab driver to drive a Black fare from the airport. Perkins was told he needed to call a Black taxi with a Black driver in order to get a ride. It didn't stop there. Perkins found many challenges when it came to locating adequate living accommodations in Dallas. Blacks were limited to one part of town, Oak Cliff, which was on the south side of the city, away from the practice facility. White players lived close to the practice facility while Blacks had a long commute to a home that didn't feel much like home. When his patience had run dry, Perkins told the media how Black Cowboys "do not feel a part of the team or the city." Renting a place in north Dallas was almost impossible for a Black man. Home ownership was the only sure path to the nice part of town as Pettis Norman, Jethro Pugh, Mel Renfro, Mike Johnson, and Bob Hayes learned.

"Perk called me to help find him housing for the season," said Pettis Norman who lived in South Dallas. "So far, I haven't found him anything. The sad thing or the sad part about it is everyone shakes your hand and pats you on the back and yet when you come to look for an apartment they say, 'Why did you have to pick my place?'" The disconnect puzzled Bob Hayes. "It's tough after game when the white players head north and the colored players had south," he said. "We play together and love one another, why not live together?" Mel Renfro said, "I could write a book about what I've been through."[286]

Renfro recalled, "I wasn't in Dallas three days when I got a dose of Jim Crow. It was borderline Oak Cliff, South Dallas, where there were a lot of white businesses. There was a white restaurant and a Black restaurant right next door. It looked like the white restaurant was a little nicer, so I walked in there to have breakfast. I was refused service. I was told, 'We don't serve coloreds here. You go eat next door.' I said, 'I didn't order a color. I ordered breakfast.' That didn't stand too well with them. And I went next door and had a great breakfast. I learned my lesson. I remembered what my dad said, 'If they don't want you, get away from it. Don't rock the boat, because you'll get hurt.' So, I started looking for places where I knew I would be accepted. Mostly Black restaurants. Very few times would I go to North Dallas or a white area unless it was a team thing, or somewhere where we knew we could go."[287]

Mel Renfro was born in Houston, Texas in 1941, but his brother's health issues prompted the family to leave the rigid segregation of Texas for the better climate and opportunities of Portland, Oregon when he was young. His father found employment as an elevator operator at the Montgomery Ward department store in the northwest section of Portland. The war effort had provided a boom to the local economy, helping all other industries. His mother found work in the shipyards. The return to Texas for professional football did not go well for Renfro. He faced segregation at restaurants and was equally bothered by his new team's racial attitude toward its minority players. When he first arrived, Cowboys management directed him to the apartments in the Oak Cliff district in south Dallas, some 26 miles from the North Dallas practice facility. Mel and wife Pat moved into the Sutherlin Apartments in Cedar Crest. They joined the other Black Cowboys football players—[Amos] March, Cornell Green, Pettis Norman, and Frank Clarke. The living arrangements worked for team camaraderie despite the extended commute to the practice facility. The restaurant discrimination didn't bother Mel. He expected as much, as he remembered the words of his father, "'Melvin, don't make a scene; it will only cause you trouble.' It's funny, because when I first moved to Dallas as a rookie in 1964, the first place I drove to was the Cowboys office and they directed me to an apartment complex in South Dallas where four or five other Black ballplayers were living. It was just automatic. It was okay. It wasn't a slum. It was the Cedar Crest Apartments, one of the nicer apartments for Blacks in that area. But just to automatically say, 'This is where you go . . .'"288

Pettis Norman spent his first decade in rural Georgia, working with his nine brothers and sisters to help his father sharecrop the land. After his father passed, the family moved to Charlotte, North Carolina. The adjustment from a rural two-room schoolhouse to a bigger school was difficult, but he slowly made it. It was in Charlotte where he played organized football for the first time. His athletic ability caught the attention of the coach at Johnson C. Smith University, which was located near the family home in Charlotte. They offered a full scholarship. He ran track and played football in college. After the AFL Dallas Texans spread the word that Norman signed a contract with them, no NFL team drafted him. After the negotiations with the Texans fell apart, Norman signed a free agent contract with the Cowboys. He started at tight end from 1962 to 1970 before moving to San Diego as part of the deal that sent Lance Alworth to Dallas.

"I would find an apartment or duplex that had a For Rent or For Lease sign on it and I would go up and immediately it was not available," continued Renfro. "Several times when we would call on the phone and we would get there, it was always leased or it wasn't available. I understood what it was and I didn't want the problem of fighting it. I would just go on to the next thing. But then, in 1968 when my wife and went and looked at a duplex and there were ads in the paper and For Lease signs and we actually went in and talked to the people and they actually said there were three or four units available, and did we want to sign up? We said no because the rent was kind of high. At that time $375 a month was a little more than we wanted to pay. I had a game that weekend, so I flew to Philadelphia and she went home. And while I was in Philadelphia I told my wife, 'Aw, what the heck. You only live once. We want to live in a nice place out near the practice field. Go back in and make the deal.' So, she went in and from the time we had been there, all the signs had been pulled out of the ground and there were no more units for lease, just for sale and I was so livid I could hardly play the game."[289]

Teammate Mel Renfro and his wife, Patricia, had had enough with the problem of segregated housing in Dallas. Like many other Black players, they had been turned down repeatedly for apartments once their race had been revealed, so they took legal action. Patricia recalled an incident in which she was about to sign the lease when the agent they were dealing with declared no more than two children could live in the house. The Renfros had three children at the time. "I was refused a place to live, a personal place to live," said Renfro. "It was blatant. It was unfair."[290]

Texas State Senator Oscar Massi from Dallas heard what was happening and reached out to Mel Renfro. The two agreed to fight the issue. They took a fair housing lawsuit to federal court. Tex Schramm called Renfro and asked him to stop the lawsuit. He said it would hurt him. "Actually, I got a lot of good letters, a lot of good phone calls from people saying, 'We are glad you are doing this, because they're not messing with us anymore. Now we can get a place and not be denied,'" recalled Renfro. "Then on the other side of the coin the hate mail came. It was ugly. I told my wife one time, 'Don't ever open a letter that looks strange and has no return address on it.' It scared her to death. I took a couple of them and put them on the bulletin board at the practice field and they weren't up five minutes before someone took them down. Never found out who. But they came off in a hurry."[291]

The courts ruled in Renfro's favor and the builder told him he could move into any unit in the complex. Renfro decided he would not move in, as he feared for his family's safety if the public knew where he lived. Good came out of the lawsuit, however, as housing opened up in Dallas. "In those days, I did not live in that great a neighborhood, but where the Blacks lived was far worse." recalled Pete Gent, a wide receiver for the Cowboys and author of *North Dallas Forty*. "When we went on the road Dick Daniels and Mike Johnson were afraid to leave their personal belongings in their apartments where they lived because it was in the paper they were out of town, so they would load up their stereos, TVs, and radios in their cars and drive over to my house and park them in my driveway, because we had firemen next door so there was always somebody watching the house. At the time, the Blacks still had problems finding hotels. I remember the first time we went to New Orleans in 1966, we stayed at the airport hotel, because no hotel downtown would take us. It was horrible. Those guys had such a tough time. They had to try and act like it wasn't happening."[292]

Steve Perkins of the *Dallas Times Herald* took an informal survey of the African American players on the team and concluded "none believes there is a racial problem on the Cowboys (but) they are nevertheless bitter about many aspects of their off-the-field life in Dallas and are 100 percent in agreement with Perkins bringing matters into the open. One facet of the team arrangements irks them plenty. This is the practice, on the road, of using separate rooms for Negro and white athletes who wind up without roommates." As an example, they said if the number of Blacks and whites was uneven, players were booked into singles rather than mixing the races.[293]

"Very few times would I do North Dallas or a white area unless it was a team thing or somewhere we knew we could go," said Mel Renfro. "I can remember when the team would go to an area where there was segregation, Coach Tom Landry used to say, 'Fellas, we know what's going on here. We don't particularly agree with it, but that's the way it is, so we have to do what we can so we don't create unnecessary problems.' And sometimes we would joke about it. I'll never forget Willie Townes. He called Coach Landry 'Presbyterian Tom.' We'd say, 'There goes Presbyterian Tom again.' Here's a guy who supposed to be a Christian and yet he's condoning segregation. He is saying, 'This stuff is happening and though we may not agree with it, we'll ignore it and stay in our lane.' I'm still a very sensitive person to things like that. But the way I was brought up, my dad told me, 'Just get away from it. Don't challenge it.' But still, you have to be a man. Be a man. Ande after being denied housing three or four times, the fifth time I said, 'I'm not going to stand for this.'"[294]

When Perkins searched for housing, he made calls to apartment owners. He had no problem when he phoned real estate agents to schedule appointments to see available houses or apartments. Perkins possessed a strong speaking voice with a dignified speech pattern, much like a professional announcer. White real estate agents were happy to show their listings to a caller they assumed to be white. Perkins noticed that their welcoming manner evaporated quickly when Black Don Perkins arrived in person. Agents claimed that their properties had been rented in the short time between when "white sounding" Perkins hung up the phone and when dark-skinned Perkins arrived at the house or apartment. As he later recalled, "It's always been the same story. The apartment selector service refers us to an out-of-town owner and then the owners won't even talk to us."[295]

The discrimination extended to eating establishments, too. After his time with the College All-Stars ended, Perkins returned to Dallas and Cowboys' Scouting Director Gil Brandt took Perkins and quarterback Don Meredith to lunch at Dallas' Highland Park Cafeteria. As they got in line to be served, a cafeteria employee told Perkins, "I'm sorry. You can't eat here." Perkins was speechless. The group immediately left the cafeteria and found another restaurant in which to eat. Perkins had lost his appetite after his first encounter with race in Dallas. He went back home to New Mexico to rest and rehabilitate his broken foot.

Like Perkins, teammate Cornell Green did not live year-round in Dallas, which was primarily due to housing. He said it took him two months to find a place before the start of every season. But Green insisted he got along with his teammates. In the locker room, Green was best buddies with Dan Reeves and Walt Garrison. "His locker was there with Walt and I," Dan Reeves said in agreement. "He was thirty-four, we were thirty, thirty-two. Whichever one of us got to the dressing room first would light the other one a cigarette and hand it to them when we got there, we were just close, close friends." It seemed like Don Perkins' public complaint got results. A newspaper reader and Cowboys fan helped the Perkins family find what they were looking for. Then Tex Schramm reached out to real estate agents and city leaders on behalf of the Black players who wanted to live closer to where they practiced. "It's a problem in all cities and it is difficult on our players," Schramm admitted. "If the problem is as acute as Don indicates, then we will do more."[296]

Don Perkins played basketball, football, and ran track in high school in Waterloo, Iowa where he frequently was the only Black on the team. Asked about racism growing up, he felt like there was not much of an impact on him. "I was an exceptional athlete, so I didn't have any problems," he said. "I didn't have any problems with coaches or with students. You always have problems with people when you are not in the majority, but I'm sure I had fewer problems than most, because, after all, I was a super jock."[297] The closest Don Perkins may have come to any issues during his high school days came with dating. Interracial dating and marriages were still taboo during this period, but Perkins attended a largely white high school, so his prospects were limited. When he dated white girls, he needed to do it quietly and not in public.

Cowboys teammate Frank Clarke, who grew up in Wisconsin, shared the concerns of racism in the South, especially the segregated businesses. "You could walk into a 5-and-10 cent store and see (water) fountains marked 'colored' and 'white,'" he said. "I had never seen this, it kind of takes your breath away. You go, 'Holy smokes. How far away are we from lynchings?'" Author John Eisenberg, who grew up in Dallas, observed, "Black and white Cowboys . . . were cheered as heroes on Sundays, but once the game was over the Blacks were subjected to the same discrimination that all Blacks in Dallas endured."[298]

Dallas had a reputation as being a segregated city. Pete Gent, who never played college football, came to the Cowboys after a solid basketball career at Michigan State. He is well-known as the author of *North Dallas Forty*. A white receiver with the Cowboys, Gent took note of how casual people in Dallas seemed to maintain discrimination despite the passage of the Civil Rights Act in 1964. "I was shocked that in 1964 America, Dallas could have an NFL franchise and the Black players could not live near the practice fields in North Dallas, which is one of the reasons I titled the book *North Dallas Forty*," said Gent. "I kept asking why the white players put up with their Black teammates being forced to live in segregated south Dallas, a long drive to the practice field."[299]

In Renfro's view, Hall of Fame coach Tom Landry deployed a strategy of ignoring Jim Crow practices throughout the South. Landry wanted to let social change play out on its own and did not want any of the Cowboys to lead it. "Tom was aware of racism," said Renfro. "When we played an exhibition game in 1965 in Birmingham, Alabama, Tom warned the Black players that there were some places that we perhaps should not go. It was like he was saying: don't make waves, don't cause problems. To me, that was capitulation. I was insulted by it. My feeling was: Why even go to Birmingham? Did it mean anything to them that Black people were being lynched there? Some Black players thought Tom was a racist. I don't believe he was. Tom Landry was a very fine man. But I could not really defend him then because I was sensitive to the issue of segregation."[300]

Pettis Norman, tight end with the Cowboys from 1962 to 1970, offered another view of the famous coach. "The fact is, Tom would not play in cities where our players had to eat separately," said Norman. "In New Orleans, he refused to let us stay at the segregated hotels. He would find places where we could eat and stay together. Tom Landry did not condone segregation. Tom knew all about my participation in sit-down demonstrations when I was in college in Charlotte, North Carolina. He could have said, 'Why get a troublemaker?' These were the kind of things some of the Black players overlooked. There was a lot of anger and people needed scapegoats, on both sides."[301]

Most athletes witnessed protests from afar, but others found themselves right in the middle of it. Norman, who had attended Johnson C. Smith University in Charlotte, North Carolina, participated in lunch counter sit-ins that ultimately spread across the country. "My earliest hands-on involvement in civil rights occurred on February 1, 1960, with my fellow Johnson C. Smith University students," recalled Norman. "We followed the news out of Greensboro that four Black male students at North Carolina A&T State University were conducting the state's first sit-in. They sat at Woolworth's lunch counter, defying the 'Whites Only' food service policy. Ezell Blair Jr., David Richmond, Franklin McCain, and Josephy McNeil were denied service but refused to move from their seats. The police arrived but did not take action. The media was called and televised the event. The four young men stayed seated until the store closed and then came back the next day with more students. Their audacity and bravery inspired me to travel to Greensboro and join the cause."[302]

Norman's awareness of social justice deepened in college, influenced by Johnson C. Smith University's motto—"Become yourself; Change our world." This left a big impression on him. A chance meeting with young Jesse Jackson, a freshman at North Carolina A&T at Greensboro, also provided a connection that turned into a solid friendship. Norman met Jackson at a demonstration and cemented their dedication to social justice through student activation. "Our cause was just," said Norman. "Throughout the month of February, we were joined by hundreds of Black students across North Carolina who sat in at lunch counters. By March, the protests expanded into Nashville, Baltimore, Houston, and New Orleans. Today, people asked if I was worried about losing my football scholarship or ruining my chances to play in a professional league based on my participation in student protests. I tell them I did not let those thoughts bother me, not then or later in the NFL, even with a football scholarship riding in the balance. We were encouraged, not discouraged, to protest by our university administrators."[303]

"For me, football was never an end in itself," said Norman. "It was an opportunity to provide an example to others that we can all make a difference, regardless of the unrelenting problems in our path. Civil rights demonstrations, specifically the lunch counter sit-ins, taught me the impact of peaceful but powerful action."[304] Norman put action to his words. The first issue he wanted to challenge was the Cowboys practice of separating players by race. He went to Coach Landry and Tex Schramm and requested a change to the team's practice of segregation. He said the team's segregation sent the wrong message to the community. A couple of months later, training camp opened and Schramm told him he would be rooming with Dave Manders, who was white and the next name on the roster alphabetically. After success with the Cowboys and King's "I Have a Dream" speech, Norman felt motivated to do more. "I focused on the concept of equal rights and inclusion in my community through open dialogue and joined causes off the field that I believed could address the anger and outrage that still simmered, sometimes boiling over. In the midst of this turmoil, Dick Nolan named me the 'Fastest Tight End' in the league in 1964, but this did not affect my salary. I continued to work multiple off-season jobs and in my case, the cause of civil rights became a 'job' of its own."[305]

Players from visiting teams shared stories of bad experiences playing road games in Dallas. Lenny Moore of the Baltimore Colts recalled the team landing at the Dallas airport for an exhibition game against the Giants in 1960. "When we arrived at Love Field, the plane wouldn't taxi to the gate, because the airport did not allow Black people," said Moore. "Buses had to be sent to pick us up. When they arrived at the tarmac, the white players boarded them while the Black players had to walk all the way to the airport. The airport's taxi wouldn't take us to the hotel, so general manager Don Kellett talked to management and had them send three cabs out to take us. We stayed at the Peter Lane Hotel in the Black section of town. The same thing happened to the Black Giants players who roomed just around the corner from us at the Green Motel. All of us met to discuss whether or not we should boycott the game because of the way we were treated. We felt Jackie Robinson would have played no matter how poorly he had been treated, so we decided not to boycott. Some of us had second thoughts, though, as we Black players were herded on yet another 'Black-only' bus to get to the stadium."[306]

Moore recalled in his autobiography, "By the time I arrived in Baltimore, the city was alive with debate about MLK's boycott of Montgomery, Alabama's bus system and Rosa Parks' refusal to give up her seat on a Montgomery bus. Needless to say, these events gave impetus to a domino effect. For the Black population, there had always been a dilemma: the fear of inciting physical harm at the expense of abrogating our rights. For centuries, Blacks have had to think carefully about their every move. Given the bravery of MLK and Rosa Parks, though, Blacks were determined to keep the issue of racial injustice in the forefront of society's collective mind—it was all about keeping the pot on the stove, as it were. The Montgomery Blacks were putting their lives on the line. They had stuck their necks out to be agents of social change. Still, the order of the day was nonviolence, even when violence was occurring everywhere, by virtue of white policemen and their German shepherds, their billy clubs, and their firehoses."[307]

Moore said the situation was worse when the team went to summer camp at Western Maryland College (now McDaniel College) in Westminster, Maryland, which is about 36 miles northwest of Baltimore. "It was a blatantly racist town where, outside of going to practice once or twice a day, there was nothing for a Black person to do," said Moore. "We couldn't go to the movies or the restaurants; the only thing we could do was walk the streets. There was one food stand, way out on the outskirts of town, that wasn't afraid to serve the Black players on the team. It wasn't a restaurant in the sense that there was no place to sit, but that didn't bother us. It was just a relief to get out of the dorm rooms we were relegated to and eat food that wasn't served cafeteria style for a change. Thinking back, it was dehumanizing and we hated it, but we didn't have much of a choice. Most of us let the restrictions roll off of us like the rest of the treatments we received, but once in a while the pressure got to be unbearable for us each individually. As Milt Davis said once, 'I cannot endure the mental punishment. Being Black, there are so many pressures.'"[308]

Moore thought the experience was different for his white teammates. One introspective white athlete who understood the plight of the Black athlete has an impressive resume. Bill Bradley was a Rhodes Scholar, played ten seasons in the NBA, and represented New Jersey in the United States Senate for eighteen years. "I have struggled with the issue of race for most of my adult life," admitted Bradley. "On its face, racism is stupid. Common sense tells us that no one person is exactly like any other person. Each is unique. Race as a category in a multiracial society should ideally have very little meaning. America is not yet such a society. Cursed by two hundred and forty years of slavery and more than one hundred years of systematic and degrading discrimination against Blacks and buffeted by generations of Black survival techniques, white guilt and denial and racist assumptions and actions, America is a nation obsessed with the interplay between African Americans and white Americans."[309]

Bradley continued, "When I was fourteen, Central High School in Little Rock, Arkansas, was forcibly integrated by order of President Dwight Eisenhower. On television, I saw the federalized National Guard troops, helmeted and uniformed, escort Black students into the high school through taunting white mobs. It all seemed so foreign from Crystal City, where I had been playing Little League baseball with Black friends since I was nine, where an African American was vice president of his newly integrated high school class and where every afternoon for three hours alone in the high school gym, I practiced my basketball moves, pretending I was Elgin Baylor. But, as I reflected later, I didn't have one Black female friend at the time. I had never danced with a Black partner. No one in the town had declared interracial dating an issue; such associations were simply taboo. I had been as brainwashed as anyone when it came to the question of who was beautiful and who was not and in Crystal City the issue was buried so deeply that it never surfaced."[310]

Bradley further recalled, "I remember one hot July evening in 1967, walking into the common room of our barracks at Air Force Officer Training School in San Antonio. The news was on TV and there were shots of tanks in the streets and soldiers with guns and helmets. 'Where is this?' I asked, wondering if we were at war somewhere other than in Vietnam. 'It's Detroit,' someone said. I stood in a state of shock. Detroit? I had read about and seen pictures of the Watts riot in Los Angeles two years earlier and also of disturbances in Harlem, Jersey City, Birmingham, Jacksonville, Chicago, Cleveland, and Milwaukee, but now American tanks were patrolling the streets of Detroit and the National Guard was occupying Newark. The march toward greater equality seemed stalled, or maybe even derailed. The war in Vietnam had sucked up the country's resources and now, with urban riots in which people broke the law not as a moral act of civil disobedience to bring about a greater good but simply in defiance of the state, I feared the disappearance of political consensus for reform."[311]

While the country was struggling with civil rights, sports became an opportunity for change. "Basketball, perhaps above all other sports, affords a unique perspective on a fundamental moral issue of our times: the need for racial unity," wrote Bill Bradley. "Bill Russell once said that the reason he liked the game was because it was about numbers, while much else in life was politics. The implication was that given the politics of life in America, a Black man would not be able to rise with his ability, because somewhere along the line racist thinking and racist acts would subvert his achievement, whereas in basketball you got the rebound, or you didn't. The ball went in, or it missed. There were no artificial barriers between ability and reward."[312]

Bradley spent time with all of his Black teammates and came to understand the issues they faced growing up Black in America. His teammate Dick Barnett grew up in a Gary, Indiana slum that was surrounded by more prosperous white neighborhoods. The air smelled from the factories in his part of town. "The Atlanta of Walt Frazier's childhood was a world of separate and unequal societies for white and Black people," observed Bradley. "The wrestling matches, the buses, and the ballparks had special Black sections; even the drinking fountains were segregated. Clyde and his friends called whites 'crackers.' They often played with them in pick-up games or swam with them in creeks, but, as Clyde recalls, 'Once you left that field, you went your separate ways.'"[313]

Knicks team captain Willis Reed was the only child on his grandfather's 200-acre farm ten miles east of Bernice, Louisiana. He learned the practice of hard work at an early age tending watermelons, picking cotton, and cutting grass.

Earl Monroe grew up in a rough gang-infested part of Philadelphia where life was dangerous. "When Earl was eight years old," Bradley shared, "he saw a stabbing in which the assailant literally cut the heart out of his victim and threw it on the street in front of twelve petrified onlookers. It was the first of three killings he was to witness."[314]

"You can't play on a team with African Americans for very long and fail to recognize the stupidity of our national obsession with race," continued Bradley. "The right path is really very simple: Give respect to teammates of a different race, treat them fairly, disagree with them honestly, enjoy their friendship, explore your common humanity, share your thoughts about one another candidly, work together for a common goal, help one another achieve it. No destructive lies. No ridiculous fears. No debilitating anger."[315]

"Being Black in America at that time was not the greatest thing in the world, let me tell you," recalled basketball star Oscar Robertson about his childhood years.

"At the time I did not know we were poor. I did not know we were being discriminated against. The only time I even saw white people was at a very early age back in Tennessee—those farmers that my dad worked for. Otherwise, I never had any contact with white people. I never thought about them. There were places my parents said we could go and places that we knew not to go and that was fine with me. My brothers and I had a roof over our heads. We had enough to eat. Yes, there were craps games floating through the neighborhood. Yes, the streets could be rough. Yes, there were druggies, drunks, and people doing all sorts of wrong things. But we were happy in our home."[316]

"Although I am not writing this book to relate every injustice I've suffered, it's simply impossible to tell my story without talking about race," Robertson wrote in his autobiography. "As much as I am an American, I am a Black American. And to tell you about growing up in the Jim Crow South and a segregated Klan-infested Midwest, I must acknowledge the influence of race. Similarly, it's impossible to discuss my experiences with basketball without mentioning race, Black and white. Otherwise, you might as well think about America's history during the second half of the twentieth century without acknowledging the civil rights movement. Or consider the Civil War without mentioning slavery. The subjects are intertwined . . ." He continued, "It wasn't until Attucks won our initial state title in my junior year that I had my first meal in a restaurant. I was seventeen years old and before that, I hadn't so much as set foot in downtown Indianapolis, much less eaten there, except to catch the bus to Tennessee. Being a champion basketball player opened the restaurants' doors to me. Maybe there were some white high school basketball champs who had never been in a restaurant until they won it all, rural kids out on a farm or whatever. But they at least would have been welcome."[317]

Robertson further recalled, "As soon as the (1962) season ended, I packed my bags and headed for Camp Pickett, Virginia. I'd been sworn into the Army during the regular season, at halftime of a televised game against the Celtics. I spent my whole off-season in the Army Reserves that year. I wasn't thrilled about it, but being on reserve was much better than going on active duty. It was a seven-year commitment, but it only required active duty for six months and you didn't get shipped overseas. In those days they were drafting Blacks left and right and putting them on the front lines. Of course, the military denies it. But America has a history of offering Black military personnel great peril and minimal recognition. My peril was Fort Jackson, South Carolina. During a summer camp, I went in uniform with two white soldiers into a restaurant for some sandwiches. No sooner had we sat down than the manager walked over and said that I couldn't eat there." Robertson explained that he was assigned to an Army camp outside town. "'If you want to eat here, go on back to camp and get your general. Then we'll see.' When he said that, it was like a little gear clicked into place in my head. I remember saying to myself, I can sit down and eat at the Cliff House in San Francisco or Berman's Steak House in Detroit. But this little jerk tells me I can't have a drink of water in the Virginia boondocks? Some things about this country were just insane."[318]

Bill Russell started his NBA career a few years prior to the "Big O," having played from 1956 to 1969. He grew up in Monroe, Louisiana. "Growing up in the Deep South, in the prewar period of the thirties and the early forties was not too bad," said Bill Russell, thinking back on his childhood. "I mean, it didn't seem too bad at the time. When you're a kid, you just never realize that there is a tremendous difference between mere existence and freedom. At least, I didn't realize it. I was just a kid who liked his friends and loved his mother and father and brother. I used to laugh a lot as I scuffed along the dirt road on my way to a barn that had been made into a school... The image of the Negro who always eats chicken and carries his lunch on trains and buses is part of American folklore. I can explain it best by pointing out that all trains in the South were segregated. Negroes couldn't eat in the diner and the only food that would last on a long trip was chicken. So, we took our chicken and rode in our segregated car from Louisiana to Little Rock to St. Louis before the rules changed and we could ride in any compartment of the train that took us on to California."[319]

He continued, "We moved into the north section of Oakland, sometimes known as the 'Landlord's Paradise.' It was a regular house with a regular garage. But there were eight families in the eight rooms of the house and another family was living in the garage. Pigs and sheep and chickens were raised in the backyard. The place was a rotten, filthy hold—a firetrap, with light bulbs hanging from exposed wires. It was the only place we could find. The landlord said it was because of the war. War does funny things to lots of people, but landlords it makes rich."[320]

Growing up, Russell said he and all the other Black children learned one lesson early. "The police represent society, white society. The Negro learns to hate authority. And the Negro learns to hate himself. They are taught through repetition that they are the scum of the earth and they are bad. He had nothing in common with anyone, not even with his fellow Negroes. They are all at the bottom of the heap. They have nothing in common with anyone, not even with each other. They are at the bottom of the heap, the bottom of a dung heap. They become more and more frustrated. They lose respect for themselves and they lose respect for society. Pretty soon you develop a hatred for yourself. And then you lose all association. That is what happened to the Negro in this time, in this place."[321] Russell said he began to read and found more purpose in life as he gained education and purpose. That transition help him become a leader with the Boston Celtics.

"There has never been any color line in the Celtics," said Russell. "This was one of the reasons for our success. But there was a quota system in the NBA and I said so. I said there was an unwritten law of pro basketball that no team should have more than two Negroes—three at the most—because, in the opinion of the owners, it would be bad for the box office—and money, not heart, rules pro sports . . .The arrival of two additional Negroes added a little more fuel to the flaming issues of segregation in basketball. In 1958 I had said very frankly there was a quota system. This had been denied, though it was obvious the system was still in effect. But the game was changing and more and more Negroes were being recognized as stars. Now, in this same year, we acquired a fourth Negro player, our number one draft choice, Ben Swain, of Texas State. A sportswriter finally summed up exactly what I had been talking about when he wrote: 'The Celtics will not keep four Negroes. The crowds won't stand for it and neither will the owners.' His intention was not to help the Negro cause, but unintentionally he did, because I seized on it. I brought the article to Brown and Auerbach and said, 'Now, tell me.' They told me, 'Just like before,' said Brown, who had brought in the first Negro in the NBA (Chuck Cooper). 'I look for players. Black, white, red, I couldn't care less.' Auerbach agreed with him. Now it is about equal—four or five Negroes on each team in the NBA. And no one thinks much of it anymore. But in those days, it was a big thing . . . it wasn't something the Negro manufactured. We knew damn well that we were on the spot. But we knew it was unjust. There was no reason why this kind of prejudice should interfere with a basic American sport. The years and the fans proved us right. It didn't hurt the attendance. It didn't hurt the game."[322]

Russell said the team experienced issues traveling to non-league cities for exhibition games. He recalled a trip to Marion, Indiana. "The team arrived and the mayor gave us the keys to the city," said Russell. "Much later that night, K.C. Jones, Carl Braun (who is white), and I went to a restaurant to eat. The manager told us that all the tables were reserved. The place was empty, but we said we would stand at the bar. 'That's reserved, too,' the manager said. I went to police headquarters to file a complaint. Nobody would take it. There was one Negro police officer in the back room—isn't that always the way?—and the desk sergeant asked us to talk to him. We did. He explained: 'These are nice people. Don't rock the boat.' Not for me. I fight things that I think are wrong. We asked to see that mayor. But, strangely enough, no one could remember where he lived. We finally found out and the next morning we swore out a complaint. The mayor agreed with us that the actions of the restaurant were against the law. The manager denied the whole thing. But we signed the complaint and K.C. Jones, who never gets mad, told him: 'You're a damn liar.' K.C. was right. How can you be given the keys to a city in the morning and told to go hungry in the evening?[323]

"Another time, I was going to Miami for an exhibition game," said Russell. "They told me the hotel was all right. I called up and the guy said, 'Yes.' I didn't believe it. I stayed on him. Finally, he said, 'Oh yes. You can stay here. You may use the dining room and the swimming pool. We ask only one thing. Try to be inconspicuous.' I broke up. In laughter and in anger. Six foot ten. Negro. Bearded. Can't you just see me using the swimming pool and not being conspicuous? I checked into a Negro hotel, instead."[324]

The experiences we all collect as we journey through our lives become those things that shape our beliefs and viewpoints. Senator Bradley's small town upbringing in Crystal City, Missouri, taught him to get along with people of different backgrounds, such as his future basketball teammates. Individuals with a tolerant attitude signaled the potential for change. Oscar Robertson and Bill Russell learned the hard way to deal with the trouble life brings. Those experiences make us what we become. Dallas Cowboys' Don Perkins, Mel Renfro, and Pettis Norman brought their experiences with them to racially torn Dallas Texas and worked to make it better for those that followed.

CHAPTER TEN

Life Experiences

"Our life experiences shape who we are and what we think," wrote Tom Golway, a writer and speaker who specializes in technology. "Our life's choices can create new experiences, further shaping us. Intellectual freedom is enabled by choosing to put ourselves on an unfamiliar path."

Writer BJ Neblett, author of new millennialism science fiction and contemporary fiction and life philosopher, expanded on it. "We are the sum total of our experiences," he wrote. "Those experiences—be they positive or negative—make us the person we are, at any given point in our lives. And, like a flowing river, those same experiences and those yet to come, continue to influence and reshape the person we are and the person we become. None of us are the same as we were yesterday, nor will be tomorrow."[325]

Over time, many philosophers and writers have made that or similar observations about the human condition. One could say that the civil rights movement of the early sixties was based on a set of experiences and some people's reactions to those conditions. Athletes faced their own segregation battles, but they also witnessed those strong individuals taking stands for social justice. Rosa Parks refused to give up her seat. Mamie Till demanded an open coffin so the world could see what they did to her son after he was kidnapped, tortured, and murdered in the Jim Crow South. Freedom Riders traveled the South on buses to bring attention to segregation in transportation. James Chaney, Andrew Goodman, and Michael Schwerner, the Mississippi civil rights workers, were abducted and murdered in June 1964 while attempting to help their fellow citizens register to vote. Young people endured emotional and physical torture while sitting at drug store lunch counters, hoping to change restaurant service. People witnessed young Black children being verbally abused while attempting to attend previously all-white schools.

History and African American Studies professor Charles K. Ross wrote, "Many Black Americans believed that desegregation on the sports field would promote the spirit of equality in other aspects of American life."[326] Some players, such as Walter Beach and Art Powell, took unpopular stands. Gale Sayers, a star running back at the University of Kansas, who was arrested for protesting Jim Crow at the school, captured the sentiment of many when he said, "They (white people) accept me as a football star, but not as a Negro."[327] In 1963, one Black writer argued, "If ministers and people of other professionals and even children, can take part in protest demonstrations and sit-ins and subject themselves to police dogs and fire hoses as well as arrests, Negro athletes could at least lend their active support to the campaign for racial justice."[328] Sometimes the images that stick are the ones formed in youth.

Hugh Duffy Daugherty, a white man who grew up in Pennsylvania, developed a network of coaches who sent Black athletes, primarily from the South, his direction. The Michigan State Spartans of 1965 and 1966 were a talented football team. Daugherty used the pipeline of Southern players to build a championship level program. This was a time when Southern schools refused to admit Blacks. Under Duffy Daugherty's courageous leadership, the Spartans were college football's first fully integrated rosters. His Spartans stood alone by ignoring the unwritten quotas other schools followed. Some schools did not take any recruits of color while other schools—including University of Southern California and Notre Dame—limited Black athletes to a half-dozen or so. The Spartans' 1965 and 1966 national title teams sat atop the college football world in the win column on the field and took more important strides off the field. Daugherty welcomed Black players from all over the country, even in the deep South and Texas. He successfully recruited in the Texas "Golden Triangle"—that wedge of land between Beaumont, Port Arthur, and Orange, near the Louisiana border. Future No. 1 NFL Draft pick Bubba Smith, future All-Pro wide receiver Gene Washington, and future NFL running back Jess Phillips hailed from Southeastern Texas. He went to North Carolina to sign Jimmy Raye, who would later lead the team at quarterback. "It was an integrated situation and everybody was so much nicer," said Washington. "It was refreshing to feel that people respected you regardless of your background and the color of your skin. Michigan State was a whole new world and I wanted to prove to the Texas segregation supporters, and especially to myself, that I would be successful."[329] Washington later played with the Minnesota Vikings and Denver Broncos.

If college football wasn't already aware of the Spartan program, it was on November 19, 1966, when Michigan State took on Notre Dame in a game billed the "Game of the Century." A record 33 million viewers watched the game and witnessed the contrast in rosters. Michigan State had 20 Black players, including 11 Black starters and two Black captains [George Webster and Jimmy Raye]. Notre Dame had one Black player, Alan Page. That 1966 squad was the first majority Black squad to win a title at a predominantly white institution. That game ended in a 10-10 tie. "Do you think we're going to win the national championship even if they run the clock out?" Bubba Smith asked teammates, according to author Michael Weinreb's *Season of Saturdays*. He was fearful voters would not find their roster favorable. "We got too many n-----s on this team to win the national championship. We have to find a way."[330]

There is no question the Spartans had a talented roster. The 1966 Spartans had five All-Americans: running back Clinton Jones, fullback Bob Apisa, defensive end Bubba Smith, wide receiver Gene Washington, and linebacker George Webster. The 1967 NFL Draft included four Michigan State players in the first eight selections overall and all four of them Black. While Jones, Smith, Washington, and Webster are Black, Apisa is of American Samoan decent. Smith was the first overall pick that year, which was the first year the AFL/NFL had a common draft. Clint Jones was selected second overall to the Vikings, George Webster fifth to the Oilers and Gene Washington went eighth, also to the Vikings. Four picks in the first eight choices meant the NFL was aware of the Spartans' talent. More evidence that Michigan State was ahead of its time was this little gem: one year before the University of Texas made Julius Whittier its first Black varsity football player in 1970, Michigan State named Clifton R. Wharton Jr. its first Black president. The East Lansing campus was the first major university in the country to name a Black president.

Many of those players came from rough upbringings, which may have prepared them well for football battles on Sunday afternoon. Bubba Smith, the huge defensive end on Duffy Daugherty's Michigan State Spartans football team, had such a memory. "As a boy, early in his dad's coaching career, Bubba stumbled upon a horrific sight in Orange, Texas," said Washington. "A group of white men were torturing a Black man on the north side of town. Bubba quickly hid behind a bush. The men burned the letters 'KKK' into the Black man's skin as he screamed. Smith was paralyzed as the smell of burnt flesh singed horror into his being. He had witnessed an act of hate that he was not able to stop. No matter how much love you might create and experience in your own home, he learned, the world outside its doors is filled with hatred and violence—and there is nothing you can do about it. Even Bubba's own mother, Georgia, suffered after she gave birth to a baby girl, who died a few days after she was born because they couldn't be seen at the white hospital, because they were Black."[331]

The images from the civil rights protests in southern states were graphic and emotional. Many people across the country watched in horror as Bull Connor allowed his police force to abuse child protestors. Police dogs and fire hoses were deployed against the protestors, which caused some athletes to refuse to go to Birmingham. Former heavyweight boxing champion Sonny Liston reportedly said, "I ain't got no dog-proof ass."[332] Charles "Bubba" Smith, from Texas, had never played in an integrated stadium before college and he played in the "Game of the Century" a few years later. Two days before the game, at a pep rally on Notre Dame's campus, the white, male crowd hung Smith in effigy next to a sign that read, "Lynch 'em."[333] Opposing players and coaches are often hanged in jest during these pep rallies, but the combination of the symbol and the sign suggested racism. The rosters of the two teams showed a clear but uneven picture of desegregation in sports in the 1960s. Notre Dame featured only one Black player, future Hall of Fame player Alan Page, while the 1966 Michigan State team had twenty. The 1965 and 1966 Michigan State teams were two of the best in the history of that school's football program. Over two seasons, they finished with a 19-1-1 record as well as a share of the 1965 National Championship (in those seasons, a playoff system had not been implemented and national polls named a title winner).

Herb Adderley, famous defender on Vince Lombardi's Green Bay Packers, first heard of the Spartans when he saw the team play games on television. He is evidence of Michigan State's pipeline of talented Black athletes from across the country to East Lansing, Michigan. When Adderley watched them play while growing up in Philadelphia, he "noticed that Black players could get a chance at Michigan State." He wanted to play for Duffy Daugherty because "at that time Black players could not go south. I had seen Michigan State on television. Number 26, Clarence Peaks, was my idol."[334] Adderley made his way to Michigan State to play for Duffy Daugherty and wore number 26, just like his idol. Lombardi selected Adderley in the first round of the draft, and he became the first African American to be the Packers' top choice. After playing offense primarily in college, he was moved to defense and became one of the best cornerbacks in the league almost immediately. Two years later, Lombardi selected Dave Robinson in the first round. The executive board of the Packers Board of Directors requested a meeting with Lombardi. They told Lombardi he was wasting his first choice on Black athletes, whom they figured would be available in the third round. Lombardi's reaction was strong and direct. "I am drafting football players," said Lombardi. "I am not drafting white or Black. I am drafting the best players out there. You guys run the business end of the thing and I'll run the football operations."[335]

The American Football League was generally considered the more liberal pro football league, but the Oilers played home games before segregated audiences until they were finally integrated in 1964.[336] African American columnist Lloyd Wells fought the policy in newsprint. He also helped spur the first successful boycott by African Americans of a sporting event on June 10, 1961, when some athletes refused to participate in the Meet of Champions in Houston. He continued to urge other Black athletes to follow suit.

As the sixties rolled along, other protests occurred. The Blue-Gray Football Classic was an All-Star football game for college seniors played annually in Montgomery, Alabama. NBC refused to televise the game in 1963 because the local Lions Club did not allow African American players to participate and required segregated seating in the Cramton Bowl. NBC took the stand after consulting with two of the largest game sponsors, Gillette Company and Chrysler Corporation. Alabama Governor George Wallace called the NBC action "tragic and irresponsible." Bowl game officials quickly pointed out that game proceeds had gone to local charities set up to help blind and needy children. Lions Club President Harris Dawson said the funds were distributed "without regard to race, color, or creed."[337] Local media hoped to spur social action with pocketbook actions. "If Chrysler and Gillette want to cease sponsoring the Blue-Gray Game because they practice segregation and use only white players, as a tool to penalize the people of Alabama, it would only be fair counteraction to refrain from buying the products that either have to sell," wrote the editors of *The Luverne Journal and News* after the decision was announced. "Of course, Chrysler won't be affected much in Crenshaw County because practically no one buys their automobiles anyway. Nearly everybody uses Gillette razor blades. Already their sales are changing here. Merchants are taking down their display signs. Men are going to the Schick stainless steel blades and others, leaving Gillette to lay on the shelf. If people all over this section would do what is happening here, then NBC, Gillette, and Chrysler would not take it upon themselves to judge our customs nor to try to force changes in them."[338]

"This is an example of how corporate influence can be brought to bear on the side of social justice," wrote *The New York Times* in an opposing view. "The action is taken openly and without subterfuge. It is taken on the responsibility of great enterprises which have had large financial interests in both the North and South. It is an action whose point and purpose are unmistakably clear, as evidenced by the outraged protests of Alabama's George Wallace."[339] Local newspapers weighed in. "There are many in this Deep South city (Montgomery, Alabama) who feel that the annual Blue-Gray football game is headed for oblivion if it doesn't consent to integrate its teams," wrote *The Anniston Star* in November 1964. "The prestige of the contest, whose officials have rejected all proposals that it allow Negroes to participate, is dwindling and this worries those interested in its future." The paper quoted a source who asked to be unnamed as saying "we're just hurting ourselves if we don't integrate. The Senior Bowl at Mobile is integrated as is all minor league baseball in Alabama. There is just no reason for us not to follow this course."[340] The policy changed in 1964 as Black athletes participated and the Cramton Bowl was desegregated.

"I am really surprised that the sponsors of the game would do a thing like this," said Allyn McKeen, a Hall of Fame football coach from the 1940s. "As much good as the game does for charity, it's a shame that so few people could bring pressure to the sponsor to have them stop the telecast and broadcast . . . I was told CORE (Congress of Racial Equality) was the opposition that caused the whole thing but it seems to me that there might be others behind this move."[341]

A professional exhibition game helped spur integration, too. The NFL created another playoff game in an attempt at competing with the rival AFL longer in the season. The Playoff Bowl, officially named the Bert Bell Benefit Bowl, was called the Runner-Up Bowl by many in the media. The exhibition game benefited the players' pension funds and matched the runners-up from the Eastern and Western Conferences to determine third place in the league. The Detroit Lions beat the Cleveland Browns 17-16 in the 1961 game. Packers coach Vince Lombardi hated the game; he called it the Losers Bowl because it matched the two runners-up for the title game. Miami, Florida hosted the game annually in the Orange Bowl. Several white players protested the separate accommodations in the city the week prior to the contest. "I believe pro football helped integrate every major city in the United States in the 1960s," said Roger Brown of the Detroit Lions in a 2017 interview. "After the 1960 season, we played in Miami in this new game called the Playoff Bowl. The Black players, like Night Train Lane, Danny Lewis, and myself, were sent to the Black part of town to stay in a dumpy old motel. We practiced at Dade Stadium in Miami. One day, the team bus picked up all of the white players at the Ivanhoe Hotel—a really nice place on Miami Beach—and then came over to our part of town to pick us up. Jim Gibbons, one of the white players, took a look at our motel and said, 'What the hell are you guys doing here?' The word got out that Blacks weren't allowed on Miami Beach. So later that day, Jim Gibbons, Howard Cassidy, Nick Pietrosante, and Gail Cogdill went to head coach George Wilson to complain about our accommodations. They told him, 'We want to stay as a team!' Wilson agreed and we all moved over to the Ivanhoe Hotel for the rest of our stay there in Miami. Thus, we integrated Miami Beach in 1960."[342]

Their opponents, the Cleveland Browns, also faced issues in Miami. "The white players were taken to the white hotel and all the Black players, including Jim Brown, were left standing there," recalled Bobby Mitchell. "We were told we were going to our own hotel. Well, Jim Brown and Paul Brown didn't tolerate that. Jim wouldn't stand for staying in a rundown Black hotel. Paul Brown then made sure we stayed together. Remember, he didn't schedule exhibition games in the South to avoid this kind of problem. He told the hotel, 'We're the Cleveland Browns and we stay together as a team.' The hotel gave in and we got to stay in Miami Beach. However, we had to agree not to go out to the beach area. That was tough—not being able to go to the beach (while) looking out the hotel window watching everyone have fun."[343] Maybe, with some small steps, sports was beginning to have an impact on race relations.

CHAPTER ELEVEN

Black Coaches

On February 4, 2007, Tony Dungy became the first African American coach to win a Super Bowl. It was the forty-first time that the NFL, with teams about 70 percent Black, hosted the Super Bowl contest and the first time a Black man coached the winning team as the Indianapolis Colts beat the Chicago Bears, 29-17. Ironically, two Black head coaches faced off in the contest as Dungy faced the Bears' Lovie Smith. Dungy took a long journey to get to be NFL head coach. After a short career as a professional player in the 1970s and sixteen seasons as an assistant coach, Dungy was hired as head coach of the Tampa Bay Buccaneers in 1996. Dungy coached six seasons, winning 54 games and losing 42 games with the Bucs, but was released because it was deemed that he could not win the big game. Eight days later, Indianapolis hired him as their head coach. He spent seven seasons with the Colts and never missed the playoffs with the team. In 1996, they put it all together with a victory in the big game.

Dungy grew up in Jackson, Michigan as the offspring of two teachers. His mother, Cleomae, taught high school English and his father, Wilbur, was one of the very first Black Ph.D. professors in science. Tony was the second oldest of four successful children. One of his siblings is a doctor, one is a nurse, and the other is a dentist. His father served in World War II as one of the famed Tuskegee Airmen, but he never spoke of it. Dungy learned of his father's war experience from one of his father's friends at his funeral. His father admitted he was in the service but refused to elaborate. His dad did not think one should brag about oneself and he passed that on to his son. That calm, deliberate way of handling life's events served Dungy well in his playing and coaching careers. "Our dad wasn't a man of many words, but he made it clear that getting an education and working hard were important," said Sherrilyn Sims, Dungy's older sister. "My mother was more outspoken and she would always say, 'Love is the most important thing.' She didn't just say that. She lived it and made sure we did likewise."[344]

Dungy spoke with his father and learned about the struggles being a Black man in America. "My dad fought in World War II and came home, graduated from University of Michigan, went to Arlington, VA to get his first job as high school teacher," recalled Dungy. "He could not teach and integrate the [white] schools so he had to go past the white school to teach in an all-Black school and he could not ride in the front of the bus. So, he told me, 'I wasn't going to ride in the back of the bus, so I walked to school.' And he said the way I can make things better is to make sure I teach these kids, so they know as much science as anybody else. And then when things get right, they'll be ready. And I'm like, Dad, how can you fight for this country and fight for freedom and then come back and they won't let you teach in certain schools. They won't let you ride the bus. He said, 'Yeah, it was bad, it was tough, but what I had to think about was how I could make the situation better.'"[345]

Tony Dungy recalled stories about his parents and the lessons they taught him, such as those about his dad teaching biology at a Black high school in Alexandria, Virginia. The school superintendent told his father that there wasn't a budget for books or equipment to teach Black students in his class because the budget was reserved for the white kids. "My dad's whole thing wasn't to get angry," said Dungy. "His job was to teach those kids. He scraped together what he could [in] books, microscopes. His thing was to teach those kids as much as those other kids. No use complaining. It's not what you don't have, or what's wrong, it's getting the job done."[346] Tony Dungy learned from his father's lessons, which became foundation principles, such as how can I make the situation better? That lesson came in handy numerous times during his career. He attended the University of Minnesota on a football scholarship and led the Big Ten in passing twice. Despite his level of production, NFL scouts were unconvinced he could play quarterback at the pro level. Even though the 1977 NFL draft had 12 rounds at that time, Dungy was not selected in any of the 335 choices. In Canada, he was selected by the CFL Montreal Allouettes and Dungy gave them some serious consideration since they would allow him to continue his career as a quarterback. After he got over his initial disappointment of not being selected, he decided he wanted to compete with the best, so he signed a free agent contract with the Pittsburgh Steelers and worked to learn how to play defensive back. That first season, he caught three interceptions but doubled that to six interceptions the following season (1978). He was traded to San Francisco before the next season, but he did not enjoy the same success on the West Coast. His playing career only lasted three seasons, so he returned to Pittsburgh as a member of the Steelers coaching staff.

While a Steelers player, one particular incident stuck with Dungy. After being told he was not quarterback material, he made the team as a defensive back. During that rookie season, both Steelers quarterbacks were injured in the same game. Dungy entered the game as emergency quarterback. After the game, Coach Chuck Noll approached Dungy and told him if both quarterbacks remained injured, he would start the next game at quarterback. "I said, wait a minute. How can that be?" recalled Dungy. "I wasn't good enough to be drafted six months ago but now I am going to play. For me that was all I needed to hear. I knew I could have done it if I had gotten the opportunity. I could have played. I was bitter to a certain extent. But it was the training I got from my dad . . . he said I just got to try to make the situation better. That's what I was thinking about. Okay, I'm upset about this. I think I could play quarterback. It would have been great. But right now, how can I make the situation better? The best thing I can do is play well and do what I can do on this team and help our team win the Super Bowl."[347]

By the time he finally reached the Super Bowl as a head coach, he faced his share of personal tragedies. He lost his mother January 3, 2002, a week and a half before his termination as the head coach of the Buccaneers. He lost his father on June 8, 2004, a few months after the Colts lost in the AFC title game. "You just wish that as much as my mom and dad did, as many games as they saw me play, as many practices, they really would have liked to see this one. I'd love to have them here."[348]

He lost his son, James, about a year before he took the field for the Super Bowl game. James Dungy, the 18-year-old son of Indianapolis Colts coach Tony Dungy, was found dead in a Tampa-area apartment December 22, 2005. James was frequently seen with his father at practice and games but, because James stood six-foot-seven inches, some people mistook him for one of his father's players. Authorities said James Dungy hanged himself from a ceiling fan with a leather belt and foul play was ruled out. The toxicology results were negative.

During the lead-up to the Super Bowl, reporters quickly pointed out history would be made as two Black head coaches faced off in the contest. Dungy coached the Colts and Lovie Smith coached the Bears. The two were friends with a relationship dating back to 1996 when Dungy hired Smith to coach linebackers for the Buccaneers. "I'm proud to be the first African American coach to win this," said Dungy as he held the Lombardi Trophy after the game. "But again, more than anything, Lovie and I are not only African American but also Christian coaches, showing you can do it the Lord's way. We're more proud of that."[349]

"If you know Tony Dungy, the one word you're always going to use is 'character' and a person who is very, very humble," said former defensive back Deron Cherry, who played for him with the Chiefs. "He has a strong faith in God and his religion and that kept him grounded and humble and when you're a humble person, there's not a person you can't get along with. I think through his actions and how he treated people every single day—that allowed him to have personal relationships with every guy he came across. He was strong enough to be a disciplinarian and tell you when you were doing something wrong, but also kind of build you up, not necessarily tear you down, but build you up in a way that a father would build up a son."[350]

Flash forward to February 4, 2019, as the Miami Dolphins introduced Brian Flores, former defensive coach with the Patriots, as the 13th head coach in team history. "The day had all the trappings that such a moment deserved: pictures with a team helmet and a happy owner, three precious kids adorably interrupting Dad while he met with reporters and talked of building things the right way, with cooperation and respect," reported the *Miami Herald* in their story about the introduction.[351] Flores came to South Beach fresh off a victory in Super Bowl LIII, in which his Patriots defense took apart the Los Angeles Rams offense led by Sean McVay in route to a 13-3 victory. In other words, he was a hot commodity among coaching prospects, despite spending his entire professional coaching career with the Patriots and not having any head coaching experience.

On January 10, 2022, with much less fanfare, the Dolphins fired Brian Flores. "After evaluating where we are as an organization and what we need going forward to improve, I determined that the key dynamics of our football organization weren't functioning at a level I want it to be and felt that this decision was in the best interest of the Miami Dolphins," said owner Stephen Ross in a statement. "I believe we have a talented young roster in place and have the opportunity to be much better in 2022."[352] Flores' firing came largely as a surprise across the league. He was 24-25 in three seasons with the Dolphins. The first season they won five games when some observers predicted a winless season followed by ten wins and nine wins. Some in the media suspected Flores disagreed with keeping quarterback Tua Tagovailoa on the roster, which prompted his firing. Stephen Ross said the firing was a result of what he described as lack of synergy between Flores and the front office, which might have been the politically correct way of saying the coach disagreed with the choice of quarterback. After three years, the honeymoon was over. This time, as media members gathered around the coach, the scene lacked all the nice touches of the earlier visit. Flores was explaining that he understood "the risk" he was taking in filing a lawsuit against his former employer alleging racial discrimination in its hiring and firing practices. He insisted that he "absolutely" wanted to coach again but added, "I also know I'm not the only story here. There are people of color before me and I know there are others who have similar stories and it's hard to speak out. It is. You're making some sacrifices, but again, it's bigger than coaching."[353]

The NFL instituted a policy commonly called the Rooney Rule in 2003 in hopes of improving opportunities for minorities. Initially, the rule required each team to interview at least one, later revised to two, minority candidates for an open head coach position. In 2021, the league expanded the rule to general manager and other high-level positions. A year later, the league added women to the policy. The rule was named after the then-chairman of the committee, Dan Rooney, the late owner of the Pittsburgh Steelers, who was a driving force behind the directive. That rule was implemented decades before Flores filed his lawsuit against the Dolphins, the Giants, and the Broncos. In the lawsuit, Flores said he became aware of an issue when the Patriots head coach Bill Belichick texted him to congratulate him on getting the Giants' head coaching job. The Patriots' head man meant to send the text to another candidate, Brian Daboll, instead of Brian Flores. Both men had coached for him previously in New England and both men were in competition for the Giants' head coaching job. According to the lawsuit, Belichick meant to text Daboll about the Giants' head coaching job. Flores was a candidate for that job but had not yet been interviewed. That convinced Flores that he was only granted the interview to meet the Rooney Rule requirements. Flores figured the Giants had already selected Brian Daboll and said he felt "humiliation, disbelief, anger" when he found out he was traveling to New York for "a sham interview." That made the decision to file a lawsuit easy for the former Dolphins head coach.

Brian Flores "is done trying to get a job the expected way for a Black head coaching candidate, the way that requires a man to smile through all the lies and sham interviews, the way that makes his dignity bleed out one insulting little cut at a time," wrote Jerry Brewer in a stinging commentary on the situation.[354] Brewer, a sports columnist since age 25, worked for the *Orlando Sentinel*, *The Seattle Times*, *The Philadelphia Inquirer,* and *The Washington Post.* At forty years old, many were surprised that the assistant coach was killing any chances of gaining another head coaching job by filing a lawsuit. Flores was fearless and ready to fight. Quietly, the NFL should fear the lawsuit because it seems to be stating in clear type what many had believed for a long time. It is difficult for minority candidates to get a meaningful interview despite the fact that the league fields teams comprised of 70 percent minority players. "God has gifted me with a special talent to coach the game of football, but the need for change is bigger than my personal goals," said Flores in a statement. "In making the decision to file the class action complaint, I understand that I may be risking coaching the game I love and had done so much for my family and me. My sincere hope is that by standing up against systematic racism in the NFL, others will join me to ensure that positive change is made for generations to come."[355]

In addition to the discrimination claims, the lawsuit contained stories that discredit Dolphins' ownership and explain how difficult it would be for a minority candidate to get a fair opportunity with the club. Flores, who lost his job after back-to-back winning seasons, alleged team owner Stephen Ross offered to pay him $100,000 for every defeat during the 2019 season when many in the media were thinking the team would purposely lose games in order to gain a higher draft pick, as the team desperately needed an upgrade at quarterback. The media deployed a catchy phrase, "Tank for Tua," which meant losing games to improve the draft position in order to select the quarterback from Alabama. In another incident, the suit alleges that Ross attempted to get Flores to commit tampering in order to recruit another team's star quarterback. Ross set up a meeting with a star quarterback, reportedly Tom Brady, also a former Patriot, and Flores on his yacht. Neither knew the other would be there. When Flores found out, he immediately left. The Dolphins began circulating stories that Flores was fired because he was difficult to work with, which for decades was code for Black employees who dared to voice their opinions. In this case, Flores was unwilling to break the tampering rules. For a long time, Black players and coaches were expected to do their jobs and keep their mouths shut. Flores' courage may help minorities gain some foothold.

The New York Giants, in a statement from the team, denied that they had already decided to hire Brian Daboll prior to interviewing Brian Flores. "Brian Flores has raised serious issues in the filing of his complaint," it read in part. "The specific claims against the Giants and Mr. Flores' allegations about the legitimacy of his candidacy for our head coaching position are disturbing and false . . . The allegation that the Giants' decision had been made prior to Friday evening, January 28, is false. And to base that allegation on a text exchange with Bill Belichick in which he ultimately states that he 'thinks' Brian Daboll would get the job is irresponsible. The text exchange occurred the day before Coach Daboll's in-person interview even took place."[356] The Giants insisted they did not make a coaching decision until after Flores' second interview and daylong visit with the Giants. "Giants ownership would never hire a head coach based only on a 20-minute zoom interview, which is all Mr. Daboll had at that point," said the Giants in a statement. "In addition, Mr. Belichick does not speak for and has no affiliation with the Giants. Mr. Belichick's text exchange provides no insight into what actually transpired during our head coaching search."[357]

The Denver Broncos were another team named in the lawsuit. Flores alleged that Broncos' President of Football Operations John Elway and President & Chief Executive Officer Joe Ellis "showed up an hour late to the interview. They looked completely disheveled and it was obvious that they had been drinking heavily the night before."[358] The interview had been scheduled to be conducted in a Providence, Rhode Island hotel. "While I was not planning to respond publicly to the false and defamatory claims by Brian Flores, I could not be silent any longer with my character, integrity, and professionalism being attacked," said Elway in a statement released by the team. Elway said Flores was considered one of the five candidates for the head coaching position that ultimately went to Vic Fangio. "For Brian to make an assumption about my appearance and state of mind early that morning was subjective, hurtful, and just plain wrong," added Elway. If he appeared disheveled, it was because he had just flown in from Denver with Ellis, "and we were going on a few hours of sleep to meet in the only window provided to us." Elway said he enjoyed the interview with Flores and was "prepared, ready, and fully engaged as Brian shared his experience and vision for our team. It's unfortunate and shocking to learn for the first time this week that Brian felt differently about our interviews with him."[359]

With Flores' lawsuit going forward, media members sought Tony Dungy's opinion on the situation. Dungy, who coached the Buccaneers and the Colts for 13 seasons, brought it back to the Rooney Rule, which he said had a goal of slowing the hiring process down so that more candidates could be considered. "He wanted to create a process to search for candidates, not an interview quota," he said. "My hope would be for owners to spell out very specifically what they are looking for and then have them research a variety of people before making a decision."[360] Since Dungy cited league rules, how successful has the Rooney Rule been? A study by three researchers said the rule had little impact on hiring.[361] Doug Williams, the first Black Super Bowl winning quarterback, doesn't think so. If asked to give the program a school grade, he said he would give the effort a D. "But it's not the rule that's not working, it's the people," he said. "It's not just football, it's America as a whole."[362]

According to an exhaustive 2022 investigation by *The Washington Post*, Black coaches face a narrower set of opportunities than their white counterparts to get top coaching jobs, have to serve longer as assistants, are more likely to get interim jobs than full-time jobs, and are held to higher standards when it comes to keeping those jobs. *The Post* studied the league's coaching transactions from 1990 until 2022 and found that Black coaches, "have been twice as likely as others to be fired after leading a team to a regular season record of .500 or better."[363] Despite the "END RACISM" pledge spelled out in end zones across league stadiums, the league has struggled implementing that stated goal. "Black coaches tend to perform about as well as white coaches," wrote *The Washington Post*. "But while white candidates are offered a vast and diverse set of routes to the league's top coaching jobs, Black coaches face a much narrower set of paths. They have had to serve significantly longer as mid-level assistants, are more likely to be given interim jobs than full-time ones, and are held to a higher standard when it comes to keeping their jobs."[364]

The Washington Post found Black coaches continue to be underrepresented in NFL hiring. At the time of their report, *The Washington Post* counted 20 Black men have served as NFL head coaches. This is 11% of the total, with the other 154 coaches being white men. If they get the head coaching job, they are more likely to be fired than their white counterparts. Black coaches follow a much narrower path to the top job. On average, Black men spend much longer in mid-level coaching jobs. Lately, ownership across the NFL has pushed for young, offensive-minded coaches with experience coaching quarterbacks for the head job. Black men have been steered away from those jobs for decades. The Rooney Rule has failed to overcome team owners' bias. "Several Black coaches, including Hall of Famer Tony Dungy, described interviews in which they were tacitly told they had no chance," according to *The Washington Post*. "Racist comments were kept to themselves, coaches said, amid concerns about being labeled as difficult." Black coaches are more likely to be named as "interim head coach" than for full-time roles. In these positions, they are often named to succeed a white coach who was fired for poor performance. At the time of the 2022 study, Black coaches have held 13 percent of full-time head coaching jobs since 1990—and 31 percent of the interim stints.

"*The Post* found that the NFL, buoyed by the Rooney Rule's apparent initial success, touted it to corporate America as a model policy," according to *The Washington Post*. "But as the number of Black head coaches plunged back to pre-Rooney-Rule levels and research piled up that the rule was growing obsolete, the league rejected calls for it to significantly modify or overhaul its signature diversity policy. The Rooney Rule's familiar flaws—allegations of sham interviews, a lack of enforcement, and illusory results—then surfaced in versions of the policy that were adopted by corporations and governments, a nationwide trend that culminated shortly after George Floyd's murder in 2020.[365]

"At the end of the day, we don't make the hires," said Troy Vincent, a former All-Pro cornerback who played for four NFL teams and now is the league's executive vice president of football operations. "We've exhausted ourselves with programs, initiatives, making sure that [owners] are aware of who's out there [as candidates]. But we don't make the hire. And so, it has been a difficult challenge for us, but we have got to keep pushing. And we believe that what we're doing is the right thing until hearts change ... We're still dealing with America's original sin — slavery—and the misconception of who Black men are. So, we're just trying different things."[366]

"The NFL doesn't have a diversity problem. The NFL has a Black problem," said Dennis Thurman, a former defensive coordinator for the Jets and Bills who left pro football in 2020 to join Deion Sanders' coaching staff at Jackson State, a historically Black university. "There aren't that many Hispanics playing in the NFL. There aren't that many Asians. There aren't women on the field in the NFL. I understand them wanting to be inclusive and I applaud what they're doing for those groups . . . But the issue is not women. It's not Asians. It's not Hispanics. The majority of players in the NFL are Black. They use the word 'diversity.' It's real slick. But, no, uh-uh. That's not the issue." A long-time coach offered additional insight. "The owners of these teams predominantly grew up in different environments," Hall of Fame coach Bill Parcells, a white man with a track record of nurturing and promoting Black assistants, told *The Washington Post*. "I don't want to say their exposure isn't too good, but really that's probably the truth."[367] Of the league's 31 majority team owners, only two identify as people of color: Bills co-owner Kim Pegula, who is Asian American, and Jacksonville Jaguars owner Shahid Khan, who is Pakistani American. Multiple business reports have called the 2024 season history making for Black ownership in the league.

Tennis stars Serena and Venus Williams have owned a minority stake in the Miami Dolphins since 2009. Magic Johnson is part of the Josh Harris ownership group that purchased the Washington Commanders. The Denver Broncos brought in the largest contingent of Black minority owners when the franchise was purchased in 2022 by a group led by Walmart heir Rob Walton. The group also includes Formula One world champion Lewis Hamiton, former Secretary of State Condoleezza Rice, and co-CEO of Ariel Investments and Starbucks Chair Mellody Hobson (both Black women). Film producer Will Packer, Walmart executive Rosalind Brewer, venture capitalist Rashaun Williams, and Olympic Gold Medalist Dominique Dawes joined the Atlanta Falcons ownership group in May 2024. Former NFL player Warrick Dunn is another Falcon owner and John Stallworth owns a portion of the Pittsburgh Steelers. In 2024, the Buffalo Bills added ten limited partners, including former U.S. National soccer team player Jozy Altidore and former NBA players Vince Carter and Tracy McGrady.

Despite the company line claiming Rooney Rule success, enforcement of potential violations is lacking. The Detroit Lions are the only team to have been fined for a violation of the Rooney Rule. The NFL fined the Lions $200,000 in

2003. Lions President Matt Millen was fined $200,000 for not interviewing any minority candidates before hiring white coach Steve Mariucci. A team spokesman said the Lions disagreed with the ruling, but media reports suggested Millen had only one candidate in mind: Mariucci.

Anthony Lynn, the former coach of the Chargers, said he interviewed with six franchises before landing that job. He was offered more interviews, he said, but refused to meet "with an organization that had not already interviewed a minority because I did not want to be a token interview." Maurice Carthon, who won two Super Bowl rings as a running back with the New York Giants, went into coaching at the urging of Bill Parcells in 1994. He served as an assistant for seven NFL teams over the next 19 seasons, three times rising to the role of offensive coordinator; in 2009, he was named assistant head coach of the Kansas City Chiefs. Carthon would interview unsuccessfully for five head coaching jobs. The most unpleasant experience Carthon faced interviewing for a head coach spot came in 2006 while interviewing with the New Orleans Saints. During his conversation with owner Tom Benson, Carthon recalled, Benson said to him, "You know, in our organization here, we let the boys wash the cars." A Saints spokesman said they never received a report of a racial comment against Benson, who died in 2018. Carthon admitted keeping the incident to himself. Many Black coaches do not want to speak out against "sham" interviews out of fear they will never get another interview opportunity. "They remain silent because they want a second opportunity," Troy Vincent said, "and to speak out when you're the minority, sometimes it can hurt you. We've seen that happen. So, we try to be a buffer where we can allow them to share in confidentiality."[368]

As of 2022, there were 13 NFL franchises that have never had a Black head coach. In recent years, two men might have been considered rising stars among the Black coaching ranks. Eric Bieniemy and Byron Leftwich are considered bright offensive minds and both have won the Super Bowl in recent years as offensive coordinators, but neither has achieved the top job. Bieniemy spent five seasons as Kansas City Chiefs offensive coordinator, including two Super Bowl victories, in 2019 and 2022. Unable to turn that into a top job, he left for a year with the Washington Commanders but was dismissed when the team changed coaching staffs. He ultimately moved to the college ranks after a single season in DC. Following his playing days, Leftwich began coaching with Bruce Arians with the Arizona Cardinals. He joined Arians' Tampa Bay staff and was offensive coordinator from 2019 to 2022, where he helped the team win Super Bowl LV.

As of 2022, Teryl Austin, a senior defensive assistant for the Pittsburgh Steelers under Mike Tomlin, interviewed for 11 head coaching jobs without being hired once. He told the Associated Press that the interviews "are invaluable experiences" and that the Rooney Rule gets Black coaches in front of owners. He said he could tell which situations were ones in which he was actually being considered and the ones that were merely attempting to meet the Rooney Rule criteria. "I could tell when I was really in it," he said. "And so, to me, that's kind of worth it."[369] After so many unsuccessful head coaching interviews, how did Austin stay positive? "It always leaves you wondering what happened, why you didn't get it," said Austin. "You can't say for sure [if race was a factor]. Maybe I'm not what the owners see when they look in the mirror and they see leadership positions." One of those interviews was with the Detroit Lions in 2018 when the team was seeking a new head coach to replace Jim Caldwell, a friend of Austin's. The Lions had a cumulative record of 36-28 under four years of Caldwell's coaching. That year, the Lions ultimately hired former Patriots assistant Matt Patricia. "Former [Lions general manager] Bob Quinn knew he was hiring Matt Patricia and used Teryl to comply with the Rooney Rule," wrote Austin's agent Eric Metz in a note to the Associated Press in 2022 after Flores filed his suit. "Didn't work out for the Detroit Lions. [They] never should have fired Jim Caldwell," said Metz.

Other experiences were different, noted Metz. After Austin lost out on the Chargers head job in 2017 to Anthony Lynn, he said he received "rave reviews of Teryl's interviews. His leadership, communication, and coaching acumen were extremely impressive." Austin started in the NFL in 2003 as a defensive backs coach with the Seattle Seahawks. Since that time, he worked with Arizona and Baltimore and took defensive coordinator roles in Detroit and Cincinnati but is still waiting for an opportunity as the head coach to open up for him. "I can't sit here and lie and say everything has gone to plan," said Austin. "There are times I thought I probably should have had an opportunity to lead a team and it didn't happen. You get disappointed with it, but you've got to pick yourself up just like you tell your players. 'You've got to pick yourself up and keep moving.'"[370]

A month after Brian Flores filed the class action lawsuit, two former NFL coaches joined the litigation: Steve Wilks, who was the Arizona Cardinals head coach for one season (2018) and Ray Horton, an NFL assistant since 1994 and a coach who interviewed for the Tennessee Titans head coaching job in 2016. At the time, the Titans, Cardinals, and Texans were added as part of the amendment. Flores' attorneys said the Texans were added because they "retaliated" against Flores by removing him for consideration for their vacant head coaching position "due to his decision to file this action and speak publicly about systemic discrimination in the NFL."[371] The amended lawsuit was filed in the Southern District of New York. Wilks "was not given any time to develop the team or culture and he was stuck with numerous burdens not of his own making," according to the lawsuit. "He had a rookie quarterback in Josh Rosen, the team general manager, Steve Keim, was suspended for five weeks following a DUI during training camp, and the Cardinals had numerous injuries to key players. Mr. Keim, a white GM, kept his job, but Mr. Wilks, a Black coach, was fired."[372]

The Cardinals finished 3-13 in Wilks' one season with the team. He was replaced by Kliff Kingsbury, who was given four years to coach the team, finishing with a 28-37-1 record as head coach. Kingsbury played quarterback at Texas Tech and served as head coach at his alma mater from 2013 to 2016. When he was hired, he became the third youngest head coach in college football. Despite a roster that included future pro prospects Davis Webb, Baker Mayfield, and Patrick Mahomes, his teams struggled to win more games as they lost. His overall record was 35 wins and 40 losses when he was released. Kingsbury was head coach of the Cardinals from 2019 to 2022. He was fired January 9, 2023. In his first season with the Cardinals, the team won five games. The best season was 2021 when they recorded 11 wins and lost their opening round playoff game. "I think he is the biggest fraud in football. Because he has not succeeded anywhere he has been to any significant degree," said CBS Sports Radio show host Damon Amendolara. "When he gets the head coach job at Texas Tech, he never had a winning record within the Big 12."[373] Amendolara continued, "Then he somehow fails upward to get the head coaching job at Arizona. Every year it is the same thing: they start out hot and collapse down the stretch. The one year they go to the postseason they are completely ill-prepared. They take on that Rams team and were down 21-0 at the half, 28-0 in the third quarter . . . His team is known for penalties, poor coaching, and sloppy play and slow starts or fades in the second half of the season."[374]

As a defensive coordinator, Steve Wilks enjoyed great success. His defensive units performed near the top of all defensive statistics. His latest stop was with the 49ers, who played in Super Bowl LVIII against the Chiefs. The game went to overtime and most observers felt the 49ers lost the game because the offense could not move the ball against the Chiefs defense. "I was sleeping on this for a few nights, trying to come up with a few tough decisions, but this morning I relieved Steve Wilks of his duties," said 49ers head coach Kyle Shanahan in announcing the decision three days after the game. "Gonna end up making a change here at defensive coordinator. Really tough decision. It says nothing about Steve as a man or football coach," Shanahan said. "He's a great football coach. But just where we're going and where we're at with our team from a scheme standpoint and things like that, looking through it all throughout the year through these last few days, I felt pretty strongly that this was the decision that was best for our organization."[375]

Wilks spent the end of the 2022 season as the interim head coach of the Carolina Panthers after the team fired head coach Matt Rhule. Despite leading the team to a 6-6 record over the last 12 weeks of the season, he was not hired for the permanent job in favor of Frank Reich, who ended up being fired midseason after a 1-10 start. "I truly don't understand!" said former Panthers safety Tre Boston. "Not one player who's played for this man has had anything bad to say about him as a man, his coaching nor schemes!"[376] Boston said it was obvious to him that Wilks had a target on his back.

After thirty years as an NFL assistant coach, Ray Horton has since retired, but still joined Flores' lawsuit with his own experiences to detail. Ray Horton served teams as an assistant coach in the NFL from 1994 to 2019. His last assignment was coaching defensive backs with Washington. From 2011 through 2015, he coordinated the defenses for the Cardinals, Browns, and Titans. His teams won two championships—the 2005 and 2008 Steelers. He interrupted his retirement in 2023 to assume the head coaching position of the Pittsburgh Maulers in the United States Football League, where he took his team to the championship game. That was a huge accomplishment for a team that finished the previous season with the worst record in the league (one win and nine losses).

Horton's "sham" experience came in Tennessee as the Titans were searching for a new head coach. Horton and Teryl Austin were the Black candidates interviewed. Horton said it was the fourth and final time he was on the head coaching interview circuit. Ultimately, the Titans hired Mike Mularkey as head coach. Mularkey played tight end for nine seasons in the NFL with the Steelers and Vikings. Aa head coach of the Buffalo Bills, his team finished with nine wins the first season (2004) but only five the second (2005). When his team regressed, Mularkey was fired. He got another opportunity in 2012 as head coach of the Jaguars but, after only two wins in 2012, he was fired. He began the season as offensive coordinator with the Titans in 2016. After the Titans suffered through one win in the first seven games under Ken Whisenhunt, Mularkey moved in as interim head coach. The win-loss record was not much different under Mularkey as they achieved only two wins in nine contests. The Titans began a full search for a new head coach after the season. Four candidates got interviews, Doug Marrone, offensive line coach with the Jaguars; Teryl Austin, defensive coordinator with the Steelers; Ray Horton, defensive coordinator with the Titans; and Mike Mularkey, interim head coach of the Titans. Horton interviewed for the head coaching job the same day that Mike Mularkey was introduced as the new head coach. After some quick interviews, the team decided to remove the interim tag and retain Mularkey as head coach. Offensively, the Titans were considered 31st overall when Mularkey took over and finished 30th overall. On defense, they were fifth overall when he started and finished at 13th overall.[377] Despite that performance, Mularkey was hired.

In a podcast interview from 2020, Mularkey revealed he was assured he had the Titans' head coaching job before the team became compliant with the Rooney Rule. The evidence seems to help the employment discrimination case according to Dan Lust, a full-time litigator and sports law professor at the New York Law School. "(Horton) has the head coach of the team—at least going on the record on a podcast—basically saying there's a world where I'm a star witness," said Lust. "Flores doesn't have the equivalent of Brian Daboll saying that or Kliff Kingsbury saying that for the Giants or Cardinals (respectively). Horton's case certainly adds teeth to the lawsuit. No other piece of evidence like that exists with any of the other (accusations against teams)."[378]

"I allowed myself, at one point, when I was in Tennessee, to get caught up in something that I regret," Mularkey said on the *Steelers Realm* podcast. "I still regret it. The ownership there, Amy Adams Strunk and her family, came in and told me I was going to be the head coach in 2016 before they went through the Rooney Rule. And so, I sat there knowing I was the head coach in '16, as they went through this fake hiring process knowing a lot of the coaches that they were interviewing, knowing how much they prepared to go through those interviews, knowing that everything they could do and they had no chance to get that job. And actually, the GM Jon Robinson, was in an interview with me. He had no idea why he was interviewing me, that I have a job already. I regret it . . . and I've regretted that since then. It was the wrong thing to do and I'm sorry I did that, but it was not the way to do that."[379]

Mularkey's admission about the 2016 Titans' coach search is considered the strongest evidence in support of the sham interview complaints. Steelers President Art Rooney II defended the rule named for his forebears but admitted that the league has not seen enough advancement. He refused to comment specifically on the lawsuit brought by Flores. "Over the past several years, our Diversity Committee has recommended and ownership has adopted a number of enhancements to the Rooney Rule as well as new policies designed to ensure that women and minorities are receiving full and fair consideration for coaching and front office positions," said Rooney in 2022. "While I acknowledge that we have not seen progress in the ranks of head coaches, we have seen marked improvement in the hiring of women and minorities in other key leadership roles, such as coordinator positions, general manager positions, and front office positions both in and out of football operations," he added. "I believe this progress has been made as a result of the implementation of many of the enhanced policies that were recently adopted."[380]

Some have called Brian Flores the Rosa Parks of the Black NFL coaching ranks for having the courage to stand up to the NFL's hiring practices. About this, Flores said, "That gives me more confidence that we made the right decision here and that we need to continue to fight for that change."[381]

CHAPTER TWELVE

Black Quarterbacks

Sometimes professional football moves along at the speed of a glacier. Things are done a certain way because that is the way they always were done. During the sixties, Black players were not "allowed" to play certain positions that were reserved for white players. "Although the NFL initiated the reintegration process in 1946, it took seventeen years to complete," wrote Charles K. Ross, history and African American Studies professor at the University of Mississippi. "And it took another nine years for Blacks to play at every position on a full-time basis. In 1960, Black players made up only 5.5 percent of the linebackers and guards, while no Blacks played regularly at center, kicker, punter, or quarterback. Black players were primarily confined to running back, defensive back and end positions. Institutional racism within the game facilitated by owners and coaches forced Black players to be 'stacked' at selected positions. Positions such as quarterback, linebacker or center, which required more responsibility and thinking, were set aside for white players only. Black players were perceived as not being smart enough to play these positions, so the league once again established an unwritten policy that created a positional system of racial quotas and set asides."[382]

The list of early quarterbacks is mostly unmemorable in football lore, except for one and he was the first. That was Fritz Pollard, one of the few Blacks in the league during that time. Listed as a halfback, he occasionally lined up as a quarterback during his seven-year career with the Akron Pros, Milwaukee Badgers, Hammond (Indiana) Pros, and Providence Steam Roller. In 1921, he became the first African American coach in the NFL. Pollard was inducted into the Pro Football Hall of

Fame in 2005, two decades after he passed away in 1986. Willie Thrower, a quarterback at Michigan State, was the first Black quarterback of the modern era and received a huge compliment from teammate George Blanda with the Bears. "You know what, Will?" asked Blanda, "If I could throw a football as good as you, I'd be playing for the next 35 years."[383] So much for Blanda's prediction! Blanda played 26 years; Thrower lasted one season. He played in one game that season (1953) against the 49ers and completed three of eight passes for 27 yards.

In 1953, George Taliaferro, a veteran halfback of seven seasons in the league for numerous teams, played quarterback for the Colts when starter Fred Enke was injured. He played two games at quarterback. Two years later, Charlie "Choo Choo" Brackins threw two passes and completed none for the Packers in his short stint at quarterback in the closing minutes of a game against the Browns. Brackins had played quarterback at Prairie View A&M University for three seasons before he became the first quarterback from a historically Black college to play in an NFL game. "Choo Choo Brackins had size, the arm and the ability to make it as a pro," said Bill Nunn, who covered football as a journalist and later was a scout for the Steelers. "Whether or not he could have is open to debate. But, based on the guys I've seen over the year, I'm certain that, given the opportunity, he would have had a very good chance of making it."[384] When the Packers cut him, it was reported that he broke some team rules, including missing curfew before a game in Chicago. After he was released, it was a decade before another African American was given a shot at pro football.

In the late sixties, there were three Black quarterbacks who had success in college football but were not given a fair chance in pro football. The three—Eldridge Dickey, Marlin Briscoe, and Jimmy Raye—all had to make the grade at a position other than quarterback. Dickey played at Tennessee State and was selected as an "athlete" by the Raiders in 1968. It is usually reported that he was selected as a quarterback, which would have made him the first African American quarterback selected in the first round, but it was clear he wasn't when the Raiders announced their second-round choice, Ken Stabler of Alabama. The team already had Daryle Lamonica as the starting quarterback with backups George Blanda and Cotton Davidson in the wings. With three quarterbacks already on the roster, why would a team pick two quarterbacks with their top selections? That season, Lamonica led the team to a 13-1 regular season record and a berth in the Super Bowl. "I played against Eldridge Dickey," said fellow Black quarterback James Harris. "I felt strongly that Eldridge Dickey would be the first Black to play quarterback in the NFL. He was a great player. When he got drafted in the first round, I jumped for joy." It was Dickey who was switched to wide receiver. "I knew he could play. There was no doubt in my mind that he would never make it. Then they drafted him in the first round, so they're not going to cut him [as a rookie]. You draft someone in the first round, you're supposed to give him a chance. But then they moved him to wide receiver. It was business as usual. He could have made it. They just didn't give him a chance. I got a chance. He didn't."[385]

Briscoe and Raye were both slated to play defensive back in the pros when drafted. Decades later, Raye became the first African American offensive coordinator and called plays for the Chiefs, Buccaneers, Rams, Patriots, Raiders, and Redskins. Jimmy Raye grew up in North Carolina during the Jim Crow era. He was one of the first Black quarterbacks to be recruited to play quarterback at a major school. He committed to Michigan State and became the starting quarterback during the 1966 season, when the team won the national championship. The team finished without a loss; the only blemish was a 10-10 tie with Notre Dame in the famous "Game of the Century." Entering the game, both teams were undefeated and ranked first and second in the country. Despite the success, he was switched to cornerback after being drafted by the Los Angeles Rams. He became a coach after his playing career ended due to injury. He served 13 years as an offensive coordinator, in a coaching career that spanned decades. He began coaching at Michigan State in 1971 and left coaching after the 2013 season with the Tampa Bay Buccaneers. He coached 36 years in the NFL for 10 different teams.

Marlin Briscoe got more opportunities than the previous two, but still his time at the position was extremely limited. Although small in stature, Briscoe was a star quarterback at the University of Nebraska at Omaha, who was drafted by the Broncos to play defensive back in the 1968 draft. During that first season, starter Steve Tensi was sidelined with a broken collarbone and the backup failed to move the team. On the verge of losing their third straight game, Denver coach Lou Saban turned to Briscoe, who entered the game with only ten minutes left and the Broncos trailing 20-7 to the Patriots. Briscoe led the team on two touchdown-producing drives and within three points of the Patriots. Even though the Broncos lost, Briscoe generated a buzz in Denver. The next week, he started at quarterback.

Briscoe went on to play quarterback in eleven games that 1968 season. "Marlin was electrifying," said former Broncos receiver Al Denson. "They could not touch him because he was so good in the backfield—better than Fran Tarkenton. Marlin was short and it was hard for him to throw over the linemen, but he was really accurate. In those days, we played straight man-to-man, bump-and-run and deep zone coverage. The defenders could go over your head and beat you half to death. If you caught fifty passes, you were great. I think Marlin completed, like, seventy percent of his passes that day and gained eighty yards scrambling. He really put us on the map."[386]

Despite being the first Black player to get extensive playing time at quarterback, he was not invited to return as quarterback in 1969. "After my rookie year, I decided to go home to Omaha and get my degree. I needed six credit hours to graduate," said Briscoe. "My cousin Bob Rose had moved to Denver with me. He called me and told me the Broncos signed Pete Liske from Canada and they are having quarterback meetings."[387] The team scheduled a quarterback camp and did not invite the most productive player from the end of the previous season. Searching for another opportunity, Briscoe agreed to play wide receiver for the Buffalo Bills. He accepted the offer and became an All-Pro receiver after one season.

By 1969, Grambling produced a college quarterback with all the attributes a pro team coveted. By then, coach Eddie Robinson had produced more than seventy professional players but none at the premier position. However, now he had a quarterback that he thought might make the grade. He was referring to James Harris, who was drafted by Buffalo in 1969. "I think he is the finest quarterback in the nation, bar none," Robinson said at the time, before addressing the elephant in the room. "I don't know about the 'unwritten law.' The only thing I ask is that they give him a chance at quarterback. Once he gets those Black hands under the center, I think they're going to see as fine a pro quarterback prospect as there is."[388]

Three years after Harris arrived, the next quarterback to challenge the white curtain came along. In 1972, the Pittsburgh Steelers drafted strong-armed Joe Gilliam out of Tennessee State despite having Terry Bradshaw at quarterback. Having led the Jets to a surprise victory in the Super Bowl, "Broadway Joe" Namath was the most famous quarterback in the country at the time. Jefferson Street is the main boulevard in Black Nashville that runs past the Tennessee State campus. People called Gilliam "Jefferson Street Joe" after he led the Tigers to consecutive

Black college national championships in 1970 and 1971. Bradshaw had been the first overall selection of the Steelers in the 1970 draft but had not exactly taken the world by a storm with 12 touchdowns and 46 interceptions in his first two seasons. As the 1972 draft commenced, most thought the Steelers were set at quarterback. Besides Bradshaw, they had backup Terry Hanratty, who had played at Notre Dame and was a second round choice of the Steelers in 1969. As the draft continued and Gilliam remained available, Steelers scout Bill Nunn convinced coach Chuck Noll that he was too good to pass up. "After a while, he was so high up on our board, we *had* to take him," recalled Nunn. "I gave him a fourth-round rating because he was really thin, didn't have much weight, but everything else was there. And he had played against big time competition. By the eleventh round, I said that the only thing preventing him from being accepted in the National Football league was him being Black. That's when Chuck Noll said, 'Let's take him.'"[389]

Gilliam won the starting job in 1974 and led the team to an undefeated 6-0 record in the preseason. By midseason, the team turned back to Bradshaw and went on to win the Super Bowl. Most observers said the quarterback played a minor role on that team that was loaded with talent, especially on the defensive side of the ball with players such as Mel Blount, Joe Greene, Jack Ham, Jack Lambert, and Donnie Shell. The offense featured Terry Bradshaw, Franco Harris, John Stallworth, Lynn Swann, and Mike Webster. The next year, Bradshaw received most of the playing time and Gilliam developed a cocaine addiction that he claimed was a result of the constant pressure to succeed as a Black quarterback.[390]

Gilliam grew up the son of a football coach as his father was longtime defensive coordinator at Tennessee State under head coach John Merritt. He grew up in the South, so he was familiar with racism, discrimination, and Jim Crow. His parents came to visit him in Pittsburgh. "I remember one time my wife Ruth and I went to visit," said the elder Gilliam. "The weather was cold up there. It was between games, during the week and we were with him in his apartment. He said, 'Come here, Daddy. Look in here.' He opens the closet and there's a huge cardboard box in there—must've been three by three—filled with letters to the very top. He said, 'read these letters, Daddy. Read some of them.' I picked one up and it's a death threat. I threw one down. I pick up another one: a death threat. I said, 'Joey, what's in here?' He said, 'Dad, the whole box is filled with death threats.' I said, I'm going to call Chuck Noll.' He said, 'No, Dad, he's on top of it. There's a guy down on the sidelines staking me out, because they say they're going to shoot me from the stands.' None of his teammates would stand next to him."[391]

Fresh off an MVP performance in the Rose Bowl with a conference Player of the Year trophy sitting on his shelf at home, the future looked rosy for Warren Moon in 1978. It appeared as if NFL teams would line up for the talented player but that didn't happen. Why? Warren Moon is Black. "Reading defenses, understanding schemes, being the face of a franchise: There were just a lot of people in pro football who didn't think we could do that," Moon said later. Pro football leadership had the perception that certain positions, quarterback, center and middle linebacker could not be manned by Black candidates. "These were 'thinking positions.' We were good for the athletic, reaction positions: run, jump, block."[392] Moon recalled what he was told as the NFL drafted players. "I found out prior to the draft that I probably wasn't going to get drafted as a quarterback, that other teams wanted to draft me at another position," he recalled. "But I had never played another position and I felt like I could play quarterback at anyone's level. I had just shown that I could do it on one of the biggest stages in college football, in the Rose Bowl, being the MVP of that game. I played in one of the top conferences in the country and was the co-player of the year in that conference. I at least deserved an opportunity to show what I could do at the next level. Did I need to be a first-round draft pick? Probably not. But even Doug [Williams], who was clearly the best player in that draft at the quarterback position, had to wait seventeen picks to get drafted by the Tampa Bay Buccaneers. [Head coach] John McKay had African American quarterbacks when he was at USC. If Tampa Bay hadn't taken Doug, who knows if he will get drafted? But I believed in myself and I was always willing to work hard to get to where I wanted to be."[393]

Warren Moon was well trained from some hard days in his lifetime. His father, also named Harold Warren Moon, died from liver and heart ailments when Warren was only seven years old. His mother, Pat, was a nurse who worked long hours while raising Warren and his six sisters in Los Angeles, California. Warren grew up right in the middle with three older sisters and three younger sisters. Wanting to help out at home, Warren only played one sport growing up: football. "I always enjoyed the position because of the leadership of it, because of everybody relying on you to make the right decision, to make the big play," he said. "I was blessed with a very good arm at a very young age. You know how they line kids up and who's the fastest is going to be running back and who throws the ball the best has a chance to be the quarterback? Well, that was me at quarterback when I was eleven. I gravitated to the position and embraced it."[394]

That choice would prove to be disappointing later in life as he found fewer opportunities than anticipated to play the sport in college due to his race. "It was a disappointment, you know? I was wondering, 'What was it going to take?'" he said. "I put the work in. I got the accolades. I had proven I was good enough to get an opportunity to play quarterback at the next level. But it just wasn't happening for me. A lot of it had to do with the color of my skin and just the stereotypes that went along with African Americans playing quarterback at the time. You had to find the right situation and the right coach who believed in you."[395] Without a major college opportunity, Moon went to junior college and worked to impress coaches at four-year colleges. He was able to attract the attention of University of Washington head coach Don James and one of his assistant coaches, Jim Mora. At Washington he needed to compete with an incumbent senior quarterback who hailed from the state. The program wasn't very good to begin with so when his starting role didn't translate into immediate victories, Moon received more than his share of the blame. Despite this, he enjoyed a successful career at Washington. When it came time for the NFL draft, his memory quickly brought him back to high school. He didn't expect to see the NFL knocking loudly on his door, so he signed a contract with the Edmonton Eskimos of the Canadian League. Soon, people were wondering why the quarterback many considered not good enough to play professionally was burning up the Canadian League.

In 1982, Moon became the first professional quarterback in CFL history to pass for more than 5,000 yards in a single season. Moon won five consecutive Grey Cups (the Canadian equivalent to the Super Bowl in the United States) and was named the game's MVP twice. He was inducted into both the American and Canadian Pro Football Halls of Fame. Can you imagine any quarterback leading his team to five straight Super Bowl victories?

Eventually, after proving his quarterback chops north of the border, Moon returned to the United States to play for the Houston Oilers in 1984. He accumulated nearly 50,000 passing yards over 17 NFL seasons. He set a club record with 3,338 passing yards that first season, which was a mark he would break four times. By 1990, the Oilers offense was running on all cylinders. He led the league in passing yards (4,689 yards), attempts (584), completions (362) and touchdowns (33). In 1994, he was traded to the Vikings and moved on to the Seahawks in 1997. He established new club records for passing efficiency at both stops before finishing up with two seasons with the Chiefs before retiring. Despite playing six seasons in Canada prior to joining the NFL, Moon ranked third all-time in passing yardage and fourth in touchdown passes thrown by his retirement date. He was inducted into the Pro Football Hall of Fame as part of the Class of 2006. "A lot has been said about me as being the first African American quarterback into the Pro Football Hall of Fame," said Moon, on the weekend he was inducted. "It's a subject I've always wanted to be judged as just a quarterback. But because I am the first and because significance does come with that, I accept that, I accept the fact that I am the first. But I also remember all the guys before me who blazed that trail to give me the inspiration and the motivation to keep going forward."[396]

During that same 1978 draft that saw Warren Moon go undrafted, the Tampa Bay Buccaneers selected Grambling quarterback Doug Williams with the seventeenth overall choice. Williams was the only quarterback selected in the first round that year. Doug Williams was born August 9, 1955, in Zachary, Louisiana as the sixth of eight children born to Robert and Laura Williams. Growing up, he played all the sports—baseball, basketball, and football—but it was football that he loved the most. He played quarterback at Chaneyville High School where he threw 22 touchdowns in his senior year. He hoped for an array of scholarship opportunities but received few.

Grambling State University head coach Eddie Robinson saw him play and offered a scholarship. After one redshirt season, Williams won the starting quarterback job and won 36 of 43 games over his tenure. During his senior season, Williams passed for 3,286 yards, 38 touchdowns, and 18 interceptions. His passing yards, touchdown passes, and total yards from scrimmage all led the NCAA that season. He finished fourth in Heisman Trophy voting the year Earl Campbell of Texas won the prize. During his tenure, Grambling won three Southwestern Athletic Conference (SWAC) championships and Williams was named Black College Football Player of the Year twice. Grambling coach Eddie Robinson spoke highly of Williams. Everybody could see his tremendous arm strength, but Robinson said Williams could make all the throws, short, middle, and deep. "But he's got more than just talent," Eddie Robinson, his football coach at Grambling

State University, said in November 1977. "He's a natural leader, he's intelligent, he's a real student of the game."[397]

"Williams has received a lot more publicity than his predecessors," wrote Ulish Carter, a sports columnist for the *Pittsburgh Courier* ahead of the 1978 draft, "so whatever team selects him must be very careful in their treatment of him . . . Once he is selected, the Black citizens in that city should start an all-out drive to make sure he isn't pressured out of the league or placed on the bench. If he doesn't make it, it should be strictly because of his ability, not because the majority of the people aren't ready or don't want a Black quarterback."[398] Carter viewed two other quarterbacks who had been drafted out of HBCUs over the previous 10 years but given minimal chances to succeed: James Harris and Joe Gilliam. Harris was picked in the eighth round by the Buffalo Bills in 1969, Gilliam in the 11th by Pittsburgh Steelers in 1972. Those two Black college quarterbacks lined up behind center but were not given much of a chance. Prior to those two prospects, other Black college quarterbacks were assigned different positions and not allowed to play quarterback.

You might think the pros would come knocking on his door. There wasn't a line at the Williams' front door, but one man was impressed. Joe Gibbs, who would become celebrated as the Super Bowl winning coach of the Washington team, was offensive coordinator of the expansion Tampa Bay Buccaneers. Gibbs visited Williams, worked with him on the field, and tested his knowledge. He left impressed with the view that Williams was the best quarterback prospect in the upcoming draft. He convinced head coach John McKay to take a chance on the Grambling quarterback. Doug Williams became the first African American quarterback selected in the NFL draft that year. Playing on an expansion team that was not overstocked with talent, Williams passed 1,170 yards, seven touchdowns, and eight interceptions. He was selected as part of the all-rookie team after the Bucs won five of fourteen games. The next season, things took off and the four-year old Bucs made the playoffs.

After leading the Bucs to the playoffs three of four seasons, Williams felt it was time for a pay increase. At the time, he was making $120,000 a year, which was less than the salary of twelve backup quarterbacks.[399] Bucs owner Hugh Culverhouse would not pay Williams what he felt was acceptable, so Williams left Tampa Bay. Many viewed Culverhouse as shortsighted and the proof might well be the team record the first season after Williams left: 2 wins, 14 losses. Williams found himself playing for a team called the Oklahoma Outlaws in the United States Football League (USFL). After two seasons, the league folded and Gibbs and Williams would reunite in Washington. "I got this phone call from Coach Gibbs. He was the only guy who called me Douglas. 'Douglas, it's Coach Gibbs,' he said. 'How you doing?' He asked me to come to Washington to be a backup. Now at this point, I don't have a job. I told him, 'Coach, I can be any type of 'up' you want me to be.' He started laughing," said Williams.[400]

He served as backup quarterback on the team to Jay Schroeder in 1986 and 1987. He stayed ready just in case and his time came late in the 1987 season when Schroeder was injured. He started playoff games against the Chicago Bears and Minnesota Vikings. Those wins put him in the position to make a little history: he would be the first Black quarterback to start a Super Bowl game. To say Williams put together a game that was historic was not hyperbole. It was the greatest offensive explosion in the history of the big game. In one quarter of football, Williams completed 9 of 11 passes for 228 yards and four touchdowns. Washington started the game trailing 10-0 and Williams was briefly hurt. He returned to action and torched the Denver Broncos secondary for four touchdowns in the second period. By halftime, Washington led 35-10. The final score was 42-10 and Williams was the easy choice as MVP. Williams said he often thinks back to the Super Bowl game in San Diego. "Not for what it meant to Doug Williams but because it was about much more than Doug Williams. It meant a lot to a whole lot of other people. All the political angles, what people would say depending on what I did, I knew all of that going into the game. But I tried not to put myself above the team and make it all about Doug Williams. I realized that no matter what happened, I was going to be a part of Black history. For me, the best way to be talked about in Black history was for the team to win the game. I didn't want to be a part of Black history and get my a– kicked. That's why I always remembered the fact that the Redskins didn't bring me to San Diego just to show off their Black quarterback. I went to San Diego as the Redskins' starting quarterback. And I went there to win."[401]

Williams retired from playing football in 1989 and worked for a time as a broadcaster and high school coach. He moved to assistant coaching jobs followed by front office positions in pro football. In 1995, he signed on as a scout for the Jacksonville Jaguars. His first college head coaching job came with Morehouse College in 1997. After one season, he followed coach Eddie Robinson at Grambling, where his team won three straight Southwestern Athletic Conference championships from 2000 to 2002. He was director of scouting with Tampa Bay, followed by a second stint as head coach at Grambling (2011-2013). He joined Washington as a scouting executive and later assistant general manager at Minnesota. His son attended Grambling State University and had to drive back and forth through some small towns in Louisiana. "If you get stopped, be compliant," Williams cautioned his son. "You've got to get out and say, 'Yes, sir.'" He was going through Mississippi and a few country towns. Don't be argumentative. He would always say, "Don't worry about me.' But I had to worry because he's Black and he's driving by himself through little towns."[402]

Williams recalled, "When I was at Grambling, all my coaches were Black and everyone I played against, their coaches were Black. I was asked a question after a game my rookie year in Tampa about what I thought about when the national anthem was playing. My dad served in World War II; I know the military. When they asked me that question, I said I was looking on the other side to see how many Black coaches were on the sideline." He said Coach John McKay called him into his office the next day and cautioned him not to say things like that. "We're talking 42 years ago, I got chastised for saying I was counting the number of Black coaches," said Williams, disagreeing with the coach, but not speaking his mind then as a rookie. "You just wanted to see somebody who looked like you be in position to make decisions. We had one Black coach on our staff, Willie Brown, who coached the running backs. I thought I had a right to count how many Black coaches were on the other side, but I got chastised.[403]

"I'm from Zachary, Louisiana. Six miles down the road is Baker. I remember stopping at a red light and the KKK was passing out pamphlets in their hoods. That was a scare tactic to Black folks, to keep them in their place . . . There were so many young people, from Emmett Till [1955] to the bombing of the little girls in Birmingham [1963] and the Freedom Riders, the two whites and a Black in Philadelphia, Mississippi, who got burned in their car [1964]. You just remember them. You go back to that, to where we are today. That's [56] years and we're still doing this. I told my wife this morning [June 8, 2020] that George Floyd will be remembered for the rest of our lives . . . Out of all the Tamir Rices and Trayvon Martins, all the other Blacks that were brutally killed in the arms of the police or what have you, George Floyd will stand out the most because we're not just talking about the United States protesting, we're talking about the world. This is the worst time with the pandemic, so there are two major issues in 2020 that should—should—change the world. Whoever thought it would be with a kneeling? There was so much controversy a few years ago about kneeling. Kneeling during the anthem is different than kneeling on the neck. Some people want to put so much emphasis on the looters. That's a small, small, small percentage out there compared to the people peacefully protesting."[404]

The player who had the biggest impact on Williams was James "Shack" Harris. They had similar background stories. Both grew up in Louisiana, attended Grambling State University, and had struggles playing professional football because they were introduced to an integrated world with tremendous outward expressions of racism. Friends called James Harris "Shack," the nickname his Baptist preacher father gave him. It is short for Meshach, a biblical figure in the Book of Daniel, who is thrown into a fiery furnace but comes out unscathed. One might say that biblical tale mirrors Harris' NFL journey. Harris grew up in Monroe, Louisiana with "Whites Only" signs posted on water fountains and public restrooms. He attended segregated schools right through high school. "Racism was a way of life in Monroe," he recalled. "My old man was a preacher and going to church every Sunday, you would pass these white churches, hear the preachers say all men are created equal. We lived close to the Little League stadium. I'd lie in my bed and hear them calling the white boys' names on this big speaker. And at second base . . . We would go there sometimes and look over the fence—see them walking around in their fine uniforms. We could not play. Those daily denials chip away at your manhood. They erode self-confidence. You saw people who challenged segregation go to jail, get beaten, or come up missing. They'd be floating down the river and you would ask yourself, how is it that all men are created equal?"[405]

Harris continued, "Until I was recruited, I really didn't have any extended contact with white people. Where I came from, we lived in our world and they lived in theirs." Coming out of high school, some Big Ten schools were interested but he didn't hear anything from Southern schools. "The SEC was out of the question back then, especially if I wanted to play quarterback. But Wisconsin, Michigan, and Michigan State all were interested." When Harris met Coach Eddie Robinson at Grambling, his mind was made up. "The minute you met him, you knew you wanted to play for him," said Harris. "There was an absolute sincerity about him, you could almost feel when he walked into a room. Once he promised my mother that I'd graduate and promised me I'd play quarterback, it was a done deal. There was no thought about going to a Big Ten school and hoping I'd get to play quarterback. At Grambling, I knew I'd get a legitimate shot to play the position."[406]

James Harris was frustrated waiting so long for his name to be called during the draft. "They didn't draft me the first day," he recalled. "All these guys I had played against in the SWAC were getting picked. What chance did I have? I decided I wasn't going to play. Coach called me and said he wanted to talk. We went down to the bleachers, just me and him sat down and I told him that being from the segregated South, understanding that no Blacks were playing quarterback, I couldn't see any reason to go to Buffalo. He said, 'I know you can play quarterback in the NFL. The decision is yours, but if you don't go, if guys like you don't go, it's going to be that much more difficult for the next guy.' That touched me."[407]

Black men who played quarterback were told they would have to play another position. Harris made it known that he would not change positions. "I kept my word by not switching," Harris said. "And they [teams in the AFL and NFL] kept their word: They didn't draft me on the first day."[408] The Buffalo Bills finally selected Harris in the eighth round with the 192nd overall selection. That was the same year the Bills selected O.J. Simpson as the first overall choice. Eddie Robinson recalled the saga of Mike Howell, a Grambling quarterback that he sent to the league in 1965. Howell was a strong-armed quarterback, but the Browns needed a defensive back, so they drafted him to play that position. He never got an opportunity to play under center in the pros. This time, Robinson and Harris were singing the same tune. "I heard Martin Luther King say that one day it will not be the color of your skin; it will be the content of your character," said Harris. "That's when I decided I wasn't going to switch. I started thinking, Blacks are going to play quarterback."[409]

Back in the sixties, training camps were long and tiring. Players found refuge from the drudgery of training camp in the daily mail received along with phone calls from home. For Harris, the mail was not helpful. Harris received piles of hate mail. Harris had come of age during the days of Jim Crow, so discrimination and hateful language was something he had not experienced before. All that did not prepare him for the hateful language in the mail he received. "I rode on the back of the bus and we could only drink from the colored water fountain, not the white one," he recalled from his youth. "So, I knew about racism. But hate mail... I had never thought about hate mail. That was something different. Here I am, twenty-one, twenty-two years old and I'm getting all this hate mail about what's going to happen to me, people saying they want to kill me. Now, I didn't take all of it seriously. But there was so much of it. It just wasn't something I expected. I don't know how anyone could expect something like that."[410]

Along with all of the hate mail, living space was a struggle. "They took me to my room," recalled Harris about his first day at Buffalo. "Had me staying at the YMCA for six dollars a night. When O.J. [Simpson, the Bills first draft choice that same year] came to town, he was staying in a suite at the Hilton. They gave me a job, working in the equipment room, putting laces in shoes. I didn't know if this was part of the game or what, but I decided not to tell Coach Robinson about it. I didn't want to put all this pressure on him. He was doing enough."[411]

His first season of professional football was one tough day followed by another. The Buffalo Bills invited eight quarterbacks to camp. Despite starting from the back of the pack, Harris showed the Bills' coaches his talents and he was named the starting quarterback in the opening game of the season against the defending champion New York Jets. "Right now, Harris is doing the best job throwing," said head coach John Rauch in announcing his decision. "He still has a long way to go, but he's come along well in handling the team. He has a fine football mind and when things go back, he doesn't seem to rattle or panic."[412] Perhaps those comments did not seem significant at the time, but they were groundbreaking. An NFL head coach was telling the assembled journalists that he had a rookie Black quarterback who was handling the requirements of the job, including the mental aspects.

Harris joined the Buffalo Bills in 1969 but was released in 1972. Without any offers from another professional team, it appeared as though his playing career might be over. He went to Washington, DC to work in the Office of Minority Enterprises inside the Commerce Department. The new career did not last long as he joined the Rams as a backup to starter John Hadl at the urging of Chuck Knox, who had scouted him coming out of college years before. Knox had always seen beyond the color of the player. Initially brought in as a backup, he did not start for the Rams until the sixth game of the 1974 season after John Hadl was traded. He finished that season as the number two passer in the NFC, completing 106 of 198 for 1,544 yards and 11 touchdowns. He led the Rams to their first playoff victory in 23 seasons and earned his only Pro Bowl appearance.

In January 1975, Harris was named the MVP of the Pro Bowl game after taking over for an injured Jim Hart in the second quarter. He passed for two fourth quarter touchdowns to lead the NFC to victory. The first was an 8-yard pass to Mel Gray of the Cardinals, which had been set up by a 57-yard bomb from Harris to Gray. The second came just one and a half minutes later with an 8-yard pass to Charley Taylor of Washington. Harris was a late replacement for Fran Tarkenton in the game and told reporters that he was glad to have had the opportunity to show his talent. "I got so disgusted at one stage that I thought I would just toss it in," he said. "I felt that people thought a Black quarterback could never make the grade. I really got the impression there was something racist in my early failures to make the grade."[413]

The next season, the Rams played multiple quarterbacks during the season. Despite the unsteady circumstance, Harris had some good days. On October 3, 1976, he passed for 436 yards and two touchdowns in leading the Rams to a 31-28 upset victory over the Miami Dolphins. As the Rams' starter, Harris went 21-6 in the regular season and 1-2 in the playoffs. Despite the record, he was traded to the San Diego Chargers, where he appeared in 26 games with 11 starts. The pressure of playing the Black quarterback in the NFL was getting to him. "Back in those days, we truly were Black quarterbacks," he recalled. "And we knew since that's the way we were looked at, we almost had to play perfectly. For many years, there was nobody in the league starting but me, I was the only one and there was always this [undercurrent in the media] that someone else should be starting ahead of me. So, I felt I couldn't make mistakes. But to play that position the best, like I did in high school and college, you have to be able to move on from a mistake, like an interception and just put it up some more. And I just didn't feel that way in the pros."[414]

Harris retired as a player in 1981. Before his career was over, Harris became the first Black quarterback to start a season opener in the modern era, the first Black quarterback to start and win a playoff game, the first to play in a Pro Bowl, and the first Black quarterback selected MVP of the Super Bowl. He had been the first Black quarterback in the NFL in the 1970s. He finished his career with 8,136 yards passing and 45 touchdown passes while playing for the Bills, Rams, and Chargers over a 12-year span.

In an 18-minute piece called "The Black Quarterback" by reporter Armen Keteyian that aired on Showtime's *60 Minute Sports*, Harris said he had to stay in a

$6 a night room in the YMCA away from his teammates in a hotel during training camp. The Bills also asked him to consider playing wide receiver and gave him a job cleaning cleats in the equipment room. "I knew it was out of line," said Harris.[415] That would have been a surprise to his legendary college coach, Grambling's Eddie Robinson, who felt Harris had the height, arm strength, intelligence, and emotional maturity to deal with anything thrown at him.

CHAPTER THIRTEEN

The Boycott, Part 2

It is generally considered that the 1965 AFL All-Star game boycott happened because several players, so-called "ringleaders," convinced the other players to go along.

ABNER HAYNES

Haynes was a poster child for the turbulent times of the sixties. The son of a minister, he was not fearful of taking a difficult stance and fighting for what he thought was right. Though Haynes played only two seasons in Kansas City after the Texans moved from Dallas in 1963, his legacy was so profound that he was inducted into the Chiefs Hall of Fame in 1991 and his number 28 jersey is one of just 10 retired by the club. Some may have called him an overnight success when he led the first-year league in rushing and became the first AFL Player of the Year as well as Rookie of the Year. He did it all for the team—rushing, receiving, and returning kicks—scoring 43 touchdowns in the first three years of the AFL and served as captain of the 1962 champion Texans. But Haynes' contribution did not stop at the white lines of the field. His outspokenness confronting the issues of the day was as much a part of the way Haynes operated as his hard running style. Haynes confronted the issues of the day just as hard as he hit defenders on inside runs up the middle.

In the end, Haynes' outspokenness may have shortened his career. He was a key figure in a threatened boycott that forced the AFL to move its 1965 All-Star Game from New Orleans to Houston because Black players were facing issues of discrimination in the Crescent City. The Chiefs traded him to Denver four days later. "Somebody had to set the tone; that's what my father kept saying and it might as well be me," said Haynes, son of a Dallas church minister, when inducted into the Chiefs Hall of Fame. "I came through the '60s. The president got killed. Dr. King got killed. The University of Mississippi was being integrated ... Central High School (in Little Rock) ... That was all affecting me while I was trying to play ball."[416]

He set new trails when he became the first Black player at what was then North Texas State and he led their team, the Eagles, in rushing for three years and was an All-American in 1959. Chiefs' owner Lamar Hunt signed Haynes under the goal posts after the 1959 Sun Bowl and recalled many good times with the running back. Hunt had a sharp sports business mind and understood Haynes would be a drawing card as a local hero playing for the Dallas Texans in the Cotton Bowl when the team competed directly with the NFL Cowboys.

In his first three seasons, Haynes piled up 4,472 yards rushing and receiving. Even though Haynes was slightly built at 6-feet, 175 pounds, he maneuvered through AFL defenses with his speed and shiftiness as he rushed for 875 yards and led the Texans in receiving with 55 catches that first season. "He was a franchise player before they talked about franchise players," said former Chiefs coach Hank Stram. "He did it all: rushing, receiving, kickoff returns, punt returns. He gave us the dimension we needed to be a good team in Dallas. When you think of the old AFL, one of the top names in the league was Abner Haynes."[417] An example of his versatile play came in a game against the New York Titans in which he rushed for 150 yards, returned a field goal attempt 92 yards, and caught eight passes—all in one game.

Haynes recalled memories of playing games in Dallas, Texas in front of numerous family and friends. "We played in the Cotton Bowl, about eight blocks from my house," he said. "That was a thrill. On Sunday mornings, I'd go off into south Dallas, where I went to high school and I'd get a charge out of seeing the guys I went to high school with. You knew the people and would get fired up to play. It was a beautiful time. I thought it was my role to show other Black kids you can achieve, you can compete, you can go to white colleges . . . you can have white friends, Black friends, green friends and get along under adversity. I think I proved that."[418]

Haynes' best season came in 1962 when he rushed for 1,049 yards and scored a record 19 touchdowns. Stram moved him to flanker for the 1962 championship game and he scored both Dallas touchdowns on a 28-yard pass reception and a two-yard run. After winning the AFL title, Hunt moved the team to Kansas City. It proved to be traumatic for Haynes, who hailed from Dallas and loved playing at home. "It not only pained me, it changed my life," said Haynes, looking back. "It cost me money and it put me in a market that was not home. In Dallas I had three jobs and had appearances. Black players had deals at home where you could make a little change, but if you were from out of the city, it wasn't the same."[419]

The 1963 season might have been the low point for Haynes. A back injury limited his carries and the season began with a tragedy. Stone Johnson, an Olympic track star from Dallas, came to the team based on Haynes' recommendation. In the final preseason game at Wichita, Johnson suffered a fractured neck and died eight days later. "It affected me a lot," said Haynes. "I was the cause of him being here. I felt responsible for him being there and getting killed. The ambulance took an hour and a half and the boy lay there on the cold ground. Now, you have ambulances at any kind of football game, but we've already blown it. Nobody wants to hear about how we got to this point, who paid the price."[420]

Haynes bounced back during the 1964 season and was selected to play in the AFL All-Star game in New Orleans. "The All-Star Game got me traded out of Kansas City . . . If you were a Black player, there was no way you were going to have the attitude of your white coach or white owner. If you were a sensitive Black guy and your dad was a minister and you had been involved in seeing your folks lead Black people in the church, you couldn't be Abner Haynes and not have a feeling about the suffering that was going on. We had 14 of us (from Kansas City). I was captain of the team and I felt responsible for those guys. We went down there as a family and we decided we'd all do the same thing, or we wouldn't. The team hung together. We had young players like Buck Buchanan and Bobby Bell. I was not going to let them get caught up in some kind of trip without taking charge."[421]

Buchanan agreed. "Thank heaven we had people like Abner who would stand up for their rights and made a difference in the league," he said. "He was right. If we were going to be a professional league, then all of the players should have access to all of the facilities and they complained about it and got it changed. He spoke his mind. There are a lot of things players in the AFL would not stand for that players let go by in the old NFL. That was one of the things Abner did for all of us when he stood up and said, 'No more of this. If we're going to be a first-class league, let's don't treat our players in a second-class manner.'"[422]

As with any relationship, the one between Abner Haynes and the Chiefs organization was mixed. Haynes spoke highly of Lamar Hunt and the opportunities the young owner of the team provided him in the 1960s, a time of much different racial views than today. It was reported that H. L. Hunt, Lamar's father, once called Chiefs coach Hank Stram and told him, "You got too many Blacks on your team."[423] Despite his father's views, Hunt was open minded toward providing opportunities to Black athletes who played at historically Black colleges and universities. Later in the decade, he hired Lloyd Wells, the first Black full-time scout in professional football, to scour Black schools in a search for talent. When the Chiefs selected Grambling tackle Buck Buchanan with the first overall selection in the 1963 AFL draft, it marked the first time a player from a HBCU was selected that high. The relationship between Haynes and Hunt was rich. In days when Blacks were unable to be served in many restaurants across the South, Hunt took Haynes to lunch. "It was wild, the places he would take me," Haynes told Vahe Gregorian, a Chiefs beat reporter. "And he would talk to you in so many ways. You really had to pay attention to Lamar Hunt. Yeah, man, you had to be alert or else you were going to miss it."[424]

Those good feelings changed a bit after the All-Star game boycott. "I sure don't appreciate your actions," Haynes said then-general manager Jack Steadman told him after the New Orleans boycott. In a Showtime documentary on the AFL, Haynes said he received a letter from Steadman, "explaining to me how a football player's role is not to help his people. All I am supposed to do is play football and keep my mouth shut." It is unclear what part Hunt and Stram had in the Denver trade, which happened days after the game. Years later, he told the reporter one thing he hoped would come across in his story. "Ain't nobody watching you but you," he said. "You can violate who you are, or you can be real to it. That's who you are. That's the journey that we are on. And the battle."[425]

Cookie Gilchrist

From an early age, Gilchrist challenged societal norms. While in high school, he was jailed for dating Betty Ann Richards, who was white.[426] Not a really good student, Gilchrist was told he would not be eligible to play his senior season, so he planned on attending Cheshire Academy in order to improve his school grades and possibly attend Michigan State University. Another player considered a ringleader, Gilchrist hailed from Brackenridge, Pennsylvania and began professional football straight out of high school. His given name was Carlton Chester Gilchrist, but his love of the sweet snack earned him the nickname "Cookie" as a youngster and it stuck. He grew up twenty-five miles northeast of Pittsburgh, where he starred on the football field while attending Har-Brack Union High School. In 1953, he led his team to the Western Pennsylvania Interscholastic Athletic League co-championship after his Har-Brack squad played to a 0-0 tie with Donora High School. Cleveland Browns head coach Paul Brown offered him $5,500 to sign a contract to play in the NFL. "That money was more than my father made in a year," said Gilchrist. "[The Browns] teased me when I joined the club. They told me they had seen all-Army, All-Pro, and all-world players, but this as the first time they had seen all-school-yard."[427] That decision proved costly. The Browns released him before the start of the season. He was prevented from attending college on an athletic scholarship since he violated his amateur status by signing a professional contract. The NFL shunned him, claiming to have a rule against the signing of underage players. Left without options, Gilchrist went north to Canada where he spent two years in the Ontario Rugby Football Union before moving to the Canadian Football League. He spent six seasons with the Hamilton Tiger-Cats, the Saskatchewan Roughriders, and the Toronto Argonauts. He dominated on both sides of the ball, running for nearly 5,000 yards, adding another 1,068 yards receiving, and recording 12 interceptions on defense. He earned All-CFL honors five seasons.

Gilchrist was fined and suspended several times during his CFL days. His CFL career might be summed up in one sentence from the *Pittsburgh Post-Gazette*: He had a near-fight with Hamilton Coach Jim Trimble but was still chosen the team's Most Valuable Player in 1956 and 1957. A reputation of highly productive on the field but a challenge off the field became his calling card. He was known as the first player to turn down nomination to the Canadian Football Hall of Fame. "I dealt with racism when I was in Canada," he said years later. "I dealt with racists. I was totally exploited. I was left with nothing, with no dignity. I was treated like an animal. My exploitation benefited everyone in Canada, except me. Canadian newspapers are full of Cookie Gilchrist stories and all are derogatory. I have all the clippings in a scrapbook and, if you read the stories, you wouldn't think that I was worthy of the Hall of Fame."[428]

While playing in Canada, Gilchrist married a white Canadian named Gwen, whom he met in Hamilton. By 1962, they had two children. When Gilchrist decided to play football in the United States, NFL teams decided not to sign him when they learned he was married to a white woman. By the time he arrived in professional football in the United States, he was a 27-year-old rookie with nearly a decade of professional experience. He took the AFL by storm, earning 1,096 yards rushing with 13 touchdowns, which led the league and finished second in total yards from scrimmage with 1,415 yards. He was named to the AFL All-Star team, first team all-league, and AFL Player of the Year honors. He added placekicking to his duties and converted 8 of 20 field goals and 14 of 17 extra points. His dominance as a powerful running back continued for two additional seasons. He was blessed with tremendous athletic abilities on his powerful 250-pound body with a 51-inch chest and 31-inch waist. "He was probably the best athlete that I have ever played ball with," said teammate Billy Shaw. "He had tremendous strength and he was exceptionally quick for a man who weighed 250 pounds. His combination of size, strength, and speed was uncommon for the time. There was no one any better than Cookie in hitting the hole from tackle to tackle. He would punish linebackers and defensive linemen. He would hit the blocker in front of him if he didn't get out of the way. I have scars on my back from when someone would stalemate me at the line and here comes Cookie from behind me. He didn't care what color jersey you had on—he was going forward. Cookie enjoyed running the ball straight ahead so he could hit somebody."[429]

On any given Sunday, Cookie Gilchrist could dominate a defense. In week 13 of the 1963 season, Gilchrist rushed for a record 243 yards on 36 carries against the New York Jets. He added five touchdowns. That rushing total was six more yards than Jim Brown ever rushed for in a single game, so Gilchrist established a new pro football record on that December afternoon in Buffalo, New York. "The game plan was to run Cookie quite a bit and we stuck to it," said Daryle Lamonica, who was making his first professional start at quarterback. "We used rollout passes to neutralize their blitzes. I faked to the halfback—they had to respect the fake—and then the pitch went to Cookie. Our interior line did some great blocking."[430] Extremely competitive, Gilchrist came to life during the biggest contests. The Buffalo Bills needed to beat the rival Patriots in Fenway Park in the last game of the 1964 season to win the division. "On the Bills' first play from scrimmage, Cookie carried the ball around the left end [and], rather than avoid cornerback Chuck Shonta, ran straight at him and hit him with a hammerlike forearm, knocking him unconscious," recalled longtime NFL reporter Larry Felser. "As Gilchrist walked past Boston's defensive huddle, he scornfully asked, 'Which one of you motherfuckers is next?' The rest of the contest seemed to be a formality. The Bills won, 24-14, and six days later Cookie played his final game as a Bill in the championship game against San Diego."[431]

That game was even more dramatic because it came against the team that had ended the Bills' undefeated season a few weeks earlier. The Bills had started the season with eight straight wins, dominating many opponents in the process. In week ten, they faced the Patriots, the team that had played in the AFL playoff game the previous season. Gilchrist, unhappy because he wasn't getting the ball, remained on the sideline when the offense took the field. Gilchrist might have had a valid point. During the game that upset Gilchrist, he only carried the ball 11 times while the Bills' quarterbacks, Kemp and Lamonica, attempted more than 50 passes. Buffalo had the ball on its own 40 with 24 seconds remaining in the first half when Gilchrist told backup Willie Ross to go in and replace him. Coach Lou Saban was hot. This incident came just weeks after an incident involving resisting an arrest accusations (the charges were later dropped). "A lot of incidents have taken place," said Saban, after waivers were announced. "I guess everybody knows about the last game."[432]

The behavior was too much for Saban and Bills' owner Ralph Wilson to take. "His only concern is himself and how much yardage he can gain," said Saban in announcing the release. At the time, Gilchrist was leading the league with 165 carries for 751 yards. "Certain incidents have taken place over the last six weeks which were uncalled for, in my opinion," added Saban. "I felt we had to go on without him. The club is more important than the individual's gain."[433] Published reports said the incidents may have been Gilchrist had reportedly missed several early season practice sessions and violated curfew. He was released, but cooler heads prevailed. The team captains, primarily led by Jack Kemp, brokered a peace so that the waivers could be recalled. Gilchrist apologized to his teammates and Coach Saban and returned committed to playing hard for the playoff push.

His teammates admired his intimidating presence on the field. "I've seen guys hit him and just bounce off," said teammate Wray Carlton. "He would hurt them.

You could tell by the way they would try to tackle him after he hit them. They didn't want to hit him head on. They'd go around and try to jump on his back and ride him. They just did not want to face up to him. When he ran for 240 yards against the Jets [in 1963], I know, in the fourth quarter of that game, they did not want to tackle him. Nobody would hit him head on. I've seen collisions made when people tried to tackle him. Ross O'Hanley, a guy who played safety with Boston, was a tough Irish kid, hard as nails. He came running up and hit Cookie one time and happened to catch him head on. [O'Hanley] was out cold and there was a crack in his helmet."[434]

Sometimes that intimidation went to the extremes. "On the football field, he was one of the nastiest sons of bitches I ever met in my life. There was absolutely no fear in that man," recalled teammate Paul Maguire. During halftime of the 1964 championship game, Gilchrist turned his enthusiasm toward his teammates as he challenged every teammate to give their all during the second half. Anyone who did not would face the wrath of Gilchrist. "Cookie stood up. 'I'm going to tell you something. If we don't win this game, I'm going to beat the s--- out of everybody in this locker room.'" At that point, Coach Saban re-entered the locker room. "'And I'm going to start with you, Coach. I'm going to kick your ass first.' I just sat back in my locker. I knew he meant it."[435]

"Everybody had a tumultuous relationship with Cookie Gilchrist," said Mike Stratton, a six-time AFL All-Star and four-time All-AFL selection at linebacker for the Bills. "It wasn't just Lou. Lou was trying to keep the team together and [team captains] Kemp and Billy Shaw did everything they could to try to keep the team together and keep Cookie in line, but it was more than a full-time job for everyone. I'm playing defense and I'm on the defensive team and in our estimation during those years, we were actually a different team from the offensive team. I didn't have a whole lot of speculation about it. We'd go along with whatever the majority of the offensive team would. They were trying to chastise Cookie and trying to bring him back into the fold, so to speak. We were for it—Cookie was a tremendous ballplayer."[436]

"I felt he didn't show good team spirit at the time that it happened," said Shaw. "But I didn't want to go into another ballgame without him lined up behind me. Selfish? Maybe so, but we had some ballgames to win and if we're going to win the whole thing, we needed him."[437]

The bottom line with Cookie Gilchrist was his unwillingness to remain quiet and just go along. He lived during the tumultuous civil rights days when Black athletes were supposed to adopt a quiet, unassuming public personality. Not Gilchrist. "There have been numerous stories about me over the years that are untrue," said Gilchrist. "Well, I haven't been the run-of-the-mill Negro athlete who accepts the crumbs offered. I felt that I produced better than the white athlete and I wanted to get paid better. Some people have been shocked at my extreme individuality and outspokenness. Canadian football game me a chance to exercise my individualism, which I think this country was founded on. America was built on individualism. America needs more individuals like me. I was selling my body for X number of dollars and when I negotiated a contract, I was negotiating my future."[438]

There were common traits between Abner Haynes and Gilchrist. Both were highly productive backs for their teams for several seasons. They led their teams in rushing and offensive production and even earned a championship for their respective teams. The other common item: both were traded from their squads shortly after the 1965 All-Star Game. Some would say that the Chiefs traded Abner Haynes to make room for the younger Mack Lee Hill and Gilchrist had long ago worn out his welcome. But the timing, coming immediately after the boycott, is questionable. In a 1963 interview, Gilchrist said, "remember a lot of things that happened when I left the states. Little Rock, Meredith, Freedom Riders, sit-ins . . . There is big change happening and I'm going to try and do my bit."[439]

"With the passage of time, there are two establishment responses to the great political rebels in sports," wrote Dave Zirin, sports editor of the progressive magazine, *The Nation*. "You either see them commodified and defanged—think Muhammad Ali—or they are simple erased from history. Count Carlton Chester 'Cookie' Gilchrist among the erased . . . His legacy as both a player and athletic rebel are well worth restoring." It is generally recognized that the AFL players boycott in New Orleans inspired Dr. Harry Edwards, Tommie Smith, and Lee Evans to call for a boycott of the 1968 Olympic Games in Mexico City and decades later, for Latino baseball players Adrian Gonzalez and Yovani Gallardo to sit out the 2011 All-Star Game in Phoenix because of harsh anti-immigrant legislation signed into law by Arizona Governor Jan Brewer. Gilchrist later said his role in leading the boycott was "better than anything I did playing football."[440]

"The truth is, New Orleans should erect a statue for Cookie," said Ron Mix, an All-AFL tackle who later became an attorney specializing in player's worker's compensation claims. He offered another viewpoint. "The city wanted an NFL team, but it was not going to get it unless it desegregated. The boycott led to change in the laws."[441]

Ultimately, a majority of Black players voted to boycott the game and transferred to Houston. Reaction across the country was immediate and heated. Many local politicians and media members reacted with strong words. After the mayor of New Orleans said the players should have "rolled with the punch," players and the media reacted. *The Louisiana Weekly* bluntly stated, "It is impossible for any white person to completely place himself in the position occupied by any Negro. Any white person who attempts to do this must allow his imagination to travel back to the days of his earliest remembrances—to childhood days to being relegated to inferior and Jim Crow schools . . . to be refused certain jobs because of race . . . to being placed in inferior, segregated housing ghettoes." The editorial continued, "If there is any white person who can pass this test, then and only then is such a person psychologically prepared to imagine how he would react if he were subjected to the indignities experienced by the 21 Negro AFL players."[442]

"We think the Negro players were right for not bowing to racial discrimination," wrote sports editor Jim Hall in *The Louisiana Weekly*. "That jive of the players should have 'rolled with the punch' is for kookaburras. For more than one hundred years, Negroes have been rolling with the punch. The case in point proves the Negroes today will not take the Sunday hate punches anymore."[443]

"All Negroes were lifted and inspired by the stand they took," observed Superior Court Judge Duke Slater and All-American football player in the 1920s at Iowa. "The city of New Orleans lost more than a million dollars in tourist trade because of the disgraceful treatment accorded these Negroes athletes. And when you hit them in the pocketbook, there is a good chance of getting results."[444]

"My grandfather and yours 'rolled with the punch' and their grandfathers before them did the same," wrote Sam Lacy of the *Afro-American*. "Today's grandfathers of the future are asking why it is that colored people are destined to be the only ones in this country showing the Christian attitude of turning the other cheek. They're interested in knowing why it is that we must content ourselves with being first class citizens only when the bugle blows for war and at income tax time."[445]

Some of the All-Stars had previous experiences of segregation that came to mind during the All-Star week. Ernie Ladd, Sherman Plunkett, and Earl Faison had been with the Chargers when they played games in Jeppesen Stadium earlier in their careers. At the time, the stadium was property of the Houston Independent School District, which set the segregation policies at the facility. Blacks were only allowed to sit in the four-dollar section behind the goal line. By 1961, only the 14,000 seats the Oilers provided were first come, first served.[446] Lloyd Wells, sports editor of the *Informer*, encouraged the three men to boycott a stadium with such racist policies in effect. Ironically, with the transfer of the game to Houston, it would be played in what some might consider the most racially segregated stadium in the AFL during its earliest days.

When white quarterback Jack Kemp entered Jeppesen Stadium for the All-Star game, his memories returned to the 1960 championship game as a member of the Chargers. He remembered his father sitting on the 45-yard line while the parents of his Black teammates were sitting in a roped-off section behind the goal posts. That visual left an impression on Kemp, who became known as the bleeding heart conservative during his political career. He pressed his party to be more inclusive to minorities and the poor. As Secretary of Housing and Urban Development, he urged revitalization of urban ghettos. Houston Antwine and Larry Garron recalled being approached by CORE and the NAACP back in 1962 when the Patriots came to New Orleans City Park for an exhibition game. Those groups asked the Black players to make an issue of the separate accommodations. The players wanted to agree to support any protest but refused to take the lead. When they saw no signs of a protest, they played in the game. When they were told the All-Star game was scheduled for New Orleans, they were apprehensive. "At that time, we realized what was waiting for us in New Orleans and we accepted it to help our team and our league," said Garron. "This time was going to be different. We were told everything had changed and we would be free to come and go like everyone else."[447] The stand taken by heroes in the sixties set the path for the stands taken today.

CHAPTER FOURTEEN

Take a Knee

When the San Francisco 49ers selected quarterback Colin Kaepernick during the second round of the 2011 draft, some in the country may not have been that familiar with the player. He played college football for the University of Nevada, which played in the Western Athletic Conference (WAC). Despite finishing the season with twelve wins and one loss for a share of the WAC championship, the school wasn't one that was featured every weekend in primetime. The San Francisco 49ers swung a trade with the Denver Broncos to move up to the 36th overall pick and selected the Nevada quarterback. Kaepernick stood six-feet-four inches, was very athletic, and possessed a strong arm. In short, he had all the tools NFL teams look for in their quarterback prospects, but many were surprised when he led the 49ers to the Super Bowl in only his second season. In fact, Kaepernick was one of the hottest names of the 2012 playoffs. In the divisional playoff game against the Green Bay Packers, Kaepernick ran for 181 yards and two touchdowns, setting both single game records for rushing yards by a quarterback and a team record for postseason rushing, regardless of position. Overall, the 49ers racked up 579 yards of total offense in a 45-31 victory. That game punched their ticket to the championship game.

Ironically, the game didn't start well for Kaepernick. Less than two minutes into the game, he threw an interception to Sam Shields, who ran it back 52 yards for a touchdown. Kaepernick rallied and led the team to victory, scoring at least one touchdown every quarter. It marked the final playoff game played at Candlestick Park. The next week, San Francisco overcame a 17-point deficit, the largest comeback in an NFC Championship Game, to return to the Super Bowl for the sixth time. Kaepernick completed 16 of 21 passes for 233 yards and a touchdown along with 21 rushing yards. The 49ers landed in New Orleans for Super Bowl XLVII against the Baltimore Ravens. Again, the 49ers fell behind early and trailed 21-6 at halftime. It appeared that the Ravens were in control of the game after dominating the first half with quarterback Joe Flacco throwing three touchdowns to take a 21-3 lead before the 49ers kicked a field goal just before halftime. Jacoby Jones returned the second half kickoff a record 108 yards that gave the Ravens a 28-6 lead before the partial power outage stalled the game for 34 minutes. When play resumed, San Francisco mounted a comeback that ultimately fell three points short by a 34-31 margin.

Over the next three seasons, Kaepernick lost and won back the starting job with the 49ers, missing the playoffs each of three seasons. Prior to the 2014 season, Kaepernick signed a six-year contract extension with the 49ers, worth up to $126 million with $13 million fully guaranteed. He played his best ball when Jim Harbaugh coached the team, but Harbaugh left to take a job at the University of Michigan after the 2014 season. The 49ers hired Jim Tomsula in 2015, but he was replaced the following season by Chip Kelly, who named Blaine Gabbert to open the 2016 season as starting quarterback. Kelly replaced Gabbert with Kaepernick midseason. The following year, Kyle Shanahan replaced Kelly as head coach. Entering the 2016 season, Kaepernick was coming off three surgeries requiring operations on his thumb and knee, in addition to a season-ending shoulder procedure. He only played in nine games during the 2015 season. Due to the physical therapy needed to recover from the injuries and as a precaution, Kaepernick was held out of the early preseason games.

Before the third preseason game against the Packers, Kaepernick sat on the bench during the anthem. His sitting didn't attract attention, perhaps because he had not been in uniform. Before the fourth game, he suited up and was slated to play in the game. Again, he sat on the bench during the playing of the anthem. Steve Wyche, a reporter from NFL Media, noticed and asked him after the game why he wasn't standing. "I am not going to stand up to show pride in a flag for a country that oppresses Black people and people of color," Kaepernick explained to a reporter after the game. "To me, this is bigger than football and it would be selfish on my part to look the other way. There are bodies on the street and people getting paid leave and getting away with murder."[448]

Just one month before the game, a police officer near Minneapolis shot a Black man named Philando Castile. When he was stopped by Officer Jeronimo Yanez due to a broken taillight, Castile told him that he had a gun and a legal permit to carry it. Diamond Reynolds, Castile's girlfriend, sat next to him in the car with her young daughter in the back seat. Diamond live-streamed the sequence on Facebook to a shocked nation. A quick sequence of events occurred after Castile told the officer that he had a gun. Yanez told him not to pull it out. Castile denied going for the gun, but Yanez fired seven shots, fatally wounding Castile. Many assumed the white police officer panicked because Castile was Black. The incident was fresh on the minds of many Americans, including Kaepernick. At the same time, the presidential race was heating up and candidate Donald Trump's speeches were laced with what many considered racial overtones, which prompted observers to label some of Trump's supporters as white nationalists.

Through a DNA test, Kaepernick learned that some of his ancestors came from Ghana and Nigeria. That news gave him a whole new perspective and a desire to learn as much as possible about his ancestry. "It changed everything for me," he said. "It helped me know that my history did not begin with being adopted. It did not begin with slavery."[449] That news spurred on the education process. Kaepernick read books such as *The Fire Next Time* by James Baldwin, *The Autobiography of Malcolm X,* and *I Know Why the Caged Bird Sings* by Maya Angelou. He took the words of those who came before to teach him how to live his life. "I've had enough of someone else's propaganda," wrote Malcolm X in his autobiography. "I'm for truth, no matter who tells it. I'm for justice, no matter who it is for or against. I'm a human being first and foremost and as such I'm for whoever and whatever benefits humanity as a whole." Kaepernick found that much of what he read contradicted what he had been taught in school as a youth. "This country stands for freedom, liberty, justice for all and it's not happening for all right now," Kaepernick said in a press conference.[450] The more Kaepernick thought of it, he found that he could not stand for the anthem that represented a country that oppressed some of its people over extended time periods.

When he heard about Kaepernick's initial protest in which he remained seated on the bench as the national anthem played, Army veteran Nate Boyer said he was disappointed. "It struck a chord with me, of course and it struck a chord with a lot of people - a lot of people in the veteran community as well - because obviously the flag and the anthem and what that stuff stands for means something, you know, very different to us," said Boyer, years later. "And I was pretty upset, you know, just because I felt like he didn't understand what those symbols really represent. Instead of letting my anger overwhelm me, I decided to relax a little bit and I wrote this open letter that was just explaining my experiences, my relationship to the flag."[451] The open letter to Colin Kaepernick was published in the *Army Times* in August 2016. Boyer had a unique perspective with a background in the military and a more recent stint—albeit short—as a college and professional football player.

Boyer doesn't look like a football player. Standing five-feet-ten inches tall and weighing 185 pounds, he looks more like an average-sized, athletically built man. He served six years as a United States Army Green Beret with tours in Iraq and Afghanistan. During his first tour of Iraq in 2009, he was awarded the Bronze Star for meritorious combat operations. When he arrived on the University of Texas campus as a 29-year-old freshman, he walked on to the Longhorn football team, despite having never played organized football. After two years, it may have looked like he was wasting his time. He played little, but during his summer deployment with the National Guard in Afghanistan, Boyer trained himself to be a long snapper. He watched YouTube videos to learn the proper technique and practiced during his off-duty hours while deployed overseas. He won the job in 2012 and held onto it for three seasons with the Longhorns.

Boyer signed a free agent contract with the Seattle Seahawks and was on the roster for a single exhibition game. It was a memorable day for Boyer. "The only time I got to stand on the sideline for the anthem was during my one and only NFL preseason game, against the Denver Broncos," wrote Boyer in his letter to Kaepernick. "As I ran out of the tunnel with the American flag, I could feel myself swelling with pride and as I stood on the sideline with my hand on my heart as the anthem began, that swelling burst into tears. I thought about how far I'd come and the men I'd fought alongside who didn't make it back. I thought about those overseas who were risking their lives at that very moment. I selfishly thought about what I had sacrificed to get to where I was and while I knew I had little to no chance of making the Seahawks' roster as a 34-year-old rookie, I was trying."[452]

Kaepernick saw Boyer's letter and the two connected. Three days later, he and Boyer met in the lobby of the team hotel before the 49ers' matchup with the

Chargers in San Diego. Kaepernick explained to Boyer his reasons for the protest, as well as his thoughts on social justice and police brutality. Boyer told him about his military service and how some might view his sitting as divisive and hurtful. Boyer listened with an open mind. Instead of sitting, he proposed kneeling. He saw it as a sort of compromise. "People—in my opinion and in my experience, kneeling's never been in our history really seen as a disrespectful act," explained Boyer. "I mean, people kneel when they get knighted. You kneel to propose to your wife and you take a knee to pray. And soldiers often take a knee in front of a fallen brother's grave to pay respects. So, I thought, if anything, besides standing, that was the most respectful. But, of course, that's just my opinion."[453] With research, Boyer found a photograph of Martin Luther King, Jr. kneeling in prayer at a protest in Selma, Alabama during the 1960s. Personally, he remembered taking a knee at Arlington National Cemetery in honor of his fallen friends who were buried there. Boyer said he personally would never take a knee during the playing of the national anthem, but he said he fought for the right of Americans to express their individual views freely. If Kaepernick found his free expression on one knee, he could not argue.

Curiously, it was kneeling that was the focus of the death of an unarmed Black man, George Floyd, at the hands of Minneapolis police. Derek Chauvin, a 44-year-old white police officer, knelt on Floyd's neck for more than nine minutes, causing his death in 2020. On April 20, 2021, a jury found Chauvin guilty of second-degree unintentional murder, third-degree murder, and second-degree manslaughter. He was given a sentence of 22.5 years in prison. Chauvin has appealed to the Minnesota Supreme Court.

As the weeks went on, more people noticed and some voiced opinions. Some observers were highly critical of Kaepernick. How could a millionaire athlete with a comfortable life know anything about oppression? If he did not like it here, they said, he could leave the country. Still others thought that it was great that an athlete cared enough to protest the mounting police violence cases across the country. As the 2016 season continued, Kaepernick continued kneeling for "The Star-Spangled Banner" and other athletes from other sports joined in. He also did not limit his activism to kneeling during the anthem. He pledged to donate $1 million to charities working in communities. His plan was to donate $100,000 every month over ten months to various small organizations. Kaepernick distributed the funds through his foundation. He also started holding free Know Your Rights Camps for children. The mission was to teach kids how to stand up for themselves. One section of the training taught kids how to interact with police to stay alive. He took it further still, teaching the children about financial literacy and tips to live a healthy life. Over a two-year period, numerous additional events played out in the media involving the deaths of unarmed Blacks at the hands of police.

July 17, 2014: Eric Garner was killed in Staten Island, New York when Daniel Pantaleo, a New York City police officer, put him in a prohibited chokehold when arresting him. Video footage of the incident generated widespread national attention. Many questioned the police use of deadly force on someone suspected of selling individual cigarettes. After Pantaleo brought Garner to the ground using a prohibited chokehold, several other officers joined in and had him pinned to the ground. When he managed a breath, he told the police, "I cannot breathe." Garner repeatedly told officers he could not breathe and eventually lost consciousness. The medical examiner ruled his death a homicide. A grand jury heard evidence for two months before issuing a ruling on December 3, 2014 of no indictment for killing Garner. As a result, protesters took to the streets to protest. A few months later, the NBA All-Star Game was held in New York with Garner's death fresh on everyone's minds. Garner's "I can't breathe" words became a rallying cry before the game.

August 9, 2014: Police officer Darren Wilson in Ferguson, Missouri, a suburb of St. Louis, shot and killed 18-year-old Michael Brown. The sequence of events is unclear. Wilson, a white police officer, said a struggle occurred between he and Brown over his service pistol and the gun fired. Dorian Johnson, a 22-year-old who had been with Brown before the shooting, said Wilson initiated the confrontation by grabbing Brown by the neck through Wilson's patrol car window, threatening him, and then shooting him. After the shots were fired, Brown and Johnson ran away with Wilson in pursuit. At that point, the stories do not align. Johnson said Brown stopped and raised his hands, giving himself up. Wilson said Brown turned as he charged him after a short pursuit. Police reports said Wilson's weapon was fired twelve times, including the two while he was still in the car and Brown was hit six times, twice in the head and four times in the arms. The event ignited protests in the St. Louis area and in Ferguson for a week afterward. Protestors would raise their hands and say, "Hands up, don't shoot." The FBI investigated and a grand jury refused to indict Wilson. A later Department of Justice investigation cleared Wilson of any civil rights violations in the shooting.

"We are seeing too many instances where people just do not have confidence that folks are being treated fairly," said President Barack Obama in an address to the nation. "And it is incumbent upon all of us, as Americans, regardless of race, religion, faith, that we recognize this is an American problem and not just a Black problem or a Native American problem."[454]

November 22, 2014: Timothy Loehmann, a 26-year-old white police officer, shot and killed Tamir E. Rice, a 12-year-old African American boy in Cleveland, Ohio. Rice was carrying a toy gun when two police officers arrived on the scene while responding to a call of a man with a gun. Loehmann shot Rice nearly immediately upon his arrival. The person who placed the call said the "male" was waving the pistol at other people in the park. The caller also said the pistol was probably a fake and that the person was probably a juvenile, but the dispatch operator did not relay this information to the responding police officers.

April 4, 2015: Michael Slager, a police officer in North Charleston, South Carolina, shot Walter Scott, a 50-year-old Black man, who was stopped for a non-functioning taillight. Slager was charged after a video surfaced that showed him shooting Scott from behind while he was fleeing. The video contradicted Slager's version of the events. Due to the difference in races of the individuals, many immediately figured the shooting was racially motivated. A grand jury indicted the officer on a murder charge and eventually Slager was sentenced to 20 years in prison when the judge determined he was guilty of second-degree murder.

April 12, 2015: Freddie Gray, a 25-year-old African American, was arrested by the Baltimore Police Department when authorities found him in possession of a knife. Gray was handcuffed and thrown into the back of a van for a trip to the police station. He suffered severe injuries to his spinal cord during the ride and died a week later. Six officers were charged with crimes. Four of the officers were put on trial but none were convicted. Gray's hospitalization and death led to a series of protests. One major protest in downtown Baltimore led to violence that resulted in arrests and injuries to police officers. Another protest led to looting and burning of local businesses and Maryland Governor Larry Hogan declared a state of emergency.

November 15, 2015: Jamar Clark, a 24-year-old African American, was shot during a scuffle with two Minneapolis police officers, Mark Ringgenberg and Dustin Schwarze. Clark died at Hennepin County Medical Center after being taken off of life support. His death was a result of the gunshot wound suffered during the scuffle. The next year (March 30, 2016), Hennepin County Attorney Mike Freeman announced no charges would be filed against the two officers. In 2019, Clark's family accepted a $200,000 settlement approved by the city council.

January 18, 2016: Police officer Philip Brailsford fatally shot Daniel Shaver of Granbury, Texas, in the hallway of La Quinta Inn & Suites in Mesa, Arizona, where he was staying while in town on business. He invited friends to his room and showed them the air rifle, which he used to exterminate birds inside grocery stores. At one point the gun was pointed outside the fifth-floor window and police were called. Bodycam footage showed Shaver in the hotel hallway on his knees, pleading for his life. The police officers told him not to move. Then the officers would alternately scream conflicting commands at him. At the four-minute mark of the video, Brailsford fired five shots from his AR-15 assault rifle, killing Shaver instantly. The jury believed the police officer who claimed he feared for his life while an unarmed man was pleading for his life while kneeling on the hallway floor of a hotel.

July 5, 2016: Two Baton Rouge police officers, Blane Salamoni and Howie Lake, shot and killed 37-year-old Alton Sterling. The police were responding to a call that Sterling was selling CDs and that he threatened a man with a gun outside a convenience store. Despite the store owner insisting Sterling was not the one causing the trouble, he was wrestled to the ground. Police said Sterling allegedly reached for a gun when they shot him. After an investigation, the Department of Justice decided not to file charges against the police officers, but the East Baton Rouge Metro Council approved a $4.5 million settlement to Sterling's family to settle a wrongful death suit.

July 6, 2016: The following night, a 32-year-old Black man, Philando Castile, was shot by a police officer in the Minneapolis-St. Paul metropolitan area during a traffic stop. Castile was driving with his girlfriend, Diamond Reynolds, and her four-year-old daughter, when he was stopped. During the traffic stop, Castile was shot by the officer. The case received national attention because Reynolds livestreamed the event. With Castile slumped in the driver's seat, Reynolds said they were pulled over for a broken taillight and the "police shot him for no apparent reason, no reason at all."[455]

That summer, Donald Trump campaigned for president. In his speeches, he often stoked fears of immigrants and minorities crossing the border and attacking citizens. While Trump expressed concern over immigrants he called criminals and rapists, other Americans were concerned about the repeated incidents by police against unarmed people. Colin Kaepernick was one of those alarmed that a century and a half after the abolition of slavery in the United States, racial injustice was still present. Kaepernick said he could not stand for a flag that represented the oppression of people of color. Consequently, Kaepernick sat during the anthem and spoke to teammates with his concerns. Safety Eric Reid was the first to join him in kneeling during the anthem.

Reid, who played college ball at Louisiana State, was a first-round selection for the 49ers in 2013, two years after Kaepernick joined the team. Reid and Kaepernick talked about what they could do to protest police brutality. After all, they reasoned, being professional football players offered them a platform to speak for those who could not speak for themselves. Reid said one incident brought him to tears. "The killing of Alton Sterling in my hometown Baton Rouge, Louisiana could have happened to any of my family members who still live in the area. I felt furious, hurt, and hopeless. I wanted to do something but didn't know what or how to do it. All I knew for sure is that I wanted it to be as respectful as possible . . . It baffles me that our protest is still being misconstrued as disrespectful to the country, flag, and military personnel."[456]

Reid continued, "It's disheartening and infuriating that President Trump has referred to us with slurs but the neo-Nazis in Charlottesville, Virginia, as 'very fine people.' His remarks are a clear attempt to deepen the rift that we've tried so hard to mend. I am nevertheless encouraged to see my colleagues and other public figures respond to the president's remarks with solidarity with us. It is paramount that we take control of the story behind our movement, which is that we seek equality for all Americans, no matter their race or gender."[457]

During a presidential town hall on CNN, President Barack Obama said he respected Colin Kaepernick's decision not to stand during the national anthem. Since the football players started the protest, other athletes in numerous sports, professional and amateur, followed suit, prompting a national debate. Jake Tapper, the moderator, asked the president what he thought of the protest. "Well, as I've said before, I believe that us honoring our flag and our anthem is part of what binds us together as a nation," said Obama. "But I also always try to remind folks that part of what makes this country special is that we respect people's rights to have a different opinion . . . The test of our fidelity to our Constitution, to freedom of speech, to our Bill of Rights, is not when it's easy, but when it's hard. We fight sometimes so that people can do things that we disagree with ... As long as they're doing it within the law, then we can voice our opinion objecting to it, but it's also their right." The president went on to ask, "everyone to listen to each other . . . I want [the protesters] to listen to the pain that that may cause somebody who, for example, had a spouse or a child who was killed in combat and why it hurts them to see somebody not standing. But I also want people to think about the pain he may be expressing about somebody who's lost a loved one that they think was unfairly shot."[458]

By the end of September 2017, about one year after the start of the sideline protests, people took their respective sides based on their political orientation. Everybody had an opinion. Many were opposed to the protests, but Republican pollster Frank Luntz recalled a 1961 Gallup poll showed that 61 percent of Americans disapproved of the Freedom Riders taking desegregated buses into the segregated South.[459]

After Trump won the presidency, the discussion took a new level. With NFL players protesting and Trump complaining about it, public opinion remained in its usual groups. A May 2018 Morning Consult poll showed 83 percent of Republicans opposed NFL players kneeling during the anthem while 43 percent of Independents and 25 percent of Democrats opposed the player protests.[460] Pollsters questioned Americans about how President Trump treated African American athletes in general. An August 2018 CBS/YouGov poll reported 65 percent of Republicans approved of the president's attitude toward African American athletes, while only 32 percent of all Americans approved.[461]

Colin Kaepernick took a knee to spotlight the violence against unarmed Black men raging across the nation. All the while he knelt, white police officers continued to kill unarmed Black citizens. Kareem Abdul-Jabbar wrote in an August 2016 guest editorial in *The Washington Post*: "What should horrify Americans is not Kaepernick's choice to remain seated during the national anthem but that nearly 50 years after Ali was banned from boxing for his stance and Tommie Smith and John Carlos's raised fists caused public ostracization and numerous death threats, we still need to call attention to the same racial inequities. Failure to fix this problem is what's really un-American here."[462]

Kaepernick's protest movement drew parallels to the stance taken by Smith and

Carlos with raised fists on the medal stand in the 1968 summer Olympic Games. After that protest, the mainstream media blasted Smith and Carlos. *Newsweek* put Smith on its July 15, 1968 cover with the headline "The Angry Black Athlete." When Ali refused to serve his country, many called him names and questioned his religious objection. "When Jim Brown quit football," wrote Howard Bryant in *The Heritage: Black Athletes, a Divided America, and the Politics of Patriotism*, "*Time* magazine ran a picture of him in fatigues, on the set of *The Dirty Dozen*, the World War II movie Brown was filming. Instead of comparing Brown to an American soldier, the magazine compared him to Che Guevara, the murdered Cuban revolutionary. Brent Musburger, who would go on to have a legendary broadcasting career despite harboring racist attitudes toward the very players he glamorized every weekend, would refer to Smith and Carlos as 'two dark-skinned storm troopers.'" When the 1965 AFL team refused to play in a city that treated them like second class citizens, they were roundly criticized. *USA Today* columnist and author Mike Freeman saw a direct comparison between the events of Smith, Carlos, and Brown in the sixties to Kaepernick. "Look at the reaction now from right-wing media to Kaepernick and the similarities are hard to ignore."[463]

"I think Trump . . . wanted to play a certain kind of race card," said Gerald Early, professor of African American Studies at Washington University in St. Louis, "because he was focusing on sports, where there are a high number of African Americans. And to his base, these African Americans who are very successful in these sports, are very highly paid and so, it's easy for him to use them to many of the disaffected whites who are Trump supporters, to say, 'Look at these ungrateful Black people.' I don't recall any incident where a sitting president went after a particular sports industry in the way that Trump did, I mean, there have been politics in sports, of course. But the idea that an entire industry, an entire sport, would be attacked in this particular way is, to my mind, unprecedented."[464]

Off the field and outside the sporting arenas, a movement was spreading across the country. It began with frustration over the lack of progress with criminal reform. In short, Black men were dying in cities across the country and some offenders were avoiding punishment. One of the first cases to attract national attention came when seventeen-year-old Trayvon Martin lived in Miami, Florida but went to Sanford, Florida, which is near Orlando, to stay with his father for a few days. People living in that gated community were worried about recent robberies.

George Zimmerman lived in that neighborhood and took part in the community watch program, where individual citizens patrolled the streets in an effort at preventing crime. Zimmerman had a license to carry a gun. On February 26, Trayvon walked to a convenience store to buy some candy and a drink. He was walking back to his father's house when Zimmerman drove by. He thought Martin looked suspicious and called the police. The dispatcher told Zimmerman to stay in his car, but he didn't listen. He got out and started following Martin, who started to run. The rest of the story is sketchy, but a struggle occurred and Zimmerman shot Trayvon Martin in the chest. Martin died. Zimmerman claimed self-defense and that he feared for his life. Six weeks later he was arrested and charged with murder. On July 13, 2013, a jury found Zimmerman not guilty. The movement that began with Trayvon Martin grew stronger the following year when a police officer killed Michael Brown and was a phenomenon in 2020 when George Floyd was murdered under the knee of Minneapolis police officer Derek Chauvin.

Three Black women—Alicia Garza, Patrisse Khan-Cullors, and Opal Tometi—created the movement to express Black political will. Garza, who is from Los Angeles and lives in Oakland, coined the phrase "Black Lives Matter" after Trayvon Martin was shot and killed. The movement spread across social media as police initially filed no charges against Zimmerman. An online petition was posted and more than two million people asked prosecutors to take action. Months later, Zimmerman was arrested and charged with second degree murder, but a jury found him not guilty. The protests took to the streets with people shouting, "No justice, no peace" and "I can't breathe."

The goal of Black Lives Matter was to focus attention not only on the killing of African Americans, but on the fact that Black lives mattered as much as any others. "We're not saying Black lives are more important than other lives, or that other lives are not criminalized and oppressed in various ways," said Alicia Garza. "When you drop 'Black' from the equation of whose lives matter and then fail to acknowledge it came from somewhere, you further a legacy of erasing Black lives and Black contributions . . . We are asking you . . . to stand with us in affirming Black lives . . . Please do not change the conversation by talking about how your life matters, too. It does, but we need less watered-down unity and more active solidarities with us, Black people, unwaveringly, in defense of our humanity. Our collective futures depend upon it."[465]

Some in the movement point out that police responses to Black protests are met with extra police, pepper spray, and rubber bullets, while largely white protestors wearing Trump paraphernalia were allowed to ransack the United States Capitol on January 6, 2021. "The events [at the Capitol showed us] that there have always been multiple Americas," said Garza. "There's been an America that we read about in history books—a romantic America that is made of fairy tales. And then there's America that some of us live in—an America where the rules have been rigged against us for a very long time. It's an America where the rules around race and gender and class are fundamental and they shape and impact people's everyday lives. It's also an America where we function under a particular sense of amnesia."[466]

"The 'Black Lives Matter' movement focuses on the fact that Black citizens have long been far more likely than whites to die at the hands of the police, and is of a piece with this history," wrote editors of *The New York Times* in 2015. "Demonstrators who chant the phrase are making the same declaration that voting rights and civil rights activists made a half-century ago. They are not asserting that Black lives are more precious than white lives. They are underlining an indisputable fact—that the lives of Black citizens in this country historically have not mattered and have been discounted and devalued. People who are unacquainted with this history are understandably uncomfortable with the language of the movement. But politicians who know better and seek to strip this issue of its racial content and context are acting in bad faith. They are trying to cover up an unpleasant truth and asking the country to collude with them."[467]

Even though many football franchise owners supported Trump with donations to his campaign, other league executives supported the players' position. "It's unfortunate that the president decided to use his immense platform to make divisive and offensive statements about our players and the NFL.," said Mark Murphy, the president and chief executive of the Green Bay Packers.[468]

On September 22, 2017, President Trump launched his harshest criticism of kneeling players. President Trump said protesting players should be "fired" for "disrespecting the flag." The first game that happened after Trump's strong words came on September 24, 2016 from Wembley Stadium in London, which was broadcast in the early morning hours on the East Coast of the United States. Twenty-seven players from both teams took a knee in protest. That was the largest number of players protesting to date. Players not protesting stood with locked arms in solidarity while standing behind the protesting players. Several days later (September 27, 2016), after receiving criticism from Republican presidential candidate Donald Trump, Kaepernick responded. "He always says make America great again," said Kaepernick. "Well, America had never been great for people of color. That's something that needs to be addressed. Let's make America great for the first time."[469] NFL observers estimated that at least 100 players participated in protests during the pre-game national anthems prior to games played on Sunday, September 24, 2017. The Pittsburgh Steelers opted to stay in the locker room while "The Star-Spangled Banner" played, although Steelers offensive tackle and former Army Ranger Alejandro Villanueva did step on the field to honor the anthem.

After Trump's blistering criticism in the September 2017 speech in Alabama, Patriots owner Robert Kraft responded on the team's Twitter account. "I am deeply disappointed by the tone of the comments made by the president," said Kraft in the statement. "I am proud to be associated with so many players who make such tremendous contributions in positively impacting our communities. Their efforts, both on and off the field, help bring people together and make our community stronger. There is no greater unifier in our country than sports and unfortunately, nothing more divisive than politics. I think our political leaders could learn a lot from the lessons of teamwork and the importance of working together toward a common goal. Our players are intelligent, thoughtful, and care deeply about our community and I support their right to peacefully affect social change and raise awareness in a manner they feel is most impactful."[470]

Stephen Ross, owner of the Miami Dolphins, also criticized the president's rhetoric. "Our country needs unifying leadership right now, not more divisiveness. We need to seek to understand each other and have civil discourse instead of condemnation and sound bites. I know our players who kneeled for the anthem and these are smart young men of character who want to make our world a better place for everyone."[471]

Some critics accused Trump of flaming racial tensions for political purposes, but he denied the accusation. "This has nothing to do with race or anything else. This has to do with respect for our country and respect for our flag."[472]

At the same Alabama rally, Trump said the protests at football games would stop if fans left when players did not stand for the anthem. "The only thing you could do better is if you see it, even if it's one player, leave the stadium," he said.[473]

After Trump said they should leave the game if someone knelt during the anthem, someone did. Trump sent his Vice President Mike Pence to an NFL game in his home state of Indiana to stage such an event. On October 8, 2017, Vice President Mike Pence and his wife, Karen, attended a game between the Indianapolis Colts and the San Francisco 49ers. White House officials selected that game on purpose as the 49ers were the NFL team most associated with the NFL protest movement. After several 49ers took a knee during the anthem, Pence and his wife walked out of the stadium. "I left today's Colts' game because President Trump and I will not dignify any event that disrespects our soldiers, our flag, or our national anthem," said Pence in a Twitter statement. "At a time when so many Americans are inspiring the nation with their courage, resolve, and resilience, now, more than ever, we should rally around our flag and everything that unites us. While everyone is entitled to their own opinions, I don't think it's too much to ask NFL players to respect the flag and our national anthem. I stand with President Trump, I stand with our soldiers, and I will always stand with our flag and our national anthem."[474]

Pence walking out of the 49ers-Colts NFL game had all the markings of a premeditated event. He had a series of tweets ready as well as an official statement issued by his office. He may have wanted it to be a quick gesture of patriotic principle, but it looked like a political stunt. "While politicians from both parties concoct situations for political gain, some criticized Mr. Pence's walkout as transparently premeditated," wrote *The New York Times* in their account of the event. "The vice president did not take a pool reporter traveling with him into the stadium; a member of Mr. Pence's staff told the reporter, Vaughn Hillyard, that the vice president might be leaving the game early."[475]

"Manipulation of faux patriotism took a new turn today with VP Pence. Preplanned early exit from Colts game after 49ers kneeled, then tweets," Norman Ornstein, a resident scholar at the conservative American Enterprise Institute wrote on Twitter. Others immediately pointed out the expense that the stunt cost taxpayers. Pence flew to Indianapolis from Las Vegas and was immediately scheduled to fly back to Los Angeles. The White House press office has a picture of Pence in a suit standing with his hand over his heart during the playing of the "The Star-Spangled Banner" ready to release to the media. Trouble is, Pence tweeted a picture before the game dressed in a Colts cap and casual clothing. Later, they admitted that the photo had been taken in 2014, when Pence was governor of Indiana.

Meanwhile Trump continued to rant over the players' actions. He said the protest was disrespectful to military and law enforcement. Further, he said the protestors were simply not grateful for all of the benefits that living in the United States provided them. With increasing clatter from the White House, owners got nervous. Fearful of losing fans and viewers, they instituted a rule requiring all players to stand for the anthem. The NFL Players Association filed a grievance in response. They said the players' right to free speech was violated. "Everyone loses when voices get stifled," said Malcolm Jenkins, a player with the Philadelphia Eagles. The rule was suspended and discussions continued behind the scenes to find a solution that worked for all.

Over time, Cowboys owner Jerry Jones' attitude, which began sympathetic, turned harsh and adamant. During 2018 training camp, he told the assembled media the Cowboys' "policy is you stand during the anthem, toe on the line." The next day, Stephen Jones, team executive vice president, elaborated. Asked during a radio interview whether he believed players would follow the team rule, Jones said, "If they want to be a Dallas Cowboy, yes." The stance was clear: any Cowboys player who protested during the playing of "The Star-Spangled Banner" would be punished to include potential removal from the roster. "We certainly are supportive of them when they have their personal issues or their personal things that they want to pursue," Stephen Jones also said. "And we'll help them pursue them on Tuesdays. But when you're wearing the Dallas Cowboy uniform and a Dallas Cowboy helmet and you're working for the Dallas Cowboys, you check the 'I' and the 'me' at the door and you're a part of a team. There are bright lines in terms of our organization."[476]

Local newspaper columnists did not agree with Jerry Jones' hardline approach. "Evidently, if Dallas Cowboys owner Jerry Jones has his way, our nation has a new litmus test for patriotism: Salute the flag or suffer," said *The Dallas Morning News'* James Ragland. "Luckily, the league won't shoot its kneeling players in the head—as one of our town's most visible preachers said might happen if the players carried on this way in North Korea. But it seems hell-bent on shaming and sullying them into submission. What we are seeing is plantation politics at its finest: A ruling class of wealthy white owners—with Jones as its front man—unwilling to meet Black players halfway."[477]

Why the change in policy? *The Wall Street Journal* reported that several NFL owners said in depositions that President Trump influenced the league's response to anthem protests. Owners were deposed at the request of 49ers quarterback Colin Kaepernick, who started the protests in 2016 to highlight police brutality and racial injustice and later claimed he was blackballed from the league due to his politics. He filed a grievance in October 2017 stating all 32 teams colluded to keep him out of the league. "Tell everybody, you can't win this one," Jerry Jones said that President Donald Trump told him. "This one lifts me," Jones quoted the president about his rants over player protests. "This is a very winning, strong issue for me."[478]

Ragland stated, "Instead of falling into President Donald Trump's trap—turning a benign and peaceful protest into cannon fodder for America's cultural war—Jones would have been wiser to use his negotiating skills to strike a substantive compromise. Why won't Jones and other team owners direct NFL Commissioner Roger Goodell to huddle up with the NFL Players Association to come up with a campaign aimed at drawing attention, in a constructive way, to the issues that compelled the players to start kneeling in the first place? . . . That's far better than allowing this issue to drive a wedge between the league and its fans, the league and its players and, worse still, induce rancor across the country."[479]

It was ironic that a bond formed between former President Donald Trump and NFL ownership over the Kaepernick matter. There was a time when ownership in the league didn't think highly of the real estate mogul. He had become owner of the New Jersey Generals of the United States Football league (USFL) in 1984 and made no secret of the fact he wanted to parlay that ownership to an NFL team. That never happened. "Mr. Trump, as long as I or my heirs are involved in the NFL, you will never be a franchise owner in the league," said NFL commissioner Pete Rozelle to Trump, according to Jeff Pearlman in *Football for a Buck*. Pearlman, author of numerous New York Times Bestselling sports books, said NFL owners held Trump in an unfavorable light. "Trump wasn't merely disliked by his fellow owners; he was loathed and abhorred and detested," explained Pearlman in 2018 in a blog about his book. "The general take: "Here was a selfish bully who desperately craved an NFL franchise and viewed the USFL as a temporary (and disposable) vehicle toward that end. Trump memorably led the USFL's suicide march away from a spring season and toward the fall and (much like now) his big words and loud voice and thuggish tendencies caused many lemming peers to follow."[480]

"The reason this is all important now is because it highlights one of Trump's defining characteristics: his world-class grudge-holding," wrote Mike Freeman. "That systematic keeping of lists of enemies was a key reason why Trump jumped into the protest fray. Before a campaign event in 2015, he told reporters at a news conference: "When people treat me unfairly, I don't let them forget it . . . It may seem odd, but Trump's grudge-holding and his attacking of Kaepernick intersect perfectly, like two interlocking puzzle pieces," continued Freeman. "Trump mainly saw the NFL player protests as an opportunity to exploit America's racial divisions for political gain. He was almost destined to dislike Kaepernick. There's another reason, however, why Trump attacked the NFL during the protests: it was payback for when the NFL rejected his attempt to purchase a team. As is his character, it was just another example of good old-fashioned score settling. He saw it as an opportunity to injure the league that had so sternly told him to fuck off."[481]

Trump pursued the purchase of NFL franchises several times, according to published reports. Among the teams he inquired about were the Dallas Cowboys, the Baltimore Colts, and the Buffalo Bills. It never happened. Just as former NFL Commissioner Pete Rozelle predicted, Trump did not get close to owning a team. All of the political discussion over the anthem had another impact. With Trump in the White House, some athletes did not welcome the traditional invitation to celebrate a championship in the nation's capital.

On Tuesday, June 5, 2018, the Philadelphia Eagles had planned a White House visit to celebrate their championship at the end of the previous season. At the very last minute, the visit was abruptly canceled by the White House. Fewer than ten players had planned on joining the Eagles contingent led by team chairman and CEO Jeffrey Lurie and head coach Doug Pederson. That news led President Trump to not so quietly rescind the invitation Monday night, the night before the scheduled visit. He took to Twitter to complain. President Trump claimed the Eagles' cancellation was due to the team's lack of patriotism. "[The Philadelphia Eagles] disagree with their president because he insists that they proudly stand for the national anthem, hand on heart, in honor of the great men and women of our military and the people of our country. The Eagles wanted to send a smaller delegation, but the 1,000 fans planning to attend deserve better."[482]

Behind the scenes, Trump was leery of the Eagles coming to the White House, according to newspaper reports attributed to confidential sources. Jeffrey Lurie had been a Trump critic and several players had been outspoken against Trump's anthem stance. In response, Malcolm Jenkins rejected the president's statement on Twitter. He said the players' social justice activism and community involvement was a sign of their patriotism and called any efforts to paint it otherwise as dishonest. "We do it [engage in symbolic protests during the anthem] because we love this country and our community," said Jenkins. "Everyone, regardless of race or socioeconomic status, deserves to be treated equally. We are fighting for racial and social equality." No member of the Eagles football team knelt during the 2017 season, Jenkins said, "Instead, the decision was made to lie and paint the picture that these players are anti-American, anti-flag, and anti-military."[483]

Jim Kenney, then mayor of Philadelphia, suggested Trump's patriotism be questioned, instead of that of the players. "When [Trump] had the opportunity to serve his country for real, his father got him out of it and I think it's really disingenuous for him to talk about patriotism in any way, shape, or form," Kenney told CNN. He was referring to military draft deferments Trump obtained that kept him out of the military during the Vietnam War.[484] "Disinviting them from the White House only proves that our president is not a true patriot, but a fragile egomaniac obsessed with crowd size and afraid of the embarrassment of throwing a party to which no one wants to attend," read Mayor Kenney's statement.[485]

The Eagles never protested by staying in the locker room during the playing of the anthem during the 2017 season. They were also one of the few teams that did not have a player kneel or sit during the anthem. Safety Malcolm Jenkins and others raised their fists and teammate Chris Long often put his arm on Jenkins' shoulder to show support, but they were not a team filled with the most outspoken, socially active players. Several Eagles took hard stances. "This is a fear of the diminished bottom line," said defensive end Chris Long. "It's also fear of a president turning his base against a corporation. This is not patriotism. Don't get confused. These owners don't love America more than the players demonstrating and taking real action to improve it." The Eagles safety pledged to keep up the cause. "I will not let it silence me or stop me from fighting," said Jenkins. "This has never been about taking a knee, raising a fist or anyone's patriotism, but doing what we can to effect real change for real people."[486] Newspapers across the country noticed. The *Pittsburgh Post-Gazette* called Trump's decision to disinvite the Eagles "petty and uncalled for" in an editorial. "Mr. Trump's decision to cancel the Eagles' White House invitation can only be seen as an act of political propaganda meant to play to his base," they wrote. "It disrespected the rights and opinion of those not of the base. For this event is not about the anthem or kneeling during the anthem. It is about sports and pride and national unity. It is about a simple, sane idea: Not everything has to be about politics, or the president . . . When a championship sports team visits the White House, it is supposed to be a moment that transcends, or at least escapes, politics," they continued. "It should either be that—and we desperately need such moments—or not happen at all. But Mr. Trump made it political and personal and diminished a nice custom. And if his cause is really the anthem and honoring the military, he cheapened that, too."[487]

Some critics say the league's hesitation cost them dearly. If they had acted quickly and decisively, they would not have been in such a difficult situation. "The league allowed players and politicians alike to hijack the brand and turn it into a platform," said public relations executive David Fouse. "And while players are private citizens and certainly entitled to political expression, they are not entitled to take the brand of a private company and expose it to the criticism of public leaders."[488]

The effects of the protest spread to the advertising and business world. Papa John's, the pizza takeout and delivery franchise, enjoyed a long history with the NFL. In 2010, the company announced its role as the official pizza sponsor of the NFL. Its marketing campaign featured Peyton Manning, a former NFL quarterback, and played prominently during games. For several years, he appeared alongside John Schnatter, Papa John's company CEO and founder. In 2017, with the continued anthem protest, the relationship grew strained. "The NFL has hurt us by not resolving the current debacle to the players' and owners' satisfaction," Schnatter said on a conference call. "NFL leadership has hurt Papa John's shareholders." Papa John's sales declined, stores missed earnings estimates, and the stock price declined. Schnatter blamed "poor leadership" at the top of the league for not acting sooner to end the protest. "This should have been nipped in the bud a year and a half ago," Schnatter said on the call. "Like many sponsors, we're in touch with the NFL. Once the issue is resolved, we're optimistic the NFL's best years are ahead."[489] Papa John's announced that Schnatter would step down as CEO in December 2017. A couple of months later, the company bowed out of its NFL sponsorship deal. In its place, Pizza Hut became the official pizza sponsor for the NFL.

Before the 2018 NFL season kicked off, Nike launched a new advertising campaign featuring Colin Kaepernick as spokesperson. The message of the ad was clear: "Believe in something. Even if it means sacrificing everything. Just do it." A close-up of Kaepernick's face accompanied those words. In response, social media posts called for a boycott of Nike products and others posted videos of Nike shoes and apparel being burned. Analysts praised the ad campaign saying Nike's demographics were young, trendy, and urban, which were just the audience that might be generally supportive of the protest. "It's an interesting decision for Nike," wrote Frank Schwab, a sports writer for Yahoo Sports for more than a decade. "No other athlete produces the same emotional response than Kaepernick. Some will rip Nike and claim they will never buy their products again. Others who support Kaepernick will gladly shift their dollars to Nike for its support of the former San Francisco 49ers quarterback, who is viewed as a hero to many for standing up for social issues even if it meant the NFL ultimately would freeze him out. If Nike wanted the maximum attention possible for its new advertising campaign, mission accomplished."[490]

When Nike released its advertising campaign featuring Colin Kaepernick's face with the quote, "Believe in something; even if it means sacrificing everything," Americans had an immediate reaction. Some liked the spokesperson selection and applauded Nike for their courageous stance. Others disagreed with the whole ad. Their opinion of the ad came from what they thought of Kaepernick as a man and his chosen method of protesting during the national anthem. Conservatives, who had adopted former NFL player Pat Tillman as a true patriotic hero for quitting the NFL in favor of serving his country, said he would have been a better "spokesman" for the campaign. After all, he sacrificed all for his country when he passed on a multimillion-dollar contract to enlist as an Army Ranger. He was tragically killed by friendly fire in combat. The Tillman family, who criticized Donald Trump when he first referenced their son's name in connection to Kaepernick, objected to his name being drawn into a political argument. Marie Tillman, the widow of the former NFL player, released a statement at the time saying her husband's service "should never be politicized in a way that divides us." She explained, "As a football player and soldier, Pat inspired countless Americans to unify. It is my hope that his memory should always remind people that we must come together. Pat's service, along with that of every man and woman's service, should never be politicized in a way that divides us. We are too great of a country for that. Those that serve fight for the American ideals of freedom, justice and democracy. They and their families know the cost of that fight. I know the very personal costs in a way I feel acutely every day."[491]

Conservatives pushed for Tillman because they favored a soldier in a military haircut and dressed in combat gear. Tillman's friends remember him as a sandals-wearing, long-haired kid from the San Francisco Bay Area, whose beliefs never lined up as a conservative on the political spectrum. He was an idealistic, voracious reader who often struggled with the meaning of military service and considered moral conviction a high virtue, said Jon Krakauer, the author of *Where Men Win Glory*, a biography of Tillman. "Pat would have found Kaepernick an extremely admirable person for what he believed in," Krakauer told *The Washington Post*. "I have no doubt if he were in the NFL today, he would be the first to kneel. So, there is irony about what is going on."[492]

"The hypocrisy of the NFL's actions in banning protests during the national anthem while simultaneously promoting the Walter Payton Man of the Year award is clear," wrote Andy Hyde, a researcher and facilitator who studies business processes and organizations. "This award recognizes players committed to serving their communities and helping those in need. However, when Colin Kaepernick protested against police brutality and racial injustice by kneeling during the national anthem, he was kicked out of the NFL and faced immense backlash. The message is clear. It is acceptable to use sports to promote social causes as long as those causes do not challenge the status quo or the power dynamics that govern sports and society.[493]

A modern day player unafraid to take controversial stands, Los Angeles Laker LeBron James will not duck from political and social issues. James volunteered for "More Than a Vote," an organization hoping to mobilize voting registration efforts in African American communities and fight voter suppression. The group formed in response to the death of George Floyd. James sees himself in the mold of Muhammad Ali, Bill Russell, and Kareem Abdul-Jabbar, who were athletes willing to take controversial political stands on the social issues of the day.

During a 2018 interview with CNN's Don Lemon, James accused President Trump of attempting to divide the country with sports, suggesting that "sports has never been something that divides people. It's always been something that brings someone together. We're in a position right now in America where this whole race thing is taking over," James said. "One, because I believe our president is trying to divide us. He's dividing us and what I've noticed over the last few months is that he's kind of used sport to kind of divide us. That's something that I can't relate to, because I know that sport was the first time I ever was around someone white. I got an opportunity to see them and learn about them and they got an opportunity to learn about me and we became very good friends. I was like this is all because of sports. And sports has never been something that divided people. It's always been something that brings someone together… At times… more often than not, I believe he uses anything that's popular to try and negate people from the positive things they could be doing. At the end of the day sport is why we all come together."[494]

CHAPTER FIFTEEN

"Shut Up and Dribble"

Some might wonder why one of the greatest basketball players in the world would use his standing in sports to cross over to politics. The way LeBron James sees it, he is a human being first and a basketball player second. So, if he sees evil spread against any of God's people, he feels it is his responsibility as a member of the global society to say something. His vocal opinions about police brutality caught the attention of Fox News personality Laura Ingraham, who told him to "shut up and dribble."

In a video released in February 2018, LeBron James, then of the Cleveland Cavaliers, was interviewed while seated next to Kevin Durant, then of the Golden State Warriors. LeBron was asked about his views on the political climate in the United States and the opposition received by sports stars, like him, when they speak out. "Well, the climate is hot," James said. "The number one job in America, the appointed person, [President Donald Trump] is someone who doesn't understand the people. And he really don't give a f--- about the people."[495] ESPN's Cari Champion conducted the interview, which was taped as part of the *Uninterrupted* program, which is available on YouTube. "What's going on in our country, it's all about leadership," Durant said in the video. "I learned that playing basketball. I learned a lot of life skills from playing basketball. You need to empower people, you need to encourage people. That's what builds a great team. And I feel like our team, as a country, is not run by a great coach."[496]

Laura Ingraham described James' comments about President Trump as "barely intelligible" in a segment on her Fox News program, *The Ingraham Angle*. Then she showed a clip of James and Durant being interviewed on ESPN to her audience. "Must they run their mouths like that?" she mused. "You're great players, but no one voted for you," she said to James and Durant. "Millions elected Trump to be their coach. So, keep the political commentary to yourself, or as someone once said, shut up and dribble."[497] Of course she was referring to herself. Published in 2003, her book *Shut Up & Sing: How Elites From Hollywood, Politics, and the UN are Subverting America* warns liberal entertainers to stay in their lane. In this case, she was telling sports stars to stick to sports.

"Our president made it cool for people to kind of speak their truth and kind of show what they're really about," Durant told *USA Today*. "It's cool to uncover that now. So, we know it's coming. We know if we use our voice and it's not what some people may agree with, of course they're going to say ignorant things like that. But we are the American dream. We come from nothing. We rose up in our profession to be able to take care of our families forever. I think everybody in the country would want to do that, so I think more people want to be us than—I don't even know her name, whoever that lady is."[498]

"We're back to everything I've been talking about over the past few years," James said at a news conference before his next game when asked to respond to Ingraham's comments. "It lets me know that everything I've been saying is correct, for her to have that type of reaction." Then, he quickly added, "But we will definitely not shut up and dribble."[499] When reporters caught up with Kevin Durant, he did not hesitate to comment. "Ignorance is something I try to ignore. That was definitely an ignorant comment," he told *USA Today*. "To me, it was racist."[500]

Before Michael Jordan and LeBron James dominated the "best ever player" debate, there was Bill Russell. He was the centerpiece of the Celtics dynasty that won an unthinkable 11 championships during his 13-year career. He collected five NBA MVP awards. He was a winner everywhere. He won back-to-back championships at the University of San Francisco in 1955 and 1956 and he captained the USA team at the 1956 Summer Olympics, which took home the gold medal. Off the court, Russell participated in the civil rights movement during the sixties. He took part in the 1963 March on Washington for Jobs and Freedom and was in the front row of the crowd to hear Dr. Martin Luther King Jr.'s "I Have a Dream" speech. After Medgar Evers was murdered, he traveled to Mississippi to open an integrated basketball camp in Jackson, and he was present at the Cleveland Summit when many prominent Black athletes met with Muhammad Ali on his anti-Vietnam War stance. In 2011, President Barack Obama awarded Russell the Presidential Medal of Freedom at the White House as "someone who stood up for the rights and dignity of all men."[501] When Trump started calling for the firing of players who knelt during the anthem, Russell posted a photo on Twitter in which he posed taking a knee which he said meant he supported the players, like James and Durant. He took to Twitter to say he would "never shut up and dribble."[502]

On *Fox & Friends* television program, President Trump said he turned off NBA games "when I see people kneeling" and "disrespecting our flag and disrespecting our national anthem." Asked about Trump's comments after the Lakers' 105-86 loss to the Oklahoma City Thunder later in the day, James fired back. "The game will go on without his eyes on it," James said at his postgame news conference from the so-called NBA bubble at Orlando during the COVID pandemic. "I can sit here and speak for all of us that love the game of basketball: We could care less."[503]

As a league, the NBA always took a more accommodating stance toward political commentary by players and coaches than the NFL. The NBA has a long-standing rule regarding the national anthem. On page 61 of the league's rule book, under Section H: Player/Team Conduct and Dress, rule 2, reads: "Players, coaches, and trainers are to stand and line up in a dignified posture along the sidelines or on the foul line during the playing of the national anthem." Despite the written procedures, NBA Commissioner David Stern said he would not enforce the rule, which dated back to 1981 mandating all players, coaches, and staff stand in a dignified manner for the playing of the anthem. "I respect our teams' unified act of peaceful protest for social justice and under these unique circumstances will not enforce our longstanding rule," Stern said. That news prompted President Trump to appear on Fox and criticize the kneeling protest. "When I see them kneeling, I just turn off the game," Trump said. "I have no interest in the game."[504]

In a September 2017 speech, President Trump urged NFL owners to fire any players who do not stand for the national anthem before a game. He then suggested viewership was down for that very reason. President Trump went further in a campaign speech in Huntsville, Alabama. "Wouldn't you love to see one of these NFL owners, when somebody disrespects our flag, to say, 'Get that son of a bitch off the field right now, out, he's fired,'" the president said at a rally for Senator Luther Strange, who was appointed to the Senate that year and faced Roy Moore in a Republican primary runoff. The president's framing of the issue was important based on what side of the street you stood. "That there are legitimate grounds for protest is incontrovertible," said conservative journalist Paul Jenkins. "This nation had not always done right by its minorities. Even given that, why is it acceptable for multimillionaire players and coaches and team owners to denigrate the very people who served and sacrificed to protest their right to protest injustice?"[505]

Trump knew his political base well. They favored the military and patriotism and would respond when the protest was framed that way. Right from the start, he framed the issue as one of a protest against the flag, the anthem, and all that it represented, particularly the military. They also thought the mass media ignored their viewpoints and were drawn to Trump's willingness to take on big causes, playing himself off as David versus Goliath. It seemed like a questionable stance for someone who avoided military service in Vietnam during his draft-eligible years and his praise of brutal dictators like Vladimir Putin, Kim Jong Un, and Adolf Hitler. Nonetheless, Trump harped on the issue and ignored the fact that it was a protest designed to call attention to racial inequality and police violence against minorities. Instead, Trump framed it as all about patriotism. "The president's deft manipulation of that misperception [that the protesters are anti-flag] is especially frustrating for Americans whose patriotism is properly grounded in the core values of the founding," wrote journalist Conor Friedersdorf. "Many regard the flag as a symbol of those values and therefore believe that the protesting NFL players have a far greater claim to the flag than does the president—that while he abuses his position by pressuring a private enterprise to punish its employees for their political speech, the NFL players, kneeling together in public protest of what they believe to be unjust killings, are acting in ways that have parallels to the founders. That is, they are pledging their honor and risking their fortunes in political protest in what they see as a government that is failing to secure the rights of Americans and failing in particular to protect their lives and liberty."[506]

"Look, I get the player protests are a highly emotional issue," wrote sports columnist Nancy Armour. "I also understand that some people will never be able to look beyond the method to hear the message. But protests aren't meant to make people comfortable—just the opposite, actually. To bring about change, people have to realize it's necessary. Democracy is hard and it's often messy, but it's worth it. That's what's gotten lost here. Respecting the symbols of our freedom is pointless if we're not willing to respect and defend the ideals they represent."⁵⁰⁷

Then San Antonio Spurs head coach Gregg Popovich criticized Commissioner Goodell's handling of the anthem protests. Popovich said Goodell was intimidated by Trump. "A smart man is running the NFL and he didn't understand the difference between the flag and what makes the country great—all the people who fought to allow Kaepernick to have the right to kneel for justice," the longtime basketball coach told *The New York Times*. "The flag is irrelevant. It's just a symbol that people glom onto for political reasons." Popovich said he has no patience with the seven NFL owners who donated $1 million to Donald Trump's campaign in 2016. Jerry Jones of the Dallas Cowboys and Robert Kraft of the New England Patriots were among the seven. "It's just hypocritical," he told the *Times*. "It's incongruent. It doesn't make sense. People aren't blind. Do you go to your staff and your players and talk about injustices and democracy and how to protest? I don't get it. I think they put themselves in a position that's untenable."⁵⁰⁸

Popovich continued, "I've been amazed and disappointed by so much of what this president had said and his approach to running this country, which seems to be one of just a never-ending divisiveness. But his comments today about those who have lost loved ones in times of war and his lies that previous presidents Obama and Bush never contacted their families are so beyond the pale, I almost don't have the words . . . This man in the Oval Office is a soulless coward who thinks that he can only become large by belittling others. This has of course been a common practice of his, but to do it in this manner—and to lie about how previous presidents responded to the deaths of soldiers—is as low as it gets. We have a pathological liar in the White House, unfit intellectually, emotionally, and psychologically to hold this office and the whole world knows it, especially those around him every day. The people who work with this president should be ashamed because they know better than anyone just how unfit he is and yet they choose to do nothing about it. This is their shame most of all."⁵⁰⁹

Steve Kerr, head coach of the NBA Golden State Warriors, also expressed criticism with the president. Kerr was born in Beirut, Lebanon to a Malcolm H. Kerr, a Lebanese-born American academic who specialized in the Middle East. Young Kerr spent most of his childhood in Lebanon and other Middle Eastern countries. He was in Beirut during the summer of 1983 when he met several U.S. Marines who were later killed in the Beirut barracks bombings. Steve Kerr's father was killed in

1984 by members of the Islamic Jihad when he was 52 years old and serving as president of the American University of Beirut. Steve was only 18 years old at the time and a college freshman. "Before my father was killed, my life was impenetrable," he said. "Bad things happened to other people."[510] But that changed on the day his father died. Kerr said he saw a difference between the brand image of the NFL and the NBA. "I think it's just typical of the NFL," he said. "They're just trying to play to their fan base and basically trying to use the anthem as fake patriotism, nationalism, scaring people. It's idiotic, but that's how the NFL has handled their business. I'm proud to be in a league that understands that patriotism in America is about free speech and about peaceful protesting."[511]

In September 2017 (the same week as Trump's fiery speech in Huntsville, Alabama), Stephen Curry, star player on Kerr's Warriors, said he didn't want to visit the White House. "I don't want to go," Curry said when asked about visiting the White House during Warriors media day on Friday. "That's kind of the nucleus of my belief. It's not *just* me going to the White House. If it was, this would be a short conversation."[512] The next day, the president tweeted that his invitation had been withdrawn.

After Steph Curry said the team did not want to visit the White House, Kerr weighed in. "I've been fortunate enough to meet President Reagan, both Bushes, Clinton, and Obama," said Kerr. "I didn't agree with all of them, but it was easy to set politics aside because each possessed an inherent respect for the office, as well as the humility that comes from being a public servant in an incredible position of power, representing 300 million people. And that's the problem now. In his tweet to Steph, Trump talked about honoring the White House but, really, isn't it you who must honor the White House, Mr. President . . . Would we have gone? Probably not. The truth is we all struggled with the idea of spending time with a man who had offended us with his words and actions time and again. But I can tell you one thing: it wouldn't have been for the traditional ceremony, to shake hands and smile for cameras. Internally, we'd discussed whether it would be possible to just go and meet as private citizens and have a serious, poignant discussion about some of the issues we're concerned about. But he's made it hard for any of us to actually enter the White House because what's going on is not normal. It's childish stuff: belittling people and calling them names.[513]

"Instead, we get Trump's comments over the weekend about NFL players, calling them 'sons of bitches' for kneeling during the anthem," said Kerr. "Those just crushed me. Crushed me. Just think about what those players are protesting. They're protesting excessive police violence and racial inequality. Those are really good things to fight against."[514] Kerr said leaders should react diplomatically and maintain a level of "respect and dignity" and not lash out when criticized. "No matter how many times a football player says, 'I honor our military, but I'm protesting police brutality and racial inequality,' it doesn't matter," Kerr said in a September 2017 interview with ESPN. "Nationalists are saying, 'You're disrespecting our flag.' Well, you know what else is disrespectful to our flag? Racism. And one's way worse than the other... The idea of civil discourse with a guy who is tweeting and demeaning people and saying the things he's saying is sort of far-fetched. Can you picture us really having a civil discourse with him?"[515]

In the Women's National Basketball Association (WNBA) championship series, the Los Angeles Sparks walked out as a team during the anthem. Their opponents, the Minnesota Lynx, remained on the court with their arms linked. The Sparks said they were influenced by the Pittsburgh Steelers, who chose to remain in the locker room during the anthem. Army veteran and offensive lineman Alejandro Villanueva was the only Steeler outside the locker room. Before the game, Steelers head coach Mike Tomlin told the media that his team would not be on the sideline during the anthem as a result of a team meeting held to discuss a response to Trump's comments on NFL players. He said the team decided not to come out of the locker room for the anthem. He said the decision was not unanimous, but the goal was to have his team focus on the game and not outside discussion. "We're not going to play politics," Tomlin said. "We're football players, we're football coaches. We're not participating in the anthem today—not to be disrespectful to the anthem, but to remove ourselves from the circumstance... People shouldn't have to choose. If a guy wants to go about his normal business and participate in the anthem, he shouldn't be forced to choose sides. If a guy feels the need to do something, he shouldn't be separated from his teammate who chooses not to. But when we come out of locker rooms, we come out of locker rooms to play football games."[516]

Megan Rapinoe, co-captain of the U.S. Women's soccer team, took a knee in solidarity with Kaepernick. "I haven't experienced over-policing, racial profiling, police brutality or the sight of a family member's body lying dead in the street.

But I cannot stand idly by while there are people in this country who have had to deal with that kind of heartache," Rapinoe wrote in *The Player's Tribune* in 2016. "There is no perfect way to protest. I know that nothing I do will take away the pain of those families. But I feel in my heart it is right to continue to kneel during the national anthem and I will do whatever I can to be part of the solution . . . When I take a knee, I am facing the flag with my full body, staring straight into the heart of our country's ultimate symbol of freedom—because I believe it is my responsibility, just as it is yours, to ensure that freedom is afforded to *everyone* in this country," she added.⁵¹⁷

At the 2016 ESPYs award show, LeBron James, Chris Paul, Carmelo Anthony, and Dwayne Wade took the stage in Los Angeles to speak from the heart. Days before the show, James contacted ESPN President John Skipper to request that the four sports stars have some time on stage to speak about the violence that was raging across the country, especially in Black communities, in response to the police violence. In recent days, Philando Castile was shot and killed by a police officer for a broken taillight. Another Black man, Alton Sterling, was killed after police confronted him for selling compact discs on a sidewalk. Micah Xavier Johnson, an Army veteran, ambushed and killed five police officers in Dallas in alleged retaliation. "The four of us are talking to our fellow athletes with the country watching, because we cannot ignore the realities of the current state of America," began Anthony. "The system is broken. The problems are not new, the violence is not new, and the racial divide is definitely not new, but the urgency for change is at an all-time high," Chris Paul continued. "Decades ago, legends like Jesse Owens, Jackie Robinson, Muhammad Ali, John Carlos and Tommie Smith, Kareem Abdul-Jabbar, Jim Brown, Billie Jean King, Arthur Ashe, and countless others, they set a model for what athletes should stand for. So, we chose to follow in their footsteps." LeBron James picked up the story, stating, "It's not about being a role model, it's not about our responsibility to the tradition of activism. I know tonight, we're honoring Muhammad Ali, the GOAT [Greatest of All Time], but to do his legacy any justice, let's use this moment as a call to action for all professional athletes."⁵¹⁸

The protest continued with players from various sports weighing in on both sides. New Orleans Saints quarterback Drew Brees said in a Yahoo Finance interview that he would never agree with players who knelt during the national anthem to protest police brutality. A group of players, including some teammates, reacted immediately. "Drew Brees, you don't understand how hurtful, how insensitive your comments are," Malcolm Jenkins, Brees' teammate, said in a video posted on Twitter. "I'm disappointed. I'm hurt, because while the world tells you, 'You are not worthy,' that your life doesn't matter, the last place you want to hear it from are the guys you go to war with and that you consider to be your allies and your friends. Even though we are teammates, I can't let this slide."[519] Brees heard the backlash and to his credit reversed his statement. He labeled his comments "insensitive and completely missed the mark." Taking full responsibility for his words, Brees asked for forgiveness. "I recognize that I should do less talking and more listening ... and when the Black community is talking about their pain, we all need to listen," he wrote.[520] A few teammates credited Brees for his apology. Demario Davis, a Saints linebacker said Brees' apology "is a form of true leadership and I would say it because that's taking ownership. It's not easy to come out and admit when you're wrong."[521] After Drew Brees' comments and Malcolm Jenkins' reply, Ingraham supported Brees' right to express his opinion, but not Jenkins'. Despite her stance that athletes should stick to sports, Ingraham made an exception for a white NFL quarterback who agreed with her. It was okay for Drew Brees to comment on players kneeling during the anthem.

LeBron James came back on his "Uninterrupted" Twitter account with a powerful video. In the background we could hear a basketball loudly striking the court. The screen was white with words appearing every few seconds:

"Shut up and dribble.

Shut up and tackle.

Shut up and stand.

Shut up and get paid.

Shut up and just do your job.

Shut up and take off that hoodie.

Shut up and stop running.

Shut up and put your fist down.

Shut up and do you live around here?

Shut up and you fit the description.

Shut up and put your hands up.

Shut up and get out of the car.

Shut up and don't move.

Shut up and get on the ground.

Shut up and lay still."[522]

With the last words still showing on the screen, the ball sounds like it is bouncing away as if the player cannot dribble any longer. The clip is powerful—one that everyone should see—because it outlined the evolution of the phrase "shut up and dribble." It even sounds like there could have been a police interaction that did not go well happening out of view of the camera, stopping the dribble.

Laura Ingraham grew up in Glastonbury, Connecticut, attended Dartmouth, and became the first female editor of the conservative student newspaper, *The Dartmouth Review*. She earned a law degree from the University of Virginia, worked as a speechwriter in the Reagan White House, and clerked for Supreme Court Justice Clarence Thomas. She made most of these comments on her prime-time Fox News program. Over time, she developed a philosophy, which eventually became her book. "The problem is, most musicians don't stop to realize how silly they can sound when they get beyond what they do best—entertain," wrote Laura Ingraham in her 2003 book, *Shut Up & Sing*. "Imagine a political talk show hostess with no musical background going on Larry King to lecture The Boss on musical arrangements. 'Dude, you needed some bass in 'The Rising'!' But our celebrities won't be deterred."[523] She summarized her view in one line: "Because they have hit the big time in music, on screen, on stage, or on the page, they think this entitles their political views to special attention and respect."[524] Ingraham must not view herself as an entertainer, which makes her exempt from her own rule. She isn't afraid to give her opinion every evening on a cable television program. She will take on any topic, especially one likely to generate controversy.

Ingraham got into trouble in 2018 when she tweeted about a 17-year-old high school student, David Hogg, whom she said whined about being rejected by some colleges. In her tweet, Ingraham tweeted, "David Hogg rejected by four colleges to which he applied and whines about it." Hogg said it's "time to love thy neighbor, not mudsling at children." The mocking tweet prompted some advertisers to reconsider the ad dollars spent on her program. Her radio bosses talked her into taking a one-week vacation as a cooling-off period.[525] Hogg was a survivor of the Marjory Stoneman Douglas High School shooting near Parkland, Florida, where he was a senior and only 17 years old. After 17 people were murdered and another 18 injured in one of the worst school shootings in history, Hogg became a leader of the student protests seeking gun control.

The First Amendment says, "Congress shall make no law respecting an establishment of religion, or prohibiting the free exercise thereof; or abridging the freedom of speech, or of the press." Basically, the framers of the Constitution said government is not allowed to prohibit any citizens from the right to state their opinion. Whether it be LeBron James or David Hogg, Laura Ingraham was saying, "mind your place." In other words, because of their status in life, NBA star or high school senior, they should stick to their day jobs and keep the comments to themselves. As she sees it, Ingraham is allowed to go on television every night and rant about her political views without restriction. As a law school graduate, Ingraham should be at least casually familiar with the U.S. Constitution. Instead, she uses it at her convenience. She acts like the Constitution prohibits citizens from criticizing the president when it protects citizens' rights to do just that. Some might say that expressing dissent with the actions of the government is the most American thing to do. There aren't any restrictions due to the occupation of the speaker.

"For decades we've been told that sports and politics don't mix," wrote columnist Ferd Lewis. "That rarely should the twain ever meet, especially when thoughts on the subject come from the mouths of prominent pro athletes. We have been reminded of that lame threadbare line of reasoning in exchanges between Fox TV host Laura Ingraham and LeBron James in the wake of the political discourse surrounding the senseless death of George Floyd . . . The problem with that is athletes don't live in a bubble of the arena or stadium much as we have long sought to pigeon-hole them there," continued Lewis. "They have lives beyond the courts and fields. They are shaped by backgrounds and experiences where the real world tends to intrude. Just as it does for the plumber, mail carrier, or baker. And athletes should no more be required to check their social consciences at the locker room door than others do upon leaving their places of employment . . . To not avail themselves of the platform, as Ingraham would decree it, would mean voices wasted, perspectives unshared, and lessons in empathy potentially unshared."[526]

Some other sports columnists agreed with Ingraham. "The message of her book was as simplistic as its title, which was to implore actors, musicians, and other entertainment personalities to stop trying to force their own political agendas upon captive audiences who tune in for entirely different reasons," wrote *San Francisco Examiner* columnist Bob Frantz. "In other words, we pay to hear you perform, not to hear you preach, so shut up and sing. Frantz brought up the example of former NFL great Jim Brown questioning the lack of social activism of two modern sports heroes, Tiger Woods and Michael Jordan. Brown labeled Woods and Jordan as "two individuals in this country that are Black, that have been put forth of us as an example. But they're basically under a system that says, 'Hey, they're not going to do a certain thing.' Yes, that disappoints me because I know they both know better."[527] Jim Brown made the comments to Bryant Gumbel on the HBO show *Real Sports*.

"This may surprise some of you—especially if you've spent much time in traffic or walking around a Walmart, but human beings are dynamic creatures," wrote sports columnist David Weitzel in the midst of the Ingraham-James feud. "We aren't one dimensional and we are capable of having a dog in multiple fights . . . The problem to me was all about her missing the point on one of the most important characteristics that makes our Republic like no other: we have the right to disagree."[528]

Ingraham's book isn't the only place we see that title and that warning. *Shut Up and Sing* is also a documentary that tells the story of the fallout after Dixie Chicks lead singer Natalie Maines told a London concert audience in 2003 that she and bandmates Martie Maguire and Emily Strayer were ashamed that President Bush is from Texas while the commander in chief was about to send the United States to war in Iraq. Conservative commentators condemned them, their songs were banned by country stations, and fans stopped buying their records. Some people gathered in public for Chicks' merchandize destruction parties. The fall from grace was dramatic and served as a warning to any other country entertainer who threatened to publicly voice any political thoughts, especially any that sounded the least bit liberal. The group, which now goes by the more politically sensitive name, The Chicks, had been immensely popular with their first major record released in 1998 that sold 13 million copies in the United States. When they released their album *Gaslighter* in 2020, it was their first new music in 14 years. The album title comes from the psychological abuser who manipulates the truth to make another person feel crazy. Although their slide occurred before Twitter or Facebook were as prominent as today, The Chicks offer a unique viewpoint on the rise of cancel culture, when prominent people are attacked online in an almost mob mentality. "On one hand, you know it's freeing now," recalled Natalie Maines. "People just are way more vocal. But then the downside is one slip up and no publicist can make that go away . . . With a new name and new album, The Chicks' voices ring loud again." Maines still hears the "shut up and sing" line about her and her bandmates but thinks the attitude of younger population is more welcoming. "There's not a whole lot of respect anymore if you're just going to smile and entertain," she said. "They want you to have a point of view."[529]

Their new music reflects that attitude. All three band members are parents of teenagers who respect the fact that young activists are taking the lead on issues such as gun control, climate change, and racial inequality. In addition to Parkland shooting survivor David Hogg's pleas for gun control, another young person took on the environment. At 15, Greta Thunberg started spending her Fridays outside the Swedish Parliament holding a sign calling for stronger action on climate change. Those actions came after she had convinced her parents to adopt lifestyle changes that would reduce their own carbon footprint. She said she first heard about climate change when she was eight years old and could not understand why so little was being done about it. Since that time, she has been actively speaking out about climate change. She was nominated for a Nobel prize three times without winning. They do not award a prize for environmental causes. In 2019, she was awarded the Right Livelihood Award, known as the "Alternative Nobel Prize" for imploring leaders around the world to take climate change seriously.

Darrell West, author of *Celebrity Politics* and professor at Brown University, thinks the mixing of politics and entertainment figures is "part of our endless fascination with the rich and famous." Further, he offers another concept: "People are so upset with career politicians that celebrities come along and they become the white knight."[530] The United States has a long history of mixed entertainment figures with politics. Ronald Reagan was President of the United States after serving as Governor of California and president of the Screen Actors Guild. Sonny Bono, half of the Sonny and Cher duo, served as mayor of Palm Springs, California and member of the United States Congress. Arnold Schwarzenegger was the governor of California. Former professional wrestler Jesse Ventura was governor of Minnesota. Football players Jack Kemp, Heath Shuler, and Steve Largent joined the United States House of Representatives after their playing days ended. Hall of Fame defensive tackle Alan Page became an associate justice on the Minnesota Supreme Court, and Byron "Whizzer" White a United States Supreme Court justice. Conservatives might recall actor Charlton Heston, who appeared in nearly 100 films including *The Ten Commandments* and *Ben-Hur*, was a five-term president of the National Rifle Association. "The law-abiding, Caucasian, middle-class Protestant or even worse, rural and apparently straight, or even worse, an admitted heterosexual, or even worse, a male working stiff ... not only don't you count, but you are also a downright obstacle to social progress," said Heston in the speech. "Your voice deserves a lower decibel level, your opinion is less enlightened, your media access is insignificant and frankly, you need to wake up, wise up, and learn a little something from your new America. And until you do, would you mind shutting up?"[531] Laura Ingraham would agree.

CHAPTER SIXTEEN

Closing

As far as incidents in the civil rights narratives go, the ones where children are involved can generate the strongest emotions. Emmett Till's beating and open casket funeral presented such an emotional incident. The 16th Street Baptist Church bombing in 1963 was another. The church bombing occurred in the sanctuary of a religious space immediately prior to the start of the Sunday service and killed four innocent children. The teens were not protesting for a cause, as they were present for the Sunday service. It has been suggested that the bombing came as a reaction to public school integration that had started a week before. It also came about a month after the March on Washington in which Rev. Dr. Martin Luther King Jr. delivered his "I Have a Dream" speech. Regardless of the reason, it was clearly a terror attack designed to strike fear in the Black community. Those types of incidents can create a strong emotion and desire to do something to help the civil rights cause, even if children are not involved.

Abner Haynes recalled that during the players-only meeting in New Orleans, many white players, "not just one or two," supported the decision to move the game. "It was almost magical," said Haynes. "And I'm sure the other Black players who were in the room were as impressed as I was." Some wonder if the stand cost him his career. Then general manager Jack Steadman traded Haynes to the Broncos. "I sure don't appreciate your actions," recalled Haynes, saying Steadman told him.[532] Despite the trade, Haynes looked back favorably on the decision to boycott the game. "You can't fear all that. It was stand time," said Haynes with a view toward the boycott. He looks at it as "true brothers" who joined the cause.

"It ain't about getting mad. It's, 'Who do you want to be? Who are we?'" In the end, Haynes summarized his learning lessons for the reporter quizzing him. "Ain't nobody watching you but you. You can violate who you are, or you can be real to it. And that's who you are. And that's the journey that we're on. And the battle."[533]

The players thought there were things that should have been taken care of prior to their arrival. New Orleans was attempting to attract a professional team and demonstrate they could accept players of all backgrounds on their streets. That did not happen. "Football is a funny thing," said Haynes. "The key to it is you must come together and trust each other, depend on each other to throw your block, make your tackle. I noticed a very important key at the time—me being good and me trusting in my white teammates who were supposed to make the block or make the tackle. Me believing in them, they delivered and that developed a relationship."[534] The treatment, combined with years of civil rights abuse, drove the players to take a stand.

The theme of teamwork conjures memories of great athletic competition. Every four years when the nations of the world gather to celebrate the Olympic Games, one song is a regular on the playlist—John Lennon's "Imagine." The song landed as the unofficial theme song of the Olympic Games. During the 2024 games in Paris, a French artist sang the song while floating down the river. After French artist Juliette Armanet's performance in Paris, a Polish state broadcaster reacted to the performance by calling it a "vision of communism." TVP, the broadcaster, issued a statement the next day saying that the journalist and sports commentator, Przemyslaw Babiarz, would not be allowed to comment on air anymore during the Games. "Mutual understanding, tolerance, reconciliation—these are not only the basic ideas of the Olympics," said TVP in a statement. "They are also the foundation of the standards that guide the new Polish Television. There is no consent to violate them."[535] The 2024 Paris performance by Armanet was stunning as she and pianist Sofiane Pamart floated down the Seine River on a raft as flames shot out of the piano during a rainstorm, making for a dramatic performance. While she sang, the words "we stand and call for peace" appeared on the screen as the crowd cheered. A constant theme during the Paris Games Opening Ceremony centered around the concepts of inclusion, respect, and solidarity. Every time athletes gather for the Olympic games there is talk about how they can support these concepts regardless of borders.

John Lennon released his *Imagine* album in 1971. The title track encouraged listeners to imagine a world different from what Lennon saw at the time: a world with peace, without materialism or religion, and lacking borders placing walls between people. The song, which became the best-selling single of Lennon's solo career, came from content developed by his wife, Yoko Ono. Just before his death, the former Beatle said he was influenced by several poems from Ono's 1964 book, *Grapefruit*. Capitol Records reproduced a portion of "Cloud Piece" on the back cover of the album. The lyrics are misunderstood by some. Critics pointed to the line, "Imagine there's no countries, it isn't hard to do, nothing to kill or die for, and no religion" and labeled it "The Communist Manifesto." Lennon denied the connection but insisted that there isn't a pure communist society existing in the world, including in Russia or China. During an interview with David Sheff for *Playboy*, shortly before his death in December 1980, Lennon shared that Dick Gregory had given him and Ono a Christian prayer book which had inspired him to write the track. "The concept of positive prayer ... If you can imagine a world at peace, with no denominations of religion—not without religion but without this my God-is-bigger-than-your-God thing—then it can be true."[536]

The 1971 song has been performed at the Olympics dating back to 1996, when Stevie Wonder sang the classic during the Closing Ceremony of the Atlanta Games. Since that time, it has become a regular part of the Games. Using a remastered version and a choir from Liverpool, Lennon's version of the song was performed during the Opening Ceremony at the 2012 Olympics in London. Lady Gaga helped kick off the 2015 European Games in Baku, Azerbaijan with an operatic rendition of "Imagine." Due to the Covid pandemic, the Tokyo games were delayed until 2021 and then they were largely done without crowds. In a highly anticipated event, celebrities from around the world gathered—John Legend (representing the Americas), Keith Urban (Australia), Angélique Kidjo (Africa), Alejandro Sanz (Europe), and the Suginami Junior Chorus (Asia) joined forces for a powerful rendition of the seminal tune. It was arranged by Oscar-winning composer Hans Zimmer and recorded in advance.[537] International Olympic Committee President Thomas Bach invoked Lennon's memory as he argued that "our fragile world, with conflicts, divisions, and wars rising" needs the Olympics' "unifying power more than ever. The Olympic Games must always build bridges. The Olympic Games must never erect walls. You may say we are dreamers. We are not the only ones,"

Bach said, borrowing from Lennon's famous peace anthem, "Imagine."[538]

Many artists such as Elton John, David Bowie, and Liza Minnelli covered the song over the years. Queen performed the song in a tribute to Lennon the day after his death in a performance at Wembley Arena. Stevie Wonder performed it during the closing ceremony of the 1996 Summer Olympics in a tribute to the victims of the Centennial Park bombing. Neil Young performed the song during the "9/11 Tribute to Heroes" concert, and Madonna sang it during a benefit for victims of the Indian Ocean tsunami. It is hard to avoid the importance of the song. Its legacy was summarized by President Jimmy Carter, who said, "In many countries around the world—my wife and I have visited about 125 countries—you hear John Lennon's song 'Imagine' used almost equally with national anthems."[539]

The themes of inclusion and togetherness present in the song "Imagine" song evoke memories of Rev. Dr. Martin Luther King's "I Have A Dream" speech from the March on Washington in 1963. "Even though we face the difficulties of today and tomorrow, I still have a dream," proclaimed King. "It is a dream deeply rooted in the American dream. I have a dream that one day this nation will rise up and live out the true meaning of its creed: We hold these truths to be self-evident, that all men are created equal. I have a dream that one day on the red hills of Georgia, the sons of former slaves and the sons of former slave owners will be able to sit down together at the table of brotherhood . . . I have a dream that my four little children will one day live in a nation where they will not be judged by the color of their skin but by the content of their character."[540] King painted a picture of his vision of the world, which was one in which love triumphs over hate. In 1966, only 28 percent of Americans held a favorable opinion of King. Over time and after a tragic assassination, feelings mellowed and opinion changed. By 1987, 76 percent of Americans held a favorable view of the civil rights leader.[541] Ironically, those negative poll results came after a big year for King. His "I Have A Dream" speech catapulted him into the view of Americans. *Time* magazine named him "Man of the Year" for 1963 and later that year he was awarded the Nobel Prize. King was considered the most well-known leader of the civil rights movement.

Lennon's lyrics ask listeners to visualize a fictitious world where man-made barriers do not exist. For example, people are not grouped by religion and measured by wealth. Most importantly, he wants us to put aside differences and unify. It was released in 1971 with the Vietnam War dragging on and civil rights riots raging in the streets at home. He asks us all to imagine a world of peace and unity. Like Lennon, who imagined a different world, King dreamed that one day his children could sit and eat together regardless of race, color, or social status. He dreamed that his children would be judged not by the color of their skin but by the content of their character. King's dream was not an individual one but a collective dream for a better tomorrow where all people can live together without segregation nor discrimination.

Just as impressions of King have changed over the years, views of New Orleans have, too. Ironically, the airport is now called Louis Armstrong New Orleans International Airport after its favorite son who refused to return home and face discrimination in his "Big Easy" hometown. The American trumpeter and vocalist, who goes by "Satchmo" and "Pops," was born and raised in New Orleans by a single mother in a rough, poverty-stricken neighborhood located near where the Superdome stands today. He left the city in 1922 to join a band in Chicago and they traveled the world. He helped introduce the world to jazz music as he toured nationally and internationally and publicly boycotted the city since it banned integrated bands in 1956. The last time he played in New Orleans was in 1965 in an event that was a precursor to the New Orleans Jazz Fest. "Among Negroes across the country, he occupies a special position as success symbol, cultural hero, and racial cop-out," wrote journalist Andrew Kopkind in *The New Republic*. Some Blacks wanted to see Armstrong do more for the civil rights cause and called him an Uncle Tom. "My life is my music," he said. "They would beat me on the mouth if I marched and without my mouth I wouldn't be able to blow my horn . . . they would beat Jesus if he was Black and marched." These were rough times.

In 1965, Malcolm X was killed and Alabama state troopers beat marchers in what became known as Bloody Sunday in Selma, Alabama. "I don't socialize with the top dogs of society after a dance or concert," said Armstrong in a 1964 profile in *Ebony*. "These same society people may go around the corner and lynch a Negro."[542] Armstrong chose his battles wisely. In September 1957, as he watched the struggle of nine Black students attempting to attend Little Rock Central High School, he spoke out against President Eisenhower urging him to take action. He called the president "two-faced" and said he had "no guts." Later, as Eisenhower helped the students, he had a friendlier tone in his comments. As retribution for his hard emotions about Little Rock, Armstrong canceled a planned tour of the

Soviet Union for the State Department. It was risky to be a Black man during the time Armstrong toured. He was arrested by the Memphis Police Department in 1931 after he sat next to his manager's wife, a white woman, on a bus. Armstrong and his bandmates were thrown in jail, but his manager got him out in time to put on a show the next evening. His social commentary was veiled. When he started to play that evening, some police officers were in the audience, so he dedicated a song to them and the band started playing "I'll Be Glad When You're Dead, You Old Rascal You." Some feared he would be arrested again, but he survived to play another day.[543]

Many of the 21 who protested during the AFL All-Star game were proud of what they accomplished. "I got hate mail and was invited to go back to Africa," admitted the Bills' Ernie Warlick. "But when I look back, it was one of the thrills of my life. We were a unified group. Every time we get together as a group, we talk about how unified we were. We hung out together and got along. It's a great thrill that I've carried with me ever since."[544] Others agreed. "We did it because someone had to take a stand and stop the Black players from being treated as second-class citizens," said Ernie Ladd. "We didn't do it for publicity. We did it because of what was right and what was wrong."[545]

After passage of the Civil Rights Act of 1964 and the All-Star Game boycott, the racial climate in Southern cities such as New Orleans improved. Black patrons didn't need to be served out of the back door of kitchens or restaurants, were able to take public transportation and sit anywhere, and could shop at stores and enter clubs in the French Quarter. In short, they were able to access the same services that their white brothers took for granted daily. The players' sacrifice came at a cost. "Just a few days after the game, I was traded to Denver as punishment," said Abner Haynes. "Cookie Gilchrist, one of the other leaders, was traded there too. They [the Broncos] were the worst team in the league. The owners would try to do things like this sometimes, to try to make you uncomfortable. It was a form of intimidation. This happened to a lot of players and many of them were out of the league in a few years. Jack Steadman, the Chiefs GM, wrote me a two-page letter explaining that he thought I helped lead the boycott. He claimed it was not a football player's role to help out his people—his job was to play football and keep his mouth shut."[546]

In sports, a common question fans ask is, "Who won?" The answer to who won during the AFL boycott or the NFL kneeling protest cannot be easily answered.

The players who knelt did so to protest social injustice. The protest attracted much attention, especially after President Trump got involved and called attention to the protestors.

Ethan Poskanzer of the University of Colorado began studying, in 2016, the career trajectories of the first 50 NFL athletes to join the protest. He found that most of those players subsequently left their teams. They left in various ways: a team released the player or traded the player to another team; the player's contract expired and he chose to move to another team, or the player retired. Interestingly, the players often received a better offer to leave the original team. "Protesting players were more likely to get a better offer elsewhere than similar players who didn't protest," said Poskanzer. "When a player who protested leaves a team that was not supportive of the protests, when the other teams are looking at who to hire, that player might get a relatively better offer from the teams that are supportive of this kind of protest."[547] The study, published in May 2023 in the journal *Organization Science*, was conducted by Poskanzer and Alexandra Rheinhardt, Assistant Professor of Management and Entrepreneurship at the University of Connecticut's School of Business and co-authored by Forrest Briscoe, professor of management and organization in the Smeal College of Business at the Pennsylvania State University. The study's implications reach beyond football to any workplace, according to the researchers.

Similarly, some players involved in the New Orleans protest left their teams. Abner Haynes and Cookie Gilchrist both joined the Denver Broncos soon after the protest concluded. It is easy to say the players won because the game was moved and much attention was received on the negative racial standing of New Orleans. At first, it was feared that the city's hope of landing a professional team was dim. New Orleans, whose inhabitants discriminated against visitors in 1965, won. The New Orleans Saints began play as an NFL expansion team two years later. Politics being the strange world they are, Louisiana was home to some of the most powerful leaders in Congress at the time and they were able to seize on political opportunity and win a franchise for the Crescent City. The city hosted its first Super Bowl game in 1970 and became a regular host city: four times in the '70s, twice in the '80s, twice in the '90s, and single times in the '00s, '10s, and '20s.

Kaepernick was a clear loser in the situation. Within seven months of his initial protest, he was out of the league. This came three years after leading his team to the

Super Bowl and his teammates recognizing him for his "inspirational and courageous" play. Eric Reid, who soon joined Kaepernick, played three more seasons but his career appeared to end sooner than expected for a talented player. Commissioner Goodell admitted four years later that "I wish I would have listened." Later on, Goodell told Emmanuel Acho on "Uncomfortable Conversations with a Black Man" that, "I wish we had listened earlier, Kaep, to what you were kneeling about and what you were trying to bring attention to."[548]

One year after the New Orleans boycott, the AFL scheduled the 1966 AFL All-Star game in Houston. Ernie Wright, Earl Faison, and Dave Grayson were flying to the game site when they faced an extended layover in New Orleans. The airline promised the players an early morning flight and directed them to the Hilton Inn Motel, which was adjacent to the airport. The three players hailed an African American cab and headed to the Oyster House in the French Quarter. They were apprehensive as they climbed into the taxi. All the players wondered if this year would be any different.

Wright said the cab driver heard us talking and said, "'Oh, you're football players. What you did last year has had a tremendous effect on New Orleans. They want a pro football team here. And after you guys refused to play here and [the story] was on national press and TV again, they integrated the transportation. Blacks did not have to sit in the back anymore. You can get any cab and so on and so forth.' We had in this era of the '60s where they had all this civil rights stuff and the marches and sitting at the counters, we had an effect too. And we had an effect in a different way because everybody wanted sports franchises and athletes around. So, in many ways we had as equally powerful an effect as students did, but it took all of us to change."[549]

ENDNOTES

Chapter One

1   Gilchrist, Cookie and Chris Garbarino, *The Cookie That Did Not Crumble*, U Are Superstar LLC, 2011, 35.

2   Gilchrist, Cookie and Chris Garbarino, *The Cookie That Did Not Crumble*, 35.

3   Harmon, Pat (Sports Editor). "The Controversial Cookie Gilchrist," *The Cincinnati Post and Times Star (Cincinnati, Ohio)*, March 2, 1965.

4   Sapp, Erin Grayson. *Moving the Chains: The Civil Rights Protest that Saved the Saints and Transformed New Orleans*, Louisiana State University Press, 2022, 142.

5   *Washington Afro-American*, December 29, 1964; *Houston Informer*, January 2, 1965.

6   Graves, Neil. *The Undefeated*. "When Racism Drove the AFL All-Star Game Out of New Orleans," *The Undefeated*, January 27, 2017.

7   Graves, Neil. *The Undefeated*. "When Racism Drove the AFL All-Star Game Out of New Orleans," *The Undefeated*, January 27, 2017.

8   Miller, Jeffrey J. *Rockin' the Rockpile: The Buffalo Bills of the American Football League.* ECW Press. 2007. 272.

9   Graves, Neil. *The Undefeated*. "When Racism Drove the AFL All-Star Game Out of New Orleans," *The Undefeated*, January 27, 2017.

10   Farrar, Doug. "How the 1964 AFL All-Star Game Player Boycott Struck a Blow for Civil Rights." *USA Today*, August 26, 2020.

11   Farrar, Doug. "How the 1964 AFL All-Star Game Player Boycott Struck a Blow for Civil Rights." *USA Today*, August 26, 2020.

12   *Fitchburg Sentinel* (Fitchburg, Massachusetts). "The AFL Rebellion: Star Gilchrist Gives Version of 24 Hours," January 26, 1965.

13   *The Historic New Orleans Collection*. "David F. Dixon's Account of the All-Star Walk Out." https://www.hnoc.org/interactive-lesson/crescent-city-sport/david-f-dixons-account-all-star-walk-out

14   Miller, Jeffrey J. *Rockin' the Rockpile*, 272.

15   Miller, Jeffrey J. *Rockin' the Rockpile*, 272.

16   Boyles, Brian W. *New Orleans Boom & Blackout: One Hundred Days in America's Coolest Hot Spot*, History Press Library Editions, 2015, 290.

17   Associated Press. "New Orleans Pro Football Dreams Now a Nightmare." *The*

Indianapolis News, January 12, 1965.

18   AP and UPI Dispatches. "A.F.L Game Moved to Houston." Courier Journal (Louisville, KY), January 12, 1965.

19   Miller, Jeffrey J. *Rockin' the Rockpile*, 272.

20   Associated Press. "Negro Players, Protesting Racial Discrimination, Quit AFL Affair," *The Gazette and Daily (York, PA)*, January 11, 1965.

21   Valli, Bob, "Clem Cites Racial Slurs in South." *Oakland Tribune,* January 11, 1965, and Graves, Neil. "When Racism Drove the AFL All-Star Game out of New Orleans." *The Undefeated,* January 27, 2017.

22   Valli, Bob, "Clem Cites Racial Slurs in South." *Oakland Tribune,* January 11, 1965.

23   Lamarre, Tom. "Inside the Raiders: 1965 AFL All-Star Game Boycott," *The Black Hole Plus*, March 22, 2021.

24   *Fitchburg Sentinel* (Fitchburg, Massachusetts), "The AFL Rebellion: Star Gilchrist Gives Version of 24 Hours," January 26, 1965.

25   Clayton, William. "Game Shifted to Houston," *The Billings (Montana) Gazette,* January 12, 1965.

26   Trosclair, Carroll. "Negro Players Claim Discrimination in New Orleans; AFL Game Switched." *The Sheboygan Press (Sheboygan, Wisconsin),* January 11, 1965.

27   Associated Press. "Negro Players Leave New Orleans; AFL All-Star Game is Off." *The Charlotte News (Charlotte, North Carolina),* January 11, 1965.

28   Kendle, Jon. "Players Boycott AFL All-Star Game," ProFootballHOF.com. February 18, 2010.

29   Associated Press. "Fuss Over New Orleans Race 'Bias' Switches Game to Houston," *The Journal Times (Racine, Wisconsin),* January 11, 1965.

30   DeArdo, Bryan. "Five Fascinating AFL Facts Ahead of Monday Night's Game Between the Raiders and Chargers," *CBS Sports,* October 4, 2021.

31   Farrar, Doug. "How the 1964 AFL All-Star Game Player Boycott Struck a Blow for Civil Rights." *USA Today*, August 26, 2020, and Tom Lamarre. "Inside the Raiders, 1965 AFL All-Star Game Boycott," *SI.com,* March 22, 2021.

32   Valli, Bob. "Clem Cites Racial Slurs in South." *Oakland Tribune,* January 11, 1965.

33   DeArdo, Bryan. "Five Fascinating AFL Facts Ahead of Monday Night's Game Between the Raiders and Chargers." *CBS Sports,* October 4, 2021.

34   Trosclair, Carroll. *The Sheboygan Press (Sheboygan, Wisconsin).* "Negro Players Claim Discrimination in New Orleans; AFL Game Switched." January 11, 1965.

35   Young, Dick. "Young Ideas." *Daily News (New York, New York),* January 13, 1965.

36   Miller, Jeffrey J. *Rockin' the Rockpile,* 273-4.

37   *Fitchburg Sentinel* (Fitchburg, Massachusetts), "The AFL Rebellion: Star Gilchrist Gives Version of 24 Hours," January 26, 1965.

38   Miller, Jeffrey J. *Rockin' the Rockpile,* 274-5.

39   United Press International. "'Should Have Rolled with Punch' -- Mayor." *The*

Billings (Montana) Gazette, January 12, 1965, and Associated Press. "AFL Houston Shift Called Hasty." *The Boston Globe,* January 12, 1965.

40   *Jet.* "Police Foundation is the Big Loser in Boycott," January 28, 1965.

41   Associated Press. "Negro Players, Protesting Racial Discrimination, Quit AFL Affair," *The Gazette and Daily (York, PA),* January 11, 1965.

42   Associated Press. "Buoniconti Raps Negro Star Walkout," *Fitchburg (Mass) Sentinel,* January 26, 1965.

43   Associated Press. "AFL Players Endorse All-Star Game Boycott," *Fort Worth Star-Telegram (Fort Worth, Texas),* January 15, 1965.

44   Associated Press. "Houston Move Saves Pension," *Corpus Christi (Texas) Times,* January 12, 1965.

45   Associated Press. "Houston Move Saves Pension," *Corpus Christi (Texas) Times,* January 12, 1965.

46   AP and UPI Dispatches, "A.F.L. Game Moved to Houston," *Courier Journal (Louisville, KY),* January 12, 1965.

47   Associated Press. "New Orleans Pro Football Dreams Now a Nightmare." *The Indianapolis News,* January 12, 1965.

48   Steele, David. "Missouri Players Walked Path Blazed by 1965 AFL All-Star Boycotters." *The Sporting News,* November 17, 2015.

49   Steele, David. "Missouri Players Walked Path Blazed by 1965 AFL All-Star Boycotters." *The Sporting News,* November 17, 2015.

50   Kendle, Jon. "Player's Boycott AFL All-Star Game." *Pro Football Hall of Fame,* February 18, 2010.

51   Smith, Wendell. "New Orleans Still Ranks as a Tank Town." *Pittsburgh Courier,* January 23, 1965.

52   *Times-Picayune.* January 13, 1965.

Chapter Two

53   *New Orleans States-Item,* January 11, 1965 and *Times-Picayune,* January 13, 1965.

54   Jacobus, Robert D. *To Live and Play in Dixie: Pro Football's Entry into the Jim Crow South.* Prometheus Books, 2021, 182-3.

55   The National Academy of Sports Poll Found 51 Percent of the Editors Favored the Matchup, 42 Percent Opposed with 7 Percent Indifferent.

56   McIntyre, Bill. "AFL 'Fix' in New Orleans?" *The Times (Shreveport, Louisiana),* January 12, 1965.

57   McIntyre, Bill. "Authority is Absent in AFL." *The Times (Shreveport, Louisiana),* January 12, 1965.

58   Young, Dick. "Young Ideas." *Daily News (New York, New York),* January 13, 1965.

59   *The New York Times,* January 12, 1965.

60   Jacobus, Robert D. *To Live and Play in Dixie,* 184.

61   Jacobus, Robert D. *To Live and Play in Dixie,* 184-5.

62   Editor. "New Orleans Gets Another Black Eye." *The Louisiana Weekly*, January 16, 1965.
63   Editor. "New Orleans Gets Another Black Eye." *The Louisiana Weekly*, January 16, 1965.
64   Hall, Jim. "Time Out." *The Louisiana Weekly*, January 23, 1965.
65   Hall, Jim. "Time Out." *The Louisiana Weekly*, January 23, 1965.
66   Hall, Jim. "Time Out." *The Louisiana Weekly*, January 23, 1965.
67   Hall, Jim. "Time Out." *The Louisiana Weekly*, January 23, 1965.
68   Curry, Ernest (Butch). "New Orleans Must Accept Blame for Negro Walkout." *Pittsburgh Courier*, January 23, 1965.
69   Given, Kyle. "Monday's Lecture." *Daily News-Post (Monrovia, California)*, January 11, 1965.
70   McIntyre, Bill. "AFL 'Fix' in New Orleans?" *The Times (Shreveport, Louisiana)*, June 26, 1965.
71   Associated Press. "AFL Houston Shift Called Hasty," *The Boston Globe*, January 12, 1965.
72   Nassif, Al. "Dixon's Decision Popular One." *The Town Talk (Alexandria, Louisianan)*, July 6, 1965.
73   Associated Press. "Criticism of AFL Move Mounts in New Orleans," *Lake Charles American-Press (Lake Charles, Louisiana)*, January 12, 1965.
74   Oriard, Michael. *Brand NFL: Making & Selling America's Favorite Sport*. The University of North Carolina Press, 2010, 213.
75   Oriard, Michael. *Brand NFL: Making & Selling America's Favorite Sport*. The University of North Carolina Press, 2010., 214.

Chapter Three

76   Vernon, John. "Jim Crow, Meet Lieutenant Robinson: A 1944 Court-Martial." *Prologue Magazine*, Spring 2008.
77   Dixon, Randy. "Uncle Sam Ignores Negro Footballers," *Pittsburgh Courier*, September 5, 1942: 16.
78   Ross, Charles K. *Outside the Lines: African Americans and the Integration of the National Football League*. New York University Press. 1999. 44.
79   Conte, Andrew. *The Color of Sundays: The Secret Strategy That Built the Steelers' Dynasty*. Blue River Press, 2016. 68.
80   Branch Rickey signed Robinson to a Brooklyn contract in the summer/fall 1945 before Strode, Washington, Motley, and Willis, but they played games in the big leagues because Robinson played pro ball in Triple A in 1946.
81   Rhoden, William C. "When Paul Brown Smashed the Color Barrier." *The New York Times*, September 25, 1997.
82   Rhoden, William C. "When Paul Brown Smashed the Color Barrier." *The New York Times*, September 25, 1997.
83   *The New York Times*. "Lafayette Declines Sun Bowl Invitation Because Texas Law Bans Negro Back." November 24, 1948, 27.

84 See Martin, Charles H. "Integrating New Year's Day: The Racial Politics of College Bowl Games in the American South," in Patrick B. Miller, *The Sporting World of the Modern South*, University of Illinois Press, 2002.

85 See Martin, Charles H. "Integrating New Year's Day: The Racial Politics of College Bowl Games in the American South," in Patrick B. Miller, *The Sporting World of the Modern South*, University of Illinois Press, 2002, 187-8.

86 See Martin, Charles H., "Integrating New Year's Day: The Racial Politics of College Bowl Games in the American South," in Patrick B. Miller, *The Sporting World of the Modern South*, University of Illinois Press, 2002, 189.

87 Bird, David. "Marvin Griffin, 74, Former Governor." *The New York Times*, June 14, 1982.

88 *College Sports Television (CSTV)*. "Uninvited: The 1951 USF Football Team." February 14, 2007.

Chapter Four

89 *Brown v. Board of Education of Topeka*, 349 U.S. 294 (1955).

90 Myers Asch, Chris. *The Senator and the Sharecropper: The Freedom Struggles of James O. Eastland and Fannie Lou Hamer*. The University of North Carolina Press, 2008, 150.

91 Till-Mobley, Mamie. *Death of Innocence: The Story of the Hate Crime that Changed America*. One World Ballantine Books, 2003, 257.

92 Hampton, Henry and Steve Fayer. *Voices of Freedom: An Oral History of the Civil Rights Movement from the 1950s through the 1980s*. Bantam Books, 1990, 19-20.

93 Theoharis, Jeanne. *The Rebellious Life of Mrs. Rosa Parks. Young, Readers' Edition*, 101.

94 Hampton, Henry and Steve Fayer, *Voices of Freedom*, 19.

95 Sitkoff, Harvard. *The Struggle for Black Equality, 1954-1980*. Hill and Wang, 2008, 49.

96 Kimble, Lindsay. "Emmett Till's Accuser Recants Part of Her Story—60 Years After His Beating Death Stoked Civil Rights Movement." *People*, January 27, 2017.

97 Weller, Sheila. "How Author Timothy Tyson Found the Woman at the Center of the Emmett Till Case." *Vanity Fair*, January 26, 2017.

98 Italie, Hillel (Associated Press). "Key Till Witness Gave False Testimony, Historian Says." *Clarion-Ledger (Jackson, Mississippi)*, January 29, 2017.

99 Strong, Catherine. "Congressional Gold Medal Presented to Rosa Parks." *The Times* (Shreveport, LA), June 16, 1999.

100 Theoharis, Jeanne. *A More Beautiful and Terrible History: The Uses and Misuses of Civil Rights History*. Beacon Press, 2018, 83.

101 Till-Mobley, Mamie. *Death of Innocence: The Story of the Hate Crime that Changed America*. One World Ballantine Books, 2003, 257.

102 Bell, Gregg. "NFL Premiers on MLK Day a Video by Metcalf on Murder of Till." *The Olympian* (Olympia, WA), January 20, 2021.

103 Bell, Gregg. "NFL Premiers on MLK Day a Video by Metcalf on Murder of

Till." *The News Tribune* (Tacoma, WA), January 20, 2021.

104 Bell, Gregg. "NFL Premiers on MLK Day a Video by Metcalf on Murder of Till." *The Olympian* (Olympia, WA), January 20, 2021.

105 Smith-Llera, Danielle. *Lunch Counter Sit-In: How Photographs Helped Peaceful Civil Rights Protests*. Compass Point Books, 2018, 31.

106 Kareem Nittle, Nadra. "How the Greensboro Four Sit-in Sparked a Movement." History.com, July 28, 2020.

107 Kareem Nittle, Nadra. "How the Greensboro Four Sit-in Sparked a Movement." History.com, July 28, 2020.

108 Herr, Melody. *Sitting for Equal Service: Lunch Counter Sit-Ins, United States, 1960s*. Twenty-First Century Books, 2010, 137.

109 Bond, Julian. *Julian Bond's Time to Teach*. Beacon Press, 2021, 124.

110 O'Brien, M.J. *We Shall Not be Moved: The Jackson Woolworth's Sit-In and the Movement it Inspired*. University Press of Mississippi, 2014, xi.

111 "Dr. King Leaves Montgomery for Atlanta." *King Encyclopedia* as quoted in Smith-Llera, Danielle. *Lunch Counter Sit-In: How Photographs Helped Peaceful Civil Rights Protests*, 28.

112 Schlosser, Jim. "Four Men Summon Courage to Alter Course of History," *Greensboro News & Record*, January 27, 1985.

113 McAdam, Doug. *Freedom Summer*. Oxford University Press, 1988. 12.

114 Gates, Verna. "Condoleezza Rice Recalls Racial Blast that Killed Childhood Friend." *Reuters*, September 14, 2015.

115 Rice, Condoleezza. *Extraordinary, Ordinary People*. Three Rivers Press, 2010. 92.

116 Rice, Condoleezza. *Condoleezza Rice: A Memoir of My Extraordinary, Ordinary Family and Me*. Delacorte Press, 2010, 96-97 and Condoleezza Rice. *Extraordinary, Ordinary People*. Three Rivers Press, 2010, 95.

117 Rice, Condoleezza. *Extraordinary, Ordinary People*, 78.

118 Rice, Condoleezza. *Extraordinary, Ordinary People*, 78-9.

119 Rice, Condoleezza. *Extraordinary, Ordinary People*, 79..

120 Rice, Condoleezza. *Condoleezza Rice: A Memoir of My Extraordinary, Ordinary Family and Me,* 98, and Condoleezza Rice. *Extraordinary, Ordinary People,* 97.

121 Rice, Condoleezza. *Condoleezza Rice: A Memoir of My Extraordinary, Ordinary Family and Me,* 99, and Condoleezza Rice. *Extraordinary, Ordinary People,* 98.

122 Rice, Condoleezza, *Condoleezza Rice: A Memoir of My Extraordinary, Ordinary Family and Me,* 100, and Condoleezza Rice. *Extraordinary, Ordinary People,* 99.

123 Rice, Condoleezza. *Condoleezza Rice: A Memoir of My Extraordinary, Ordinary Family and Me,* 103.

124 Morrie, Williesha. "16th Street Baptist Church Bombing 60th Anniversary: Why Church Bells Rang at 10:22 a.m." *al.com*, September 15, 2023.

125 Kiszla, Mark. "Condoleezza Rice, Once a Child Deemed Unworthy of Sitting on Santa's Knee, Now Sits in Owners' Box at Broncos Games." *Denver Post*, November 23, 2022.

Chapter Five

126 A copy of Marion Motley's AAFC contract is in the Pro Football Hall of Fame and shows an annual salary of $4,000 and is dated August 10, 1946. He had been signed a week after Bill Willis, according to the Cleveland Browns.

127 Associated Press. "Kenny Washington to Have Knee Surgery." *Chippewa Herald-Telegram (Chippewa Falls, Wisconsin)*, April 11, 1946.

128 Murray, Jim. "Kenny Washington Still Fighting Hard." *Corpus Christi Times (Corpus Christi, TX)*, September 29, 1970.

129 Murray, Jim, "Long Career of 'Almosts.'" *Corpus Christi Times (Corpus Christi, TX)*, September 29, 1970.

130 Johnson, Keyshawn and Bob Glauber. *The Forgotten First: Kenny Washington, Woody Strode, Marion Motley, Bill Willis, and the Breaking of the NFL Color Barrier.* Grand Central Publishing, 2021, 61.

131 Johnson, Keyshawn and Bob Glauber. *The Forgotten First*, 71-2.

132 Johnson, Keyshawn and Bob Glauber. *The Forgotten First*, 74.

133 Myers, Bob. "Kenny Washington Called 'Best I Ever Saw' by Bob Waterfield." *The Los Angeles Times*, May 7, 1970.

134 Johnson, Keyshawn and Bob Glauber. *The Forgotten First*, 181.

135 Johnson, Keyshawn and Bob Glauber. *The Forgotten First*, 155-7.

136 Lahman, Sean. *The Pro Football Historical Abstract: A Hardcore Fan's Guide to All-Time Player Rankings,* 25.

137 Christl, Cliff. "Bob Mann Endured for His Opportunity." Packers.com, September 27, 2018.

138 Jacobus, Robert D. *To Live and Play in Dixie,* 30-1.

139 Vandermause, Mike. "'I Never Had Any Problems.'" *Green Bay Press-Gazette*, October 24, 2006, and Christl, Cliff. "Oral History: Bob Mann, Packers' First African American," Packers.com, July 10, 2014.

140 Vandermause, Mike. "'I Never Had Any Problems.'" *Green Bay Press-Gazette*. October 24, 2006.

141 Piascik, Andy. *Gridiron Gauntlet: The Story of the Men Who Integrated Pro Football in Their Own Words.* Taylor Trade Publishing, 2009, 45.

142 *WBAY (Green Bay, Wisconsin)*. "'Delay of Game' Exhibit Captures History of African American Packers Players," August 7, 2018.

143 Piascik, Andy. *Gridiron Gauntlet,* 47-8.

144 *Pittsburgh Courier (Pittsburgh, Pennsylvania)*. "Bears Sign Eddie Macon," July 12, 1952.

145 Piascik, Andy. *Gridiron Gauntlet,* 160-1.

146 Jacobus, Robert D. *To Live and Play in Dixie,* 32.

147 Piascik, Andy. *Gridiron Gauntlet,*162-3.

148 Piascik, Andy. *Gridiron Gauntlet,* 163.

149 Piascik, Andy. *Gridiron Gauntlet,* 164.

150 Jacobus, Robert D. *To Live and Play in Dixie,* 33.

151 Piascik, Andy. *Gridiron Gauntlet*, 215.
152 Piascik, Andy. *Gridiron Gauntlet*, 219-222.
153 Murray, Jim. "Recognition For Milt Campbell." *Indian River Press Journal (Vero Beach, Florida)*, July 17, 1991.
154 Dehman, Elliott. "Greatest of State's Olympians." *Asbury Park Press (Asbury Park, NJ)*, July 5, 1992.
155 Jacobus, Robert D. *To Live and Play in Dixie*, 33-4.
156 Murray, Jim. "Forgotten Decathlete Speaks Out." *Los Angeles Times*, July 16, 1991.
157 Swartz, Jimmy. "The Life and Career of Walter Beach (Complete Story)." *Browns Nation*, August 28, 2021.
158 Jacobus, Robert D. *To Live and Play in Dixie*, 38.
159 Swartz, Jimmy. "The Life and Career of Walter Beach (Complete Story)," *Browns Nation*, August 28, 2021.
160 Jacobus, Robert D. *To Live and Play in Dixie*, 36.
161 Jacobus, Robert D. *To Live and Play in Dixie*, 36.
162 Simers, T. J. "Art Powell: Wide Receiver Paid Price for His Strong Convictions." *The Los Angeles Times*, February 9, 1992.
163 Jacobus, Robert D. *To Live and Play in Dixie*, 156.
164 Jacobus, Robert D. *To Live and Play in Dixie*, 157-8.
165 Simers, T. J. "Art Powell: Wide Receiver Paid Price for His Strong Convictions." *The Los Angeles Times*, February 9, 1992.
166 MacDonald, Jerry. "Art Powell and his Raiders Legacy." *The Mercury News (San Jose, CA*, April 8, 2015.

Chapter Six

167 Somers, Dale A. *The Rise of Sports in New Orleans, 1850-1900*, 3.
168 Souther, J. Mark. "Making 'America's Most Interesting City': Tourism and the Construction of Cultural Image in New Orleans, 1940-1984" in Starnes, Richard D. *Southern Journeys: Tourism, History, and Culture in the Modern South*. University of Alabama Press, 2003, 115.
169 ExperienceNewOrleans.com, "Why is New Orleans Called the Big Easy?" February 7, 2023.
170 Schwam, Diana & Lavinia Spalding. *Frommer's Easy Guide to New Orleans. 8th Edition*, Frommer Media, 2022.
171 Lewis, Peirce F. *New Orleans: The Making of an Urban Landscape*. Center for American Places, 2003, 42.
172 THNOC Visitor Services. *HNOC.org*. "New Orleans History Starter Pack: A Beginner's Guide to Understanding the Crescent City." January 21, 2022, and *United Teachers of New Orleans*. "Some New Orleans Black History You Should Know."
173 THNOC Visitor Services. *HNOC.org*. "New Orleans History Starter Pack: A Beginner's Guide to Understanding the Crescent City." January 21, 2022.
174 Beyer, Scott. "The Quirks of New Orleans Culture: Everything Else." *Forbes*,

February 12, 2016.

175 NewOrleans.com, "America's First City of Opera."

176 https://www.neworleans.com/things-to-do/history/history-of-new-orleans-by-period/

177 *United Teachers of New Orleans*. "Some New Orleans Black History You Should Know."

178 *United Teachers of New Orleans*. "Some New Orleans Black History You Should Know."

179 Souther, J. Mark. "Into the Big League: Conventions, Football, and the Color Line in New Orleans." *Journal of Urban History* 29, no. 6. September 2003, and Schreiber, Casey. *Saints in the Broken City*. 9.

180 Dixon, Dave. *The Saints, the Superdome, and the Scandal*. Pelican, 2008.

181 Detillier, Mike. "How New Orleans Got an NFL Team, by Mike Detillier - Part 3." *Saints News Network*, June 27, 2020.

182 Associated Press. "Oakland's AFL Club New Orleans-bound?" *Star-Gazette (Elmira, NY)*, November 21, 1962.

183 Associated Press. "Oakland's AFL Club New Orleans-bound?" *Star-Gazette (Elmira, NY)*, November 21, 1962.

184 Nadeau, Rene. "Before There Were Saints, Raiders and Chiefs Almost Moved to New Orleans." *Crescent City Sports*, October 15, 2018.

185 Detillier, Mike. "How New Orleans Got an NFL Team, by Mike Detillier - Part 3." *Saints News Network*, July 12, 2020.

186 Detillier, Mike. "How New Orleans Got an NFL Team, by Mike Detillier - Part 2." *Saints News Network*, June 28, 2020.

187 Detillier, Mike. "How New Orleans Got an NFL Team, by Mike Detillier - Part 2." *Saints News Network*, June 28, 2020.

188 Covitz, Randy. "The Big Uneasy," *The Kansas City Star*, August 29, 2004.

189 *The Louisiana Weekly*. May 5, 1962, as quoted in Haas, Edward F. *Mayor Victor H. Schiro: New Orleans in Transition, 1961-1970*, 182.

190 *The Louisiana Weekly*. August 25, 1962, as quoted in Haas, Edward F. *Mayor Victor H. Schiro: New Orleans in Transition, 1961-1970*, 183.

191 Dixon, Dave. *The Saints, the Superdome, and the Scandal*. Pelican Publishing Company, 2008. 43.

192 *The Louisiana Weekly*. September 14, 1963, as quoted in Haas, Edward F. *Mayor Victor H. Schiro: New Orleans in Transition, 1961-1970*, 183.

193 Katz, Allan. "How Football Saved a City," *New Orleans*, January 1990. 86.

194 United Press International. "President Johnson Signs Bill 4 Hours after Passage," *The Louisiana Weekly*, July 11, 1964.

195 Associated Press. "Cards, Colts Ready for Orleans Clash," *The Times (Shreveport, LA)*, August 14, 1965.

196 Christl, Cliff. "The 1960s Packers: A Product of Vince Lombardi's Prejudice-free Culture." Packers.com, February 4, 2021.

197 Ryczek, William J. *Crash of the Titans: The Early Years of the New York Jets and

the AFL, McFarland, 2009, 99.

198 Ford, Mark L. *A History of Preseason and Exhibition Games: 1960 to 1985,* 38.

199 Detillier, Mike. "How New Orleans Got an NFL Team, by Mike Detillier - Part 3." *Saints News Network,* July 12, 2020.

200 Detillier, Mike. "How New Orleans Got an NFL Team, by Mike Detillier - Part 3." *Saints News Network,* July 12, 2020.

201 Stern, Walter. *Race & Education in New Orleans: Creating the Segregated City, 1764-1960.* Louisiana State University Press, 2018.

202 Bridges, Ruby. *Through My Eyes.* New York: Scholastic Books. 1999. 15-6.

203 Steinbeck, John. *Travels with Charley in Search of America.* New York: Penguin Books. 1980. 189.

204 Steinbeck, John. *Travels with Charley in Search of America.* Penguin Books. 1980. 193.

205 Steinbeck, John. *Travels with Charley in Search of America,* 1980. 186.

206 Bridges, Ruby. *Through My Eyes,* 18-20.

207 Bridges, Ruby. *Through My Eyes,* 22.

208 Steinbeck, John. *Travels with Charley in Search of America,* 187.

209 Bridges, Ruby. *Through My Eyes,* 26-8.

210 *Good Housekeeping.* April 1962 as quoted in Bridges, Ruby. *Through My Eyes,* 29.

211 *The New York Times.* November 15, 1960.

212 *U.S. News & World Report.* November 28, 1960. 31.

213 Bridges, Ruby. *Through My Eyes,* 50.

214 Richman-Abdou, Kelly and Margherita Cole. "Norman Rockwell's 'The Problem We All Live With,' a Groundbreaking Civil Rights Painting." MyModernMet.com, August 5, 2022.

215 Solomon, Deborah. *American Mirror: The Life and Art of Norman Rockwell.* Farrar, Straus, and Giroux. 2013, 3.

216 *Look.* January 14, 1964. 21-23.

217 Pastan, Amy. "Norman Rockwell + The Problem We All Live With." *Kennedy Center,* July 31, 2022.

218 Coles, Dr. Robert. "Southern Children Under Desegregation." *American Journal of Psychiatry,* Volume 120, Number 4. October 1963, 332-44.

219 Solomon, Deborah. *American Mirror: The Life and Art of Norman Rockwell,* 372-3.

220 Marling, Karal Ann. *Norman Rockwell.* Library of American Art. 145.

221 Richman-Abdou, Kelly and Margherita Cole. "Norman Rockwell's 'The Problem We All Live With,' a Groundbreaking Civil Rights Painting," MyModernMet.com, August 5, 2022.

Chapter Seven

222 Samuels, Gertrude. "Little Rock Revisited—Tokenism Plus." *The New York*

Times, June 2, 1963.

223 Associated Press. "Louis Armstrong Sounds Off at Way Integration Handled." *The Burlington Free Press*, September 19, 1957.

224 Associated Press. "Louis Armstrong Sounds Off at Way Integration Handled." *The Burlington Free Press,* September 19, 1957.

225 Associated Press. "Louis Armstrong Sounds Off at Way Integration Handled." *The Burlington Free Press*, September 19, 1957.

226 Reynolds, Christopher (*Los Angeles Times*). "The Mother Church of Country Music." *Detroit Free Press,* November 25, 2018.

227 *Down Beat*, January 7, 1960.

228 *Jet.* November 26, 1959, as quoted in James Lincoln Collier. *Louis Armstrong: An American Genius.* New York: Oxford University Press, 1983. 318-9.

229 *Harper's.* November 1967 as quoted in James Lincoln Collier. *Louis Armstrong: An American Genius.* New York: Oxford University Press, 1983, 319.

230 Clark, William E. "Bombs Don't Stop 'Satchmo' in South." *The News-Herald (Franklin, Pennsylvania)*, February 20, 1957.

231 Clark, William E. "Bombs Don't Stop 'Satchmo' in South." *The News-Herald (Franklin, Pennsylvania)*, February 20, 1957.

232 United Press International. "Louis Armstrong Raps Segregation Group in Selma." *Enterprise-Record (Chico, California),* March 11, 1965.

233 Ostwald, David H. "Louis Armstrong, Civil Rights Pioneer." *The Anniston Star (Anniston, Alabama)*, August 29, 1991.

234 Ostwald, David H. "Louis Armstrong, Civil Rights Pioneer." *The Anniston Star (Anniston, Alabama)*, August 29, 1991.

235 Collier, James Lincoln. *Louis Armstrong: An American Genius*. Oxford University Press, 1983, 317.

236 Lewis, Andy. "L.A.'s Ugly Jim Crow History: Nat King Cole's Dog Poisoned in Hancock Park." *The Hollywood Reporter*, February 19, 2015.

237 *A History of Racial Injustice.* "White Men Attack Nat King Cole During Performance in Birmingham, Alabama." On this date – April 10, 1956.

238 Doherty, Thomas. "Assault in Alabama." *Quillette*, July 22, 2022.

239 Knopper, Steve. "Racism on the Road: The Oral History of Black Artists Touring in the Segregated South." *Billboard*, November 10, 2020.

240 Brown, Deneen A. "A Real Green Book." *Edmonton Journal (Edmonton, Alberta, Canada)*, November 23, 2018.

241 Martinez, Melinda (*USA Today*). "A Lifesaving Guide." *The Town Talk (Alexandria, Louisiana)*. October 10, 2021.

242 Brown, Deneen A. "A Real Green Book." *Edmonton Journal (Edmonton, Alberta, Canada)*, November 23, 2018.

243 Ramsey, Calvin Alexander with Gwen Strauss. *Ruth and the Green Book*. Carolrhoda Books. 2010.

244 Contreras, Russell and Jay Reeves. "Follow the 'Green Book' Path." *Tampa Bay Times (Tampa Bay, Florida)*, February 24, 2019.

245 Robinson, Rachel with Lee Daniels. *Jackie Robinson: An Intimate Portrait*, 46.

246 Baird, Jonathan P. "Between 1877 and 1950, There Were More Than 4,000 Lynchings in 12 Southern States." *Concord Monitor (Concord, New Hampshire)*, September 24, 2017.

247 Baird, Jonathan P. "Between 1877 and 1950, There Were More Than 4,000 Lynchings in 12 Southern States." *Concord Monitor (Concord, New Hampshire)*. September 24, 2017.

248 *Equal Justice Initiative*. "Lynching in America: Confronting the Legacy of Racial Terror." 2017.

249 Weeks, Dan and Sindiso Mnisi Weeks. "Hiding from History: Why Are We So Afraid to Say the Word?" *Concord Monitor (Concord, New Hampshire)*. September 24, 2017.

250 Taylor, Candacy. *Overground Railroad: The Green Book and the Roots of Black Travel in America*. Abrams Press. 2020. 104.

Chapter Eight

251 Civil Rights Task Force. "Beatles Force Desegregation of Their Concert in Jacksonville." *The Florida Times-Union*, September 16, 2018.

252 Gunderson, Chuck. "The Untold Story of the Beatles Desegregation Rider." *Culture Sonar*, July 31, 2020.

253 Stolworthy, Jacob. "Paul McCartney Says The Beatles Angrily Turned Down Segregated Gig in 1964." *Independent (UK)*, June 6, 2020.

254 Gunderson, Chuck. "The Untold Story of the Beatles Desegregation Rider." *Culture Sonar*, July 31, 2020.

255 Kane, Larry. "The Beatles Fight Bigotry in America." *CBS News*, January 30, 2014.

256 Gunderson, Chuck. "The Untold Story of the Beatles Desegregation Rider." *Culture Sonar*, July 31, 2020.

257 Kielty, Martin. "How the Beatles' 'Blackbird' Took Flight from Racism." *Classic Rock and Culture*, June 29, 2020.

258 Associated Press. "New Film Shows How the Beatles Helped Fight Segregation." *Billboard*, September 18, 2016.

259 Kielty, Martin. "How the Beatles' 'Blackbird' Took Flight from Racism." *Classic Rock and Culture*, June 29, 2020.

260 Kim, Juliana. "What the Beatles and Beyonce's 'Blackbird' Means to This Little Rock Nine Member." *National Public Radio (NPR)*, April 2, 2024.

261 Adderley, Herb, Dave Robinson, and Royce Boyles. *Lombardi's Left Side*. Olathe, Kansas: Ascend Books. 2012. 14.

262 Lombardi Jr., Vince. *What It Takes to Be #1: Vince Lombardi on Leadership*. McGraw-Hill. 2001. 85-6.

263 Adderley, Herb, Dave Robinson, and Royce Boyles. *Lombardi's Left Side*, 12.

264 Adderley, Herb, Dave Robinson, and Royce Boyles. *Lombardi's Left Side*, 13.

265 Adderley, Herb, Dave Robinson, and Royce Boyles. *Lombardi's Left Side*, 12.

266 Adderley, Herb, Dave Robinson, and Royce Boyles. *Lombardi's Left Side*, 12.

267 Lombardi Jr., Vince. *What It Takes to Be #1: Vince Lombardi on Leadership*, 86-7.

268 Jacobus, Robert D. *To Live and Play in Dixie*, 138.

269 Jacobus, Robert D. *To Live and Play in Dixie*, 140.

270 Christl, Cliff. "The 1960s Packers: A Product of Vince Lombardi's Prejudice-free Culture." Packers.com, February 4, 2021.

271 Jacobus, Robert D. *To Live and Play in Dixie*, 143.

272 Jacobus, Robert D. *To Live and Play in Dixie*, 143.

273 Jacobus, Robert D. *To Live and Play in Dixie*, 138.

274 Jacobus, Robert D. *To Live and Play in Dixie*, 140.

275 Lombardi Jr., Vince. *What It Takes to Be #1: Vince Lombardi on Leadership*, 87.

276 Jacobus, Robert D. *To Live and Play in Dixie*, 139.

277 Jacobus, Robert D. *To Live and Play in Dixie*, 136-7.

278 Lombardi Jr., Vince. *What It Takes to Be #1: Vince Lombardi on Leadership*, 88.

279 Robinson, Dave & Royce Boyles. *The Lombardi Legacy: Thirty People Who Were Touched by Greatness*. Goose Creek Publishers. 2009. 229.

280 Robinson, Dave & Royce Boyles. *The Lombardi Legacy*, 230.

281 Magner, Howie. "The Long Walk Home." *Milwaukee*, December 30, 2014.

282 Robinson, Dave & Royce Boyles. *The Lombardi Legacy*, 234.

283 Jacobus, Robert D. *To Live and Play in Dixie*, 139.

284 Robinson, Dave & Royce Boyles. *The Lombardi Legacy*, 233.

285 Robinson, Dave & Royce Boyles. *The Lombardi Legacy*, 234-5.

Chapter Nine

286 Patoski, Joe Nick. *The Dallas Cowboys: The Outrageous History of the Biggest, Loudest, Most Hated, Best Loved Football Team in America*, 190.

287 Golenbock, Peter. *Cowboys Have Always Been My Heroes: The Definitive Oral History of America's Team*. Warner Books, 1997. 346-7.

288 Golenbock, Peter. *Cowboys Have Always Been My Heroes*, 347.

289 Golenbock, Peter. *Cowboys Have Always Been My Heroes*, 347-8.

290 Melzer, Richard. *Don Perkins: A Champion's Life*. University of New Mexico Press, 2023. 104.

291 Golenbock, Peter. *Cowboys Have Always Been My Heroes*, 349.

292 Golenbock, Peter. *Cowboys Have Always Been My Heroes*, 353-4.

293 Patoski, Joe Nick. *The Dallas Cowboys: The Outrageous History of the Biggest, Loudest, Most Hated, Best Loved Football Team in America*. 189-90.

294 Golenbock, Peter. *Cowboys Have Always Been My Heroes*, 347.

295 Ribowsky, Mark. *The Last Cowboy: A Life of Tom Landry*. Liveright Publishing. 2014. 310.

296 Patoski, Joe Nick. *The Dallas Cowboys: The Outrageous History of the Biggest, Loudest, Most Hated, Best Loved Football Team in America*. 191.

297 Melzer, Richard. *Don Perkins: A Champion's Life*, 15.

298 Eisenberg, John. *Cotton Bowl Days: Growing Up with Dallas and the Cowboys in the 1960s*. Simon and Schuster. 1997. 153-4.

299 Merron, Jeff. "Reel Life: 'North Dallas Forty.'" *ESPN* 2. https://www.espn.com/page2/s/closer/021101.html

300 Golenbock, Peter. *Cowboys Have Always Been My Heroes*, 18.

301 Ribowsky, Mark. *The Last Cowboy: A Life of Tom Landry*, 243-4.

302 Norman, Pettis Burch. *The Pettis Norman Story: A Journey Through the Cotton Fields, to the Super Bowl, and into Servant Leadership*. SuburbanBuss,com, 2021, 123.

303 Norman, Pettis Burch. *The Pettis Norman Story*, 124.

304 Norman, Pettis Burch. *The Pettis Norman Story*, 124.

305 Norman, Pettis Burch. *The Pettis Norman Story*, 125-6.

306 Moore, Lenny with Jeffrey Jay Ellish. *All Things Being Equal: The Autobiography of Lenny Moore*. Sports Publishing, LLC, 2005, 95-6.

307 Moore, Lenny with Jeffrey Jay Ellish. *All Things Being Equal*, 70.

308 Moore, Lenny with Jeffrey Jay Ellish. *All Things Being Equal*, 71.

309 Bradley, Bill. *Time Present, Time Past: A Memoir*, Alfred A. Knopf. 1996. 354.

310 Bradley, Bill. *Time Present, Time Past: A Memoir*, 355.

311 Bradley, Bill. *Time Present, Time Past: A Memoir*, 356-7.

312 Bradley, Bill. *Values of the Game*, Artisan, 1998, 76.

313 Bradley, Bill. *Life on the Run*. Vantage Books, 1976, 1995, 40.

314 Bradley, Bill. *Life on the Run*, 90-1.

315 Bradley, Bill. *Values of the Game*, 76-8.

316 Robertson, Oscar. *The Big O: My Life, My Times, My Game*, Rodale, 2003, 8.

317 Robertson, Oscar. *The Big O: My Life, My Times, My Game*, 55-6.

318 Robertson, Oscar. *The Big O: My Life, My Times, My Game*, 164-5.

319 Russell, Bill with Bill McSweeny. *Go Up for Glory*. Dutton, 1966, 13.

320 Russell, Bill with Bill McSweeny. *Go Up for Glory*, 13.

321 Russell, Bill with Bill McSweeny. *Go Up for Glory*, 15-6.

322 Russell, Bill with Bill McSweeny. *Go Up for Glory*, 68-9.

323 Russell, Bill with Bill McSweeny. *Go Up for Glory*, 84.

324 Russell, Bill with Bill McSweeny. *Go Up for Glory*, 84-5.

Chapter Ten

325 www.goodreads.com/author/quotes/6113119.B_J_Neblett

326 Ross, Charles K., *Outside the Lines* as quoted in Schreiber, Casey. *Saints in the Broken City*, 10.

327 *Chicago Defender*, "Grid Star in College Protest," March 17, 1965.

328 Livingston, Charles. "Raps Athletes." *Pittsburgh Courier*, July 17, 1963.

329 Young, RJ. "How Michigan State Changed the Landscape of College Football." *Fox Sports*, July 20, 2021.

330 Young, RJ. "How Michigan State Changed the Landscape of College Football." *Fox Sports*. July 20, 2021.

331 Washington, Maya. *Through the Banks of the Red Cedar: My Father and the Team That Changed the Game.* Little A. 2022. 142.

332 Moore, Louis. *We Will Win the Day: The Civil Rights Movement, the Black Athlete, and the Quest for Equality.* Praeger. 2017. 148.

333 Damer, Roy. "Frenzied Irish Fans Give Heroes Sendoff." *Chicago Tribune*, November 18, 1966.

334 Green, Jerry. "Adderley: From MSU to Hall." *Detroit News*, May 12, 1996.

335 Claerbaut, David. *Bart Starr: When Leadership Mattered.* Taylor Trade. 2007. 71-72.

336 Jacobus, Robert D. *To Live and Play in Dixie*, 149.

337 United Press International. "Wallace Hits NBC Ban on 'Bias' Bowl." *Los Angeles Evening Citizen News*, November 14, 1963.

338 *The Luverne Journal and News,* November 13, 1963.

339 Associated Negro Press. "What Other Papers Are Saying: Blue, Gray and Jim Crow." *The Call (Kansas City, Missouri),* November 29, 1963.

340 Associated Press. "Blue Gray in Danger of Oblivion." *The Anniston Star (Anniston, Alabama)*, December 28, 1964.

341 United Press International. "Blue-Gray Telecast is Killed." *The Anniston Star (Anniston, Alabama)*, November 9, 1963.

342 Jacobus, Robert D. *To Live and Play in Dixie*, 151.

343 Jacobus, Robert D. *To Live and Play in Dixie*, 152.

Chapter Eleven

344 Lage, Larry (Associated Press). "Town Takes Pride in Native Son's Moment in Super Bowl Spotlight." *The Journal News (Hamilton, Ohio)*, January 27, 2007.

345 *Beyond the Game.* "Episode 1: Cool, Calm and Composed: Tony Dungy's Life. Part One."

346 Fennelly, Martin. "Dungy's Loved Ones Are With Him Tonight." *The Tampa Tribune*, February 4, 2007.

347 *Beyond the Game.* "Episode 1: Cool, Calm and Composed: Tony Dungy's Life. Part One."

348 Fennelly, Martin. "Dungy's Loved Ones Are With Him Tonight." *The Tampa Tribune*, February 4, 2007.

349 Associated Press. "Dungy Makes His Mark." *The News-Star (Monroe, Louisiana)*, February 5, 2007.

350 Chiefs.com. "Deron Cherry Reflects on Almost 40 Years of History with Tony Dungy," August 6, 2016.

351 Beasley, Adam H. "Rebuilding Dolphins Begins with Flores." *Miami Herald*, February 5, 2019.

352 Furones, David. "Flores Out as Head Coach." *The Orlando Sentinel*, January 11, 2022.

353 Oyefusi, Daniel and David Wilson. "'This is Bigger Than Football,' Flores Says." *Miami Herald*, February 3, 2022.

354 Brewer, Jerry (*The Washington Post*) Commentary. "Flores is Finished Pretending and the NFL is Losing Control," *Sun-Journal (Lewiston, Maine),* February 3, 2022.

355 Brewer, Jerry (*The Washington Post*) Commentary. "Flores is Finished Pretending and the NFL is Losing Control," *Sun-Journal (Lewiston, Maine),* February 3, 2022.

356 Iannazzone, Al. "Giants: It Was No 'Sham.'" *The New York Daily News,* February 4, 2022.

357 Stapleton, Arnie. "Elway, Ross, Giants Deny Claims Made in Brian Flores Lawsuit." *The Santa Fe New Mexican (Santa Fe, NM),* February 4, 2022.

358 Iannazzone, Al. "Giants: It Was No 'Sham.'" *The New York Daily News,* February 4, 2022.

359 Stapleton, Arnie. "Elway, Ross, Giants Deny Claims Made in Brian Flores Lawsuit." *The Santa Fe New Mexican (Santa Fe, NM),* February 4, 2022.

360 Walker, Teresa M. (Associated Press). "If Hired as Coach, Flores Won't Drop Lawsuit." *Portland Press Herald (Portland, Maine),* February 3, 2022.

361 Solow, Benjamin L. & Solow, John L. & Walker, Todd B. "Moving On Up: The Rooney Rule and Minority Hiring in the NFL." *Labour Economics.* Elsevier, vol. 18(3), June 2011, 332-337.

362 Neuman, Scott. "Why a 20-year Effort by the NFL Hasn't Led to More Minorities in Top Coaching Jobs." *National Public Radio,* February 3, 2022.

363 Rhoden, William C. "Steve Wilks, Kyle Shanahan and Scapegoating Black NFL Coaches." *Andscape,* February 19, 2024.

364 Sheinin, Dave, Michael Lee, Emily Giambalvo, Artur Galocha, and Clara Ence Morse. "How the NFL Blocks Black Coaches." *The Washington Post*, September 21, 2022.

365 *The Washington Post* Staff. "Key Findings from 'Black Out,' The Post's Series on Black NFL Coaches." *The Washington Post*, September 21, 2022.

366 Sheinin, Dave, Michael Lee, Emily Giambalvo, Artur Galocha, and Clara Ence Morse. "How the NFL Blocks Black Coaches." *The Washington Post,* September 21, 2022.

367 Sheinin, Dave, Michael Lee, Emily Giambalvo, Artur Galocha, and Clara Ence Morse. "How the NFL Blocks Black Coaches." *The Washington Post,* September 21, 2022.

368 Sheinin, Dave, Michael Lee, Emily Giambalvo, Artur Galocha, and Clara Ence Morse. "How the NFL Blocks Black Coaches." *The Washington Post,* September 21, 2022.

369 Walker, Teresa M. (Associated Press). "If Hired as Coach, Flores Won't Drop Lawsuit." *Portland Press Herald (Portland, Maine),* February 3, 2022.

370 Graves, Will. "For Steelers Assistant Austin, a Long and Mysterious Wait." *The Island Packet (Hilton Head Island, South Carolina),* February 4, 2022.

371 *Flores v NFL.* U.S. District Court, Southern District of New York, Case 1:22-cv-00871.Files February 1, 2022.

372 *Flores v NFL.* U.S. District Court, Southern District of New York, Case 1:22-cv-00871.Files February 1, 2022. 43.

373 Note: At the time, Kingsbury had Patrick Mahomes as his quarterback and the best record they achieved was 7-5.

374 Lambert, Ivan. "Commanders' OC Kingsbury Called 'The Biggest Fraud in Football.'" *Commanders Wire* (*USA Today*), February 12, 2024.

375 Dragon, Tyler. "San Francisco 49ers Fire Defensive Coordinator Steve Wilks Three Days After Super Bowl 58 Loss." *USA Today*, February 14, 2024.

376 WBTV Staff. "Former Panthers Safety Tre Boston Says Steve Wilks Has 'A Target on His Back.'" WBTV, February 15, 2024.

377 Glennon, John. "Do the Titans Already Have Their Head Coach?" *The Tennessean (Nashville, Tennessee)*, January 4, 2016.

378 Arthur, Ben (*Nashville Tennessean*). "Law Experts' Weigh in on Mularkey's Allegations." *The Knoxville News-Sentinel*, April 14, 2022.

379 *Pro Football Talk*. "Mike Mularkey Revealed Titans Did Sham Rooney Rule Interviews After Hiring Him as Coach." April 7, 2022.

380 Dulac, Gerry. "Team President Defends NFL Hiring Rule." *Pittsburgh Post-Gazette*, February 4, 2022.

381 Walker, Teresa M. (Associated Press). "If Hired as Coach, Flores Won't Drop Lawsuit." *Portland Press Herald (Portland, Maine)*, February 3, 2022.

Chapter Twelve

382 Ross, Charles K. *Outside the Lines*, 160.

383 *Chicago Tribune*. "In History Books, Willie Thrower Always Will Be No. 1," January 15, 1998.

384 Rhoden, William C. *Third and a Mile: The Trials and Triumphs of the Black Quarterback*. ESPN, 2007, 72.

385 Reid, Jason. *Rise of the Black Quarterback: What it Means for America*. New York: Andscape. 2022. 115.

386 Rhoden, William C. *Third and a Mile*, 88-89.

387 Rhoden, William C. *Third and a Mile*, 91.

388 Horrigan, Joe. *NFL Century: The One-Hundred-Year Rise of America's Greatest Sports League*. New York: Crown, 2019, 202.

389 Rhoden, William C. *Third and a Mile*, 29.

390 Ross, Charles K. *Outside the Lines*, 161.

391 Rhoden, William C. *Third and a Mile*, 36.

392 Powell, Michael. "Warren Moon, Who Helped Clear Way for Black Quarterbacks, Recalls His Struggles." *The New York Times*, February 5, 2016.

393 Reid, Jason. *Rise of the Black Quarterback*, 138.

394 Reid, Jason. *Rise of the Black Quarterback*, 139.

395 Reid, Jason. *Rise of the Black Quarterback*, 139.

396 Reid, Jason. *Rise of the Black Quarterback*, 145.

397 Borelli, Stephen (*USA Today*). "The Story of Doug Williams, Celebrated Now, Was Hardly a Fairy Tale: He Faced Ugly Racism." Yahoo.com, February 15, 2023.

398 Borelli, Stephen (*USA Today*). "The Story of Doug Williams, Celebrated Now,

Was Hardly a Fairy Tale: He Faced Ugly Racism." Yahoo.com, February 15, 2023.

399 Donahue, Ben. "The Life and Career of Doug Williams." *Pro Football History*, April 15, 2022.

400 Reid, Jason. "Doug Williams: The Real MVP." *Andscape,* January 31, 2018.

401 Reid, Jason. "Doug Williams: The Real MVP." *Andscape,* January 31, 2018.

402 Keim, John. "Doug Williams, the First Black QB to Win a Super Bowl, Shares 42 Years of 'Teaching Moments.'" *ESPN.* June 13, 2020.

403 Keim, John. "Doug Williams, the First Black QB to Win a Super Bowl, Shares 42 Years of 'Teaching Moments.'" *ESPN,* June 13, 2020.

404 Keim, John. "Doug Williams, the First Black QB to Win a Super Bowl, Shares 42 Years of 'Teaching Moments.'" *ESPN,* June 13, 2020.

405 Rhoden, William C. *Third and a Mile,* 101-2.

406 Feinstein, John. *Raise a Fist, Take a Knee: Race and the Illusion of Progress in Modern Sports.* Little, Brown and Company. 2021. 45-6.

407 Rhoden, William C. *Third and a Mile,* 108.

408 Reid, Jason. "James 'Shack' Harris Was an NFL Pioneer On and Off the Field." *Andscape,* February 8, 2023.

409 Horrigan, Joe. *NFL Century,* 202.

410 Reid, Jason. *Rise of the Black Quarterback,* 110.

411 Rhoden, William C. *Third and a Mile,* 110.

412 Horrigan, Joe. *NFL Century,* 204.

413 Grimsley, Will (Associated Press). "Jim Harris Scores Personal Triumph." *The Buffalo News,* January 21, 1975.

414 Reid, Jason. *Rise of the Black Quarterback,* 114.

415 Pergament, Alan. "Showtime Documentary on Racism Highlights Former Bills Marlin Briscoe, James Harris." *The Buffalo News,* August 8, 2013.

Chapter Thirteen

416 Covitz, Randy. "Former KC Chiefs & Dallas Trailblazer Who Still Holds Franchise Records Has Died." *The Kansas City Star,* July 18, 2024.

417 Covitz, Randy. "Chiefs' Haynes Left Lasting Mark." *The Kansas City Star*, February 24, 1991.

418 Covitz, Randy. "Chiefs' Haynes Left Lasting Mark." *The Kansas City Star*, February 24, 1991.

419 Covitz, Randy. "Chiefs' Haynes Left Lasting Mark." *The Kansas City Star,* February 24, 1991.

420 Covitz, Randy. "Chiefs' Haynes Left Lasting Mark." *The Kansas City Star*, February 24, 1991.

421 Covitz, Randy. "Chiefs' Haynes Left Lasting Mark." *The Kansas City Star*, February 24, 1991.

422 Covitz, Randy. "Chiefs' Haynes Left Lasting Mark." *The Kansas City Star*, February 24, 1991.

423 Gregorian, Vahe. "Why NFL Story of KC Chiefs' Abner Haynes is Relevant

Today." *The Wichita Eagle (Wichita, Kansas)*, June 28, 2020.

424   Gregorian, Vahe. "Why NFL Story of KC Chiefs' Abner Haynes is Relevant Today." *The Wichita Eagle (Wichita, Kansas)*, June 28, 2020.

425   Gregorian, Vahe. "Why NFL Story of KC Chiefs' Abner Haynes is Relevant Today." *The Wichita Eagle (Wichita, Kansas)*, June 28, 2020.

426   Ross, Charles K. *Mavericks, Money and Men: The AFL, Black Players, and the Evolution of Modern Football*. Temple University Press, 2016, 46.

427   Gruver, Ed. *The American Football League: A Year-by-Year History, 1960-1969*. McFarland, 1997, 84.

428   *Pittsburgh Post-Gazette*. "Gilchrist Still Bitter Over CFL Notoriety," July 29, 1983.

429   Cohen, Robert W. *The 50 Greatest Players in Buffalo Bills History*, 136.

430   Felser, Larry. "Lamonica Sticks to 'Game Plan' and Runs Cookie 243 Yds. To All-Time Pro Record." *The Buffalo Evening News,* December 9, 1963.

431   Felser, Larry. *The Birth of the New NFL: How the 1966 NFL/AFL Merger Transformed Pro Football*. Lyons Press. 2008. 18-9.

432   Wallace, William N. "Gilchrist Put on Waivers and Jets Claim Him." *The New York Times*, November 18, 1964.

433   Associated Press. "Buffalo Fires Gilchrist, AFL's Top Rusher." *Pittsburgh Post-Gazette*, November 18, 1964.

434   Gruver, Ed. *The American Football League: A Year-by-Year History, 1960-1969*, 84.

435   Zirin, Dave. "I'm a Negro Who Speak Up': Remembering Football Great Cookie Gilchrist." *The Nation*, January 13, 2011.

436   Miller, Jeffrey J. *Rockin' The Rockpile*, 254.

437   Miller, Jeffrey J. *Rockin' the Rockpile*, 254.

438   Gruver, Ed. *The American Football League: A Year-by-Year History, 1960-1969*, 130.

439   Leveson, Jared. "Carlton 'Cookie' Gilchrist: A Loud Voice Not Heard." *Pro Sports Fans*, February 9, 2024.

440   Zirin, Dave. "'I'm a Negro Who Speak Up': Remembering Football Great Cookie Gilchrist." *The Nation*, January 13, 2011.

441   Simonich, Milan. "Cookie Cutter." *Pittsburgh Post-Gazette,* January 19, 2003.

442   "Editorial," *The Louisiana Weekly,* January 23, 1965, as quoted in Louis Moore, *We Will Win the Day*, 96-7.

443   Hall, Jim. "Time Out." *The Louisiana Weekly*. January 23, 1965. Louis Moore. *We Will Win the Day*, 97.

444   Moore, Louis. *We Will Win the Day*, 97.

445   Hall, Jim. "Time Out." *The Louisiana Weekly*, January 23, 1965.

446   *New Journal and Guide*. June 17, 1961. *The Dallas Morning News*. December 22, 2012, and *Chicago Daily Defender*. November 29, 1961.

447   McDonough, Will. "Negro Stars, Charge Bias, Bolt Game." *The Boston Globe*. January 11, 1965.

Chapter Fourteen

448 Wyche, Steve. "Colin Kaepernick Explains Why He Sat During National Anthem." NFL.com, August 28, 2016.

449 Braun, Eric. *Colin Kaepernick: From Free Agent to Change Agent*. Lerner Publications. 2020. 29.

450 Chambers, Veronica with Jennifer Harlan. *Call and Response: The Story of Black Lives Matter*. Versify. 2021. 77-78.

451 Martin, Michel. "The Veteran and NFL Player Who Advised Kaepernick to Take a Knee." *National Public Radio*, "All Things Considered," September 9, 2018.

452 Boyer, Nate (Opinion). "An Open Letter to Colin Kaepernick, from a Green Beret-Turned-Long Snapper." *Army Times*, August 30, 2016.

453 Martin, Michel. "The Veteran and NFL Player Who Advised Kaepernick to Take a Knee." *National Public Radio*, "All Things Considered," September 9, 2018.

454 *Obama White House*. "Statement on the Grand Jury Decision in the Death of Eric Garner." December 3, 2014.

455 Pheifer, Pat and Claude Peck. *Star-Tribune*. "Aftermath of Fatal Falcon Heights Officer-involved Shooting Captured on Video," July 7, 2016.

456 Reid, Eric. "Why Colin Kaepernick and I Decided to Take a Knee," (Opinion). *The New York Times*, September 25, 2017.

457 Reid, Eric. "Why Colin Kaepernick and I Decided to Take a Knee," (Opinion). *The New York Times*, September 25, 2017.

458 Diaz, Daniella. "Obama Defends Kaepernick's Anthem Protest." CNN, September 29, 2016.

459 Freeman, Mike. *Football's Fearless Activists: How Colin Kaepernick, Eric Reid, Kenny Stills, and Fellow Athletes Stood Up to the NFL and President Trump*. Sports Publishing. 2020. 38-9.

460 Sabin, Sam. "NFL's National Anthem Policy Draws Support from 53% of U.S. Adults in One Poll." *Morning Consult*, May 31, 2018.

461 Salvanto, Anthony. "Poll: One Year after Charlottesville, Majority of Americans See Racial Tensions on the Rise." CBS News, August 12, 2018.

462 Freeman, Mike. *Football's Fearless Activists*, 61.

463 Freeman, Mike. *Football's Fearless Activists*, 146.

464 Freeman, Mike. *Football's Fearless Activists*, 145-6.

465 Garza, Alicia. "A History of the #BlackLivesMatter Movement." *Feminist Wire*, October 7, 2014, as quoted in Edwards, Sue Bradford, and Duchess Harris, JD, PhD. *Special Reports: Black Lives Matter*. Minneapolis, MN: Abdo Publishing. 2016. 68.

466 Bunn, Curtis. "Why Black Lives Matter Matters," in Bunn, Curtis, Michael H. Cottman, Patrice Gaines, Nick Charles, and Keith Harriston. *Say Their Names: How Black Lives Came to Matter in America*. 13.

467 The Editorial Board. "The Truth of 'Black Lives Matter.'" *The New York Times*, September 4, 2015.

468 Belson, Ken and Julie Hirschfield Davis. *The New York Times*. "Trump Attacks

Warriors' Curry. LeBron James's Retort: 'U Bum,'" September 23, 2017.

469 Wilner, Barry (Associated Press). "Colin Kaepernick: Timeline of a Gesture and Its Echoes." *The Denver Post*, June 7, 2020.

470 Twitter @Patriots, September 24, 2017.

471 Twitter @Miami Dolphins, September 23, 2017.

472 Tynes, Tyler. "Donald Trump Says His Comments on NFL Player Protest 'Have Nothing to Do about Race.'" *SB Nation* (Blog), September 24, 2017.

473 Belson, Ken and Julie Hirschfield Davis. *The New York Times*. "Trump Attacks Warriors' Curry. LeBron James's Retort: 'U Bum,'" September 23, 2017.

474 Haerens, Margaret. *The NFL National Anthem Protests (21st Century Turning Points)*, ABC-CLIO, 2018, 48-9.

475 Lander, Mark, Ken Belson, and Maggie Haberman. "Trump Tells Pence to Leave N.F.L. Game as Players Kneel During Anthem." *The New York Times*, October 8, 2017.

476 Reyes, Lorenzo. "Stephen Jones: 'If They Want to Be a Dallas Cowboy,' Players Better Stand for Anthem." *USA Today*, July 26, 2018.

477 Ragland, James (Opinion). "A Lesson in Plantation Politics from Dallas Cowboys Owner Jerry Jones." *The Dallas Morning News*, October 11, 2017.

478 Leah, Rachel. "Did NFL Owners Just Admit to Colluding with Trump to Punish Kneeling Players?" *Salon*, May 30, 2018.

479 Ragland, James (Opinion). "A Lesson in Plantation Politics from Dallas Cowboys Owner Jerry Jones." *The Dallas Morning News*, October 11, 2017.

480 Freeman, Mike. *Football's Fearless Activists*, 152.

481 Freeman, Mike. *Football's Fearless Activists*, 152-3.

482 Trump, Donald. "Statement by the President," June 4, 2018.

483 Jenkins, Malcolm. Twitter. June 5, 2018.

484 Associated Press. "Trump Cancels Eagles' White House Visit." *Victoria Advocate (Victoria, Texas)*, June 6, 2018.

485 Colvin, Jill and Errin Haines Whack (Associated Press), "Trump Calls Off Eagles Visit Over Anthem Dispute." Journal Tribune (Biddeford, Maine), June 5, 2018.

486 Colvin, Jill (Associated Press). "Trump Says No to Eagles." *The Morning Call (Allentown, Pennsylvania)*, June 5, 2018.

487 *Pittsburgh Post-Gazette*. "Grounding the Eagles," June 7, 2018.

488 Fouse, David. "The NFL Protests' Hidden Lesson: Don't Let Your Brand Get Hijacked by Politics." *Fox News*, October 17, 2017.

489 Giammona, Craig. "Papa John's Blames NFL 'Debacle' for Hurting its Pizza Sales." *The Florida Times-Union*, November 1, 2017.

490 Schwab, Frank. "Nike Makes Colin Kaepernick the Face of 'Just Do It' 30th Anniversary Campaign." *Yahoo Sports*, September 4, 2018.

491 McCrory, Chris. "Pat Tillman Becomes Focus of Social Media Outrage Over Nike Campaign." *The Republic (Phoenix, Arizona)*, September 3, 2018.

492 Horton, Alex (*The Washington Post*). "'He Would Be the First to Kneel': Pat Tillman Exploited to Attack Kaepernick, Biographer Says." *The Mercury News*, Septem-

ber 6, 2018.

493 Hyde, Andy. "Kaepernick: The Hypocrisy of Sports: Banning Protests While Promoting Myths." *Medium*, February 14, 2023.

494 Kaskey-Blomain, Michael. "LeBron James Says He Would Never Sit Across From President Trump." 247sports.com, July 31, 2018.

Chapter Fifteen

495 FitzSimons, Peter. "LeBron James and Laura Ingraham: War of Words Shows Why Sport and Politics Should Mix." *The Sydney Morning Herald*, February 21, 2018.

496 Letourneau, Connor. "Kevin Durant Calls Laura Ingraham's Commentary 'Racist.'" *San Francisco Chronicle*, February 16, 2018.

497 Bromwich, Jonah E. "'To Me, It Was Racist': N.B.A. Players Respond to Laura Ingraham's Comments on LeBron James." *The New York Times*, February 16, 2018.

498 Letourneau, Connor. "Kevin Durant Calls Laura Ingraham's Commentary 'Racist.'" *San Francisco Chronicle*, February 16, 2018.

499 Bromwich, Jonah E. "'To Me, It Was Racist': N.B.A. Players Respond to Laura Ingraham's Comments on LeBron James." *The New York Times,* February 16, 2018.

500 Bromwich, Jonah E. "'To Me, It Was Racist': N.B.A. Players Respond to Laura Ingraham's Comments on LeBron James." *The New York Times*, February 16, 2018.

501 Goldstein, Richard. "Bill Russell, Who Transformed Pro Basketball, Dies at 88." *The New York Times,* July 31, 2022.

502 Bird, Hayden. "Bill Russell 'Proud' of LeBron James and Kevin Durant for 'Speaking Truth Against Racism." *The Boston Globe,* February 18, 2018.

503 Bird, Hayden. "Bill Russell 'Proud' of LeBron James and Kevin Durant for 'Speaking Truth Against Racism." The Boston Globe, February 18, 2018.

504 Stein, Marc. "LeBron James Says He Doesn't Care if Trump Shuns N.B.A. Over Protests." *The New York Times*, August 6, 2020.

505 Jenkins, Paul. "NFL Players' Protest is an Insult, Period." *Anchorage Daily News*, September 29, 2017.

506 Friedersdorf, Conor. "How NFL Players Can Avoid Playing into Trump's Hands." *The Atlantic*, July 21, 2018.

507 Armour, Nancy. "Trump Has No Right Questioning Patriotism of NFL Players." *USA Today*. July 20, 2018.

508 Reuters Staff. "Popovich Blasts Goodell for Folding to Trump on Anthem Protests." *Reuters,* June 14, 2020.

509 Zirin, Dave. "'A Soulless Coward': Coach Popovich Responds to Trump." *The Nation*, October 16, 2017.

510 Galloway, Paul. "A Separate Peace." *Chicago Tribune,* October 24, 1993.

511 Beer, Jeff. "The NBA and NFL Offer Opposite Versions of American Brand Image." *Fast Company*, May 25, 2018.

512 O'Donnell, Ricky. "Steph Curry Said He Didn't Want to Go to the White House, So Donald Trump Said He Wasn't Invited." *Bleacher Reports*, September 23, 2017.

513 Kerr, Steve (as told to Chris Ballard). "Mr. President: You Represent All of Us.

Don't Divide Us. Bring Us Together." *Sports Illustrated*, September 24, 2017.

514 Rapp, Timothy. "Steve Kerr Writes Article to Donald Trump, Says Protest Comments 'Crushed' Him." *Bleacher Report*, September 24, 2017.

515 Carter, Brandon. "Warriors Coach: 'Far-fetched' to Expect Civil Discourse with Trump." *The Hill*, September 24, 2017.

516 McLaughlin, Kelly. "'We Agreed on Unity and Solidarity:' Los Angeles Sparks Leave the Court before National Anthem at Game 1 of WNBA Finals After Being Inspired by the Pittsburgh Steelers." *DailyMail.com*, September 25, 2017.

517 Moran, Lee. "Here's Why Megan Rapinoe Is Protesting During the National Anthem at the World Cup." *Huffington Post*, June 18, 2019.

518 Bryant, Howard. *The Heritage: Black Athletes, A Divided America, and the Politics of Patriotism*. Beacon Press. 2018. 223.

519 Belson, Ken. "Drew Brees's Unchanged Stance on Kneeling Is Suddenly Out of Step." *The New York Times*, June 4, 2020.

520 Belson, Ken. "Drew Brees's Unchanged Stance on Kneeling Is Suddenly Out of Step." *The New York Times*, June 4, 2020.

521 Belson, Ken. "Drew Brees's Unchanged Stance on Kneeling Is Suddenly Out of Step." *The New York Times*, June 4, 2020.

522 Uninterrupted. *Twitter* post, 6:19 PM, June 4, 2020.

523 Ingraham, Laura. *Shut Up & Sing: How Elites from Hollywood, Politics, and the UN are Subverting America*, 86.

524 Coffey, Kevin. "Political Grand Canyon Reflected in Omaha." *Omaha World-Herald*, July 30, 2010.

525 Bauder, David. "Ingraham Due Back at Fox Following Tweet Backlash." *The Spokesman-Review (Spokane, Washington)*, April 8, 2018.

526 Lewis, Ferd. "Athletes Have Earned a Spot on the Soapbox." *Honolulu Star-Advertiser (Honolulu, Hawaii)*, June 5, 2020.

527 Frantz, Bob. "It's Unfair to Expect Athletes to Double as Political Activists." *San Francisco Examiner*, June 22, 2009.

528 Weitzel, David. "I Won't Shut Up and Dcribble: Why Sports, Politics can Mix." *Sun News (Myrtle Beach, South Carolina)*. February 21, 2018.

529 Hall, Kristin M. (Associated Press). "With New Name and Album, The Chicks' Voices Ring Loud Again." *The Commercial Appeal (Memphis, Tennessee)*, July 13, 2020.

530 Loth, Rene (*The Boston Globe*). "Rockin' Politics." *South Florida Sun Sentinel (Fort Lauderdale, Florida)*, September 2, 2004.

531 Wells, Jeffrey. "Poor Gentlemanly Chuck." *Hollywood Elsewhere*, April 5, 2008.

Chapter Sixteen

532 Gregorian, Vahe. "Even Decades Later, the Story of Chiefs' Abner Haynes and Race Remains Instructive." *The Kansas City Star*, June 26, 2020.

533 Gregorian, Vahe. "Even Decades Later, the Story of Chiefs' Abner Haynes and Race Remains Instructive." *The Kansas City Star*, June 26, 2020.

534 Lattimore-Volkmann, Laurie. "What Abner Haynes Started in 1965 is Rever-

berating Through the Broncos, NFL Today." *Mile High Report*, September 14, 2020.

535   Gera, Vanessa. "Polish Journalist Suspended for Calling 'Imagine' a 'Vision of Communism' During Olympic Opening." *Associated Press,* July 27, 2024.

536   Taysom, Joe. "The Misunderstood Meaning of Iconic John Lennon song 'Imagine.'" *Far Out,* December 14, 2020.

537   JohnLennon.com. "Drones Light Up the Sky & Artists Sing 'Imagine' at the Tokyo 2020 Olympics Opening Ceremony," July 26, 2024.

538   Leicester, John. "Olympic President Invokes John Lennon's Memory as Paris Marks 1-year Countdown to War-clouded Games." Associated Press, July 26, 2023.

539   Taysom, Joe. "The Misunderstood Meaning of Iconic John Lennon song 'Imagine.'" *Far Out,* December 14, 2020.

540   King, Martin Luther. "Martin Luther King Jr.'s 'I Have a Dream' Speech in its Entirety." *National Public Radio,* January 16, 2023.

541   Theoharis, Jeanne. *A More Beautiful and Terrible History,* ix-x.

542   Schwartz, Ben. "What Louis Armstrong Really Thinks." *The New Yorker*, February 25, 2014.

543   Schwartz, Ben. "What Louis Armstrong Really Thinks." *The New Yorker,* February 25, 2014.

544   Jacobus, Robert D. *To Live and Play in Dixie,* 188.

545   Jacobus, Robert D. *To Live and Play in Dixie,* 188.

546   Jacobus, Robert D. *To Live and Play in Dixie*, 189.

547   Marquardt Hill, Katy. "The NFL's 'Take a Knee' Movement and its Impact on Workplace Protest." *CU Boulder Today*, September 14, 2023.

548   Didion, Alex. "Goodell Apologizes to Kap, Wishes NFL had Listened Earlier." NBCbayareasports.com, August 23, 2020.

549   Tobias, Todd. "Ernie Wright—November 13, 1998." *Tales from the American Football League.*

www.ingramcontent.com/pod-product-compliance
Lightning Source LLC
Chambersburg PA
CBHW070314240426
43661CB00057B/2641